Creating Client Extranets with SharePoint 2003

Mark E. Gerow

Apress®

Creating Client Extranets with SharePoint 2003

ISBN-13 (pbk): 789-159059-635-7

ISBN-10 (pbk): 1-59059-635-8

Library of Congress Cataloging-in-Publication data is available upon request.

Printed and bound in the United States of America 9 8 7 6 5 4 3 2 1

Lead Editor: Jim Sumser
Technical Reviewer: Judith Myerson
Editorial Board: Steve Anglin, Dan Appleman, Ewan Buckingham, Gary Cornell, Jason Gilmore, Jonathan Hassell, James Huddleston, Chris Mills, Matthew Moodie, Dominic Shakeshaft, Jim Sumser, Matt Wade
Project Manager: Richard Dal Porto
Copy Edit Manager: Nicole LeClerc
Copy Editor: Nancy Sixsmith
Assistant Production Director: Kari Brooks-Copony
Production Editor: Ellie Fountain
Compositor: M&M Composition, LLC
Proofreader: Nancy Riddiough
Indexer: Toma Mulligan
Artist: Kinetic Publishing Services, LLC
Cover Designer: Kurt Krames
Manufacturing Director: Tom Debolski

Distributed to the book trade worldwide by Springer-Verlag New York, Inc., 233 Spring Street, 6th Floor, New York, NY 10013. Phone 1-800-SPRINGER, fax 201-348-4505, e-mail `orders-ny@springer-sbm.com`, or visit `http://www.springeronline.com`.

For information on translations, please contact Apress directly at 2560 Ninth Street, Suite 219, Berkeley, CA 94710. Phone 510-549-5930, fax 510-549-5939, e-mail `info@apress.com`, or visit `http://www.apress.com`.

The source code for this book is available to readers at `http://www.apress.com` in the Source Code section.

This book is dedicated to my mother, who taught me to love learning in all its forms, has been my most enthusiastic supporter in this endeavor, and who has asked me expectantly every day for the past six months: "What have you written today?"

Contents at a Glance

Contents

About the Author

MARK GEROW has more than 20 years of experience in IT, professional services, and software product development, and has provided consulting to hundreds of companies throughout the San Francisco Bay area and Northern California. He currently works for Fenwick & West, LLP, where he is responsible for defining and implementing the firm's intranet and extranet strategies using SharePoint technologies.

Mark holds a Bachelor of Arts degree with majors in Computer and Information Sciences and Economics from the University of California, Santa Cruz, and an MBA from Santa Clara University. He is also a certified Project Management Professional by the Project Management Institute.

Mark lives with his family in the San Francisco Bay area.

About the Technical Reviewer

JUDITH M. MYERSON is a systems architect and engineer. Her areas of interest include middleware technologies, enterprise-wide systems, database technologies, application development, web development, software engineering, network management, security management, standards, and project management. Judith holds a Master of Science degree in Engineering and is a member of the IEEE organization.

Acknowledgments

As with any complex project, writing a book is not a solitary exercise. Authoring a technical book, in particular, requires one to draw on the expertise of others, many of whom I've met only through their blogs or user-group postings. Of all these collaborators, a few deserve special notice. First, I'd like to thank my colleagues Matt Kesner, Mal Mead, Helen Nomura, and Tammy White at Fenwick & West, LLP for their support and inspiration. I'd also like to thank Lea Ann Kjome, Jon Storchevoy, and Eric Hansen, who were fellow travelers at various points along my journey to SharePoint enlightenment. In addition, there would be no book without an editor, project manager, and technical reviewer: Jim Sumser, Richard Dal Porto, and Judith Myerson, respectively. Finally, I'd like to thank my wife Debbie and my son Mark for letting me slip off after dinner or on weekends to write; their understanding and encouragement made this book possible.

Introduction

This book is about creating client extranets with SharePoint 2003. Although there are many fine books that expand upon or clarify the material found in the various SharePoint SDKs published by Microsoft, this book is different. Most SharePoint books focus primarily on SharePoint administration or end user features, not on SharePoint as a development platform.

Creating Client Extranets with SharePoint 2003 is written to give you exactly what you need to deploy a secure, reliable, and highly usable extranet as quickly as possible. By reading this book, you can expect to acquire a wide range of skills that are both necessary to take full advantage of SharePoint as a development platform, as well as being valuable in their own right. Specifically, upon completing the book, you will be able to:

- Install and maintain SharePoint in an extranet environment.
- Use the SharePoint object model to create custom components called web parts.
- Create .NET applications that use the SharePoint object model.
- Build a framework to provide full control over content targeting.
- Customize the SharePoint look and feel to present your firm's brand to your clients.

If you want to create secure websites in which you, your colleagues, clients, vendors, and partners can share and collaborate on documents and data, you need an extranet. Extranets provide individuals inside and outside your firm with a secure online meeting place, and SharePoint provides a robust and highly customizable platform on which you can create your extranet sites. In this book, you'll learn how to install and configure Windows SharePoint Services (WSS) to support secure access over the Internet. You will also learn how to customize SharePoint at the site and page level through CAML, the template definition language, and through .NET programming. We'll cover the creation of administration tools to aid you in supporting a large number of sites and improvements to user navigation that will make your end users happier.

Why Build an Extranet?

Because you picked up this book and read this far, I assume that you already have one or more good reasons for wanting to build an extranet. Perhaps you (or your internal "customers") want to provide better service to your clients by creating online collaborative spaces. On the other hand, your clients might have let it be known that they expect such services from their vendors. In any case, an extranet is the next logical step beyond "one-on-one" collaboration via email, or group collaboration via file shares and FTP. Extranets break down the barriers between what's inside and what's outside your firm, but do so in a controlled way. Extranets address the fact that the defining work unit at many firms is now the project and that project teams are fluid and made up of employees, clients, vendors, and partners.

What Is an Extranet?

The word *extranet*, like many technical terms, seems to have taken on as many meanings as there are people using it, so it's worth clarifying what I mean by it in this book.

Note An *extranet* is an online collaborative space hosted on a secure web server that provides access for both internal and external users to documents, data, and applications for the purposes of collaboration on engagements, cases, deals, matters, projects, or other business activities and transactions.

An extranet is typically hosted in your data center or in a co-location facility. Ideally, internal users should be able to access the resources without needing to log in again to the extranet. Figure 1 shows a typical extranet topology.

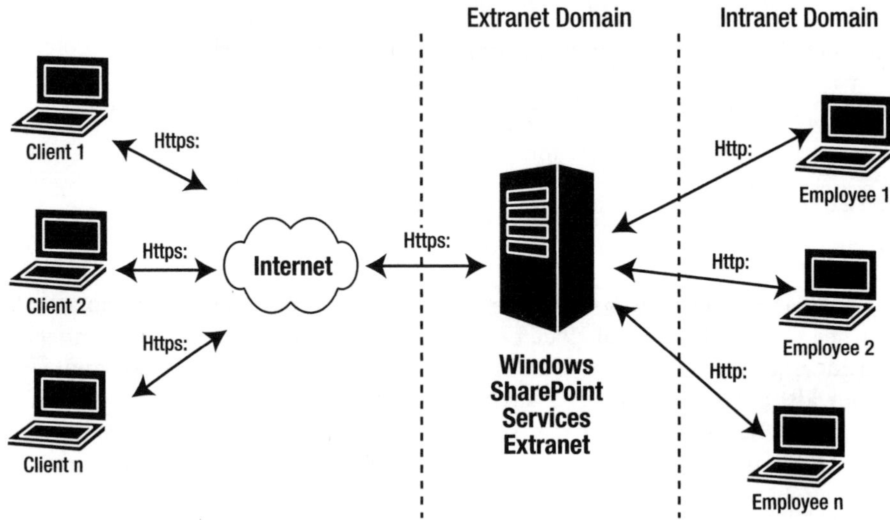

Figure 1. *A typical extranet topology*

As shown in the preceding figure, an extranet is typically composed of three domains:

- *Internet.* An unsecured environment through which external users will browse to your extranet
- *Extranet.* A secure environment that is exposed to both the Internet and accessible from your intranet, located in a special segment of your internal network, sometimes referred to as a demilitarized zone (DMZ)
- *Intranet.* A highly secure environment only accessible to individuals within your firm

The trick is to create an extranet environment that is easy for both external and internal users to access and use, without compromising security or exposing confidential data to unauthorized access. In this book, you'll learn how to use SharePoint to do exactly this.

Why This Book?

My first experience with SharePoint came when I was leading a team of developers responsible for creating an intranet for a global law firm. At that time, we were working with SharePoint 2001, which had some nice document handling features, and built-in security, but not much else. Because of SharePoint 2001's limited feature set, we developed more than half the intranet in ASP.NET. All the personalization and integration with back-end systems had to be coded from scratch and bolted on.

Given my experience with this earlier version, when the time came to select a platform for upgrading the extranet environment at this same firm, SharePoint was by no means a shoe-in. Fortunately, SharePoint 2003 had just been released. Its core component, Windows SharePoint Services (WSS), was now well-integrated with Windows Server 2003. More importantly, WSS provided extensive support for customization and a robust object model. With WSS, it became possible to integrate SharePoint with our core financial, document management, and Client Relationship Management (CRM) systems to provide clients with a personalized experience and to provide the professional look that our extranet users expected.

I've now come to view SharePoint as one of the three pillars of application development in a Microsoft-oriented IT environment, along with SQL Server and .NET. I find it hard to imagine a business application that isn't best delivered via a web browser or a web application that shouldn't be hosted by SharePoint. Just a few of the features SharePoint provides the extranet developer are the following:

- A hierarchical security model that is integrated with Active Directory
- Template-based site creation that can be extended through XML and .NET
- A basic document management system
- The ability to use a variety of predefined lists for data sharing, including contacts, events, tasks, issues, or links; or to create custom lists to meet unique business requirements
- A complete—and for the most part well-documented—library of .NET classes for manipulating all aspects of WSS server, sites, and pages
- A flexible framework for creating reusable components (called web parts) that can deliver virtually any SharePoint or non-SharePoint content to the web page, making it easy to target content to end users and recombine components to create new pages and applications
- Full integration with SQL Server for content storage, indexing, backup, and recovery
- A large and growing community of users, developers, and vendors working with and supporting SharePoint (most important for those responsible for deploying, customizing, and supporting SharePoint)

Note At this point, you might be thinking that I've drunk too deeply from the Microsoft well and lost my sense of perspective! Let me assure you that despite my enthusiasm for Windows SharePoint Services, I also know that there are still plenty of rough edges. In fact, a large portion of this book discusses how to smooth out those edges to present a polished, professional appearance for your extranet users. Nevertheless, it's clear that the foundation is solid, all the essentials are in place, and this is a platform you can build on with confidence.

Given this Nirvana of technology and features, why should you bother to read this book? The reason is, quite simply, that SharePoint is a very complex product built on top of many other complex technologies. Specifically, to install, configure, customize, and support SharePoint you will need to know at least a little bit about all of the following (in addition to SharePoint itself):

- Active Directory Services (AD)
- Cascading Style Sheets (CSS)
- HTML
- Internet Information Server (IIS)
- JavaScript
- .NET
- SQL Server
- Windows 2003 Server
- XML
- XSLT

Moreover, to deploy SharePoint in an extranet environment, you will probably want to learn about these:

- Internet Security and Acceleration (ISA) Server
- Windows Network Load Balancing (NLB)
- Secure Sockets Layer (SSL) encryption

In my experience, very few IT professionals, whether application developers or systems administrators, come to SharePoint with the breadth of knowledge required to take it from its out-of-the-box state to a fully tailored, professional-quality extranet solution. With a product so rich in features and composed of so many distinct technologies, it's difficult to know where to start.

- Should you use the CAML site definition language for all of your customizations?
- When (if at all) should FrontPage 2003 be used?

- Should SQL be used to access and update the configuration and context databases, or is it better to use the object model?
- When should you use the provided web services; and when should you write custom .NET code?
- Where does SharePoint store its configuration data and how do you modify it?
- What's the best way to back up and restore content?

These and a thousand other questions confront you along the path to creating a SharePoint extranet. First and foremost, then, this is the book I wish I'd had when I was building my first SharePoint extranet. This book is designed to be a roadmap to help you correctly install, configure, customize, and deploy Windows SharePoint Services to create a secure, useful, and appealing environment; an environment for collaboration between you and your colleagues, clients, vendors, and partners; and an environment for sharing documents, contacts, task lists, invoices, and just about any other electronic content that enables all parties to work together more effectively.

Who Should Read This Book?

This book was written for the IT professional who wants to quickly learn the skills necessary to install, customize, and deploy WSS as an extranet. I assume that you are comfortable with .NET programming and have some experience with SQL Server. You should also have some experience creating and administering SharePoint sites using the Windows SharePoint Services web interface. Beyond that, you need to be willing to look at application development in a new way, to learn to build on top of SharePoint's rich and multilayered framework for delivering web content.

Note Although the code examples in this book are written in VB.NET, the C# programmer will find them easy to read and convert to that language if desired. All the concepts, classes, properties, and methods described here are identical for both languages.

Windows SharePoint Services vs. SharePoint Portal Server

One point of confusion for many SharePoint users is the difference between Windows SharePoint Services (WSS) and SharePoint Portal Server (SPS). WSS is a free download from Microsoft that integrates with Windows Server 2003 to provide the core security, content management, and customization capabilities inherent in SharePoint. SPS is an application built on top of WSS by the Microsoft Office team, which provides a platform for creating corporate intranets. Table 1 highlights some of the key similarities and differences between the two platforms:

Table 1. *A Comparison of WSS and SPS*

WSS	SPS
Built on top of Windows Server 2003, IIS, and SQL Server	Built on top of Windows Server 2003, IIS, SQL Server, and WSS
Search is limited to WSS content	Search can include SPS, WSS, Exchange, file system, and Internet content
Licensed by the server, not the end user	Licensed by the server and end users
Provides basic site templates for creating websites for collaboration	Provides a platform for creating a corporate intranet
Best for creating a large number of independent sites	Best for creating a corporate intranet with areas, subareas, and pages mapped to organizational units (departments, divisions, geographies, and so on)

SPS is essentially a highly customized collection of WSS templates, sites, and applications designed to make the job of creating a corporate intranet easier. WSS, on the other hand, provides fewer out-of-the-box features, but is better suited to the task of creating numerous independent sites, which is a good match with the needs of a typical extranet environment.

Note For the remainder of this book, when I refer to *SharePoint* I am referring to *Windows SharePoint Services*.

What Software Do You Need to Deploy a SharePoint Extranet?

To deploy a SharePoint extranet, you will need, at a minimum, the following software:

- Windows 2003 Server
- Windows SharePoint Services
- SQL Server 2000
- Visual Studio 2003

Although it's possible to program in .NET without using the Visual Studio–integrated development environment, doing so is much more difficult, so you should not seriously consider developing applications in .NET without it. Other Microsoft servers and services that you will want to consider for inclusion in your extranet environment will be discussed in the chapters on installation and configuration.

How This Book Is Organized

The chapters of this book are organized into three sections:

- The first few chapters cover installing and configuring SharePoint and the related technologies you will need to deploy it in an extranet environment.
    - Chapter 1, "SharePoint Extranet Architectures," covers the nuts-and-bolts of installing SharePoint and related servers and services to support a secure extranet environment.
    - Chapter 2, "Configuring ISA, WSS, IIS with SSL," walks you through the process of configuring each of these components in detail.
    - Chapter 3, "Windows SharePoint Services Backup and Restore Techniques," provides detailed coverage of the various options and strategies for ensuring that your extranet sites are recoverable in case of human error or system failure.
- The next chapters focus on techniques for customizing SharePoint and automating common tasks such as creating new extranet sites
    - Chapter 4, "Creating the Custom Building Blocks," shows you how to create a framework for targeting content to specific classes of users.
    - Chapter 5, "Creating a TreeView Web Part," shows you how to use the SharePoint object model to provide your end users with a better way to navigate document libraries—and in doing so, shows you how to harness the object model to navigate any kind of list.
    - Chapter 6, "Integrating with Non-SharePoint Data Sources," addresses the need to extract and present structured data from databases on your extranet. This chapter shows you how to create a utility to cache data as XML on the extranet and format it using XSLT.
    - Chapter 7, "Customizing Site Navigation," addresses SharePoint's weakness in this area by showing you how to create simple and effective inter- and intrasite navigational elements.
    - Chapter 8, "Creating Custom Site Templates," focuses on how to use CAML to customize extranet sites and how to use .NET programming to take that customization to a higher level.
    - Chapter 9, "Automating Site Creation," shows you how to combine your custom templates with administrative utilities and post-creation processing to make creating new sites quick and painless.

- The final chapters integrate the topics covered in the previous chapters, and provide references for further study.
    - Chapter 10, "Putting It All Together," revisits and integrates the earlier chapters.
    - Chapter 11, "Conclusion," wraps it up and looks at the impact of a few of the developments relevant to those creating SharePoint extranets.
    - The Appendix, "Additional Resources," provides an extensive list of other resources to help you build on the topics covered in this book.

Note I've written each chapter so that it stands on its own, serving as a complete reference for the topic covered. You can therefore read this book straight through as a blueprint for creating your extranet, or pick and choose just those chapters that address a specific topic of interest.

CHAPTER 1

SharePoint Extranet Architectures and Components

There are many possible SharePoint extranet deployment scenarios, each providing a different level of security and complexity. In this chapter, I will cover several typical configurations and explain why one in particular is the best choice when data security is a paramount concern (which should be always for an extranet!). To successfully deploy SharePoint, you need knowledge of several Windows system components. With this in mind, the current and next chapters also provide the information you need to install and configure the components that make up a working SharePoint extranet environment.

Requirements of a Secure SharePoint Extranet

The efficacy of any solution must be measured against some objective criteria. In our case, we need a set of requirements that will drive the selection of the best SharePoint extranet architecture. For our purposes, I'll assume that our extranet must meet the following requirements:

- Provide user-level authentication and authorization
- Encrypt data sent over the Internet
- Hide the identity of the SharePoint server from Internet users
- Allow employees to access the extranet without re-authenticating

Provide User-Level Authentication and Authorization

We want each user to be identified via login so that access to extranet resources (sites, lists, document libraries, and web parts) can be tightly controlled. Further, identifying the user allows SharePoint to keep track of who uploaded or changed content.

Encrypt Data Sent over the Internet

Both you and your clients will want to know that the data on their extranet is safe from prying eyes while traveling between SharePoint and their browser. To achieve this, all communication should be encrypted using the industry-standard Secure Sockets Layer (SSL) algorithm.

Hide the Identity of the SharePoint Server from Internet Users

Malicious attempts to breach website and network security are an ever-increasing fact. One thing you can do to protect SharePoint is to place an intelligent proxy server between it and the outside world. Microsoft Internet Security and Acceleration (ISA) Server addresses this need by providing *reverse proxy* capabilities: all external extranet users will connect through the ISA Server and never have direct communications with SharePoint. In this configuration, ISA Server does two things: 1) checks incoming messages for malicious content, and 2) redirects nonmalicious requests to SharePoint, and SharePoint's responses back to the external user.

Allow Employees to Access the Extranet Without Re-Authenticating

An *extranet* is a point of collaboration between employees and clients. We want to ensure that the barriers to use are minimal, eliminating any process that would tend to discourage use. Therefore, your intranet users should not have to sign in to the extranet if they have already authenticated on your firm's intranet.

Extranet Configuration Scenarios

To select the best extranet configuration, it's necessary to understand the range of possible architectures. After you see the following scenarios, you'll agree that the last configuration, Windows authentication with ISA Server and SSL, provides the best solution from a security standpoint.

■ **Note** Each of the scenarios presented has an appropriate use and should not be considered inferior to the others for all purposes. However, in an extranet environment security is of primary importance, both to protect internal systems and confidential client data.

Scenario 1: No Security

Both Microsoft Internet Information Server (IIS) and SharePoint support anonymous access. If you enable anonymous access to IIS, users are authenticated using a shared account (IUSR_*servername* by default). As shown in Figure 1-1, SharePoint can be directed to allow this user account access to some or all of its resources, thus allowing anonymous users to connect.

Although it's conceivable that SharePoint could be used to create a public website, an extranet is by definition a secure portal for sharing documents and data with clients. It's clear that this scenario won't meet our requirements, as noted previously.

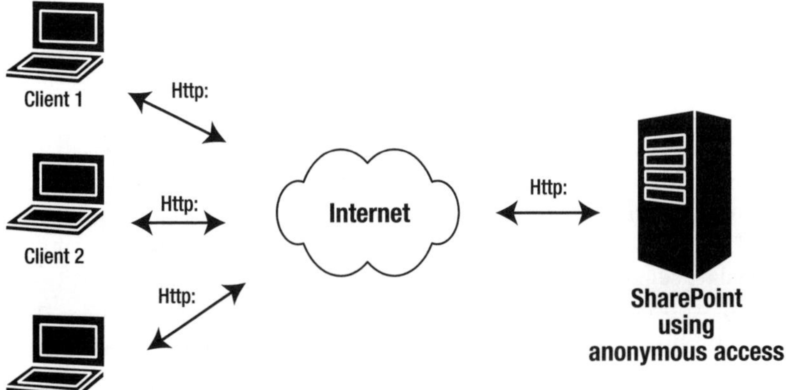

Figure 1-1. *SharePoint extranet without security*

Scenario 2: Windows Authentication Without SSL

This configuration meets our first security requirement: a user must be uniquely identified to SharePoint. This is, in fact, the default configuration for SharePoint when installed for internal use, but because intranet users are authenticated when they log in to Windows, they are not usually required to log in again unless they try to access a website in another domain without a trust relationship to the one they originally logged in to.

In an extranet environment, the first contact a user will have with the Windows domain is when the browser requests a page on the SharePoint server. At this time, the browser will display a login dialog box that requires the user to enter a valid username and password in the EXTRANET domain. The username and password are then sent in encrypted form to the Windows server. Most modern browsers support this type of authentication with no trouble, and it provides a secure and reliable means to authenticate a SharePoint user. This process is shown in Figure 1-2.

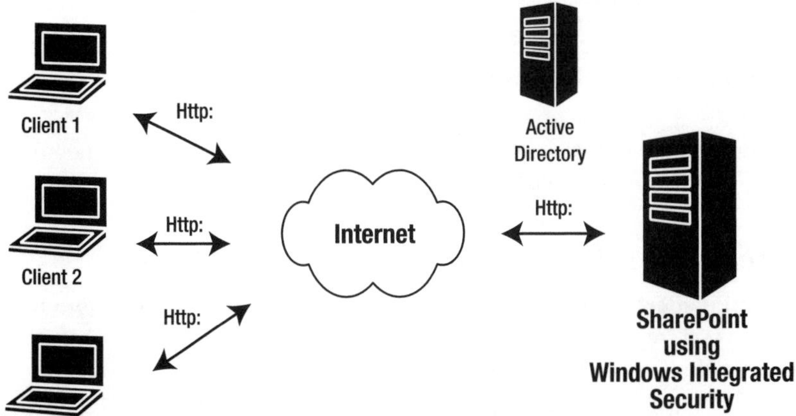

Figure 1-2. *SharePoint extranet with Windows Integrated Security*

This configuration is appropriate only when you want to make nonconfidential SharePoint data available over the Internet to a select group of users.

Scenario 3: Windows Authentication with SSL

A more secure approach incorporates SSL to encrypt all information sent between the browser and SharePoint. So even if data is intercepted during transmission, it is indecipherable by an unauthorized third party.

The details of how this works are beyond the scope of this book. But the essence is that you obtain two strings of random text, known as *keys* or *certificates*—one public that you share with authorized users, and one private that only your server has access to. Because both keys (or derivatives of those keys) are required to decipher a message, only authorized users and SharePoint can read the data sent between them. A third party such as VeriSign, referred to as a *certificate authority (CA)*, certifies that the provider of the certificate (your SharePoint server) is valid (see Figure 1-3). This prevents another party from maliciously impersonating your server as a way of capturing confidential data.

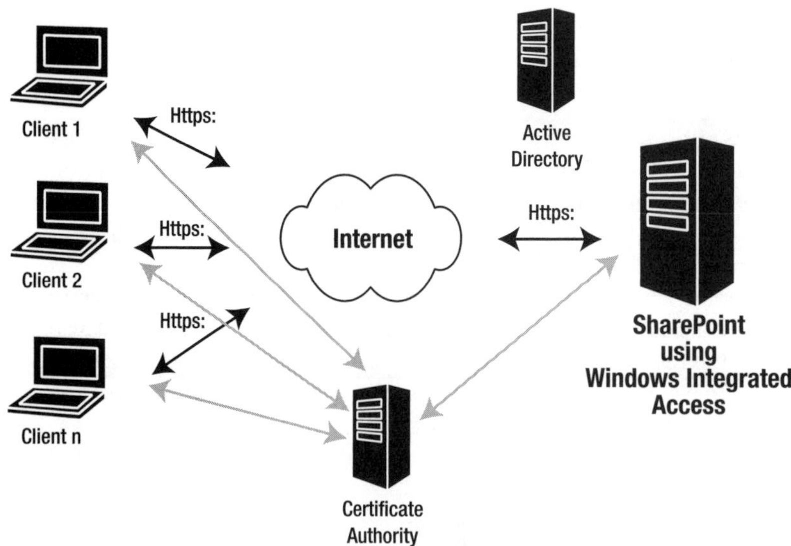

Figure 1-3. *SharePoint extranet with Windows and SSL security*

This solution is a proven and robust way to provide secure communication over the Internet, and is used by many banks and financial institutions.

Scenario 4: Windows Authentication with ISA 2004 Server

The previous two scenarios address the need to uniquely identify users and secure communications. This scenario takes a step back for illustrative purposes; it eliminates SSL encryption, but adds a proxy server in the form of Microsoft's Internet Security and Acceleration Server 2004 (ISA 2004 Server). This application server performs many functions, but the feature we're interested in is its capability to act as a reverse proxy.

A *reverse proxy* is a server that receives requests for a web resource, such as a SharePoint server, and directs that request to the appropriate location. Using this capability, we can publish just the address of the ISA Server on the Internet, preventing external users from having direct contact with our SharePoint server. This provides not only a security benefit but also flexibility in terms of server configuration because clients know only the address of the ISA Server. We can move SharePoint servers at will without breaking any links our clients might have cached in their browsers—or the need to update a public Domain Name Service (DNS) name.

You'll also notice the addition of a one-way trust from the INTRANET to EXTRANET domains, as shown in Figure 1-4. This trust relationship allows internal users, who have already been authenticated in the intranet domain, to be automatically logged in to the external domain without having to re-enter their username and password.

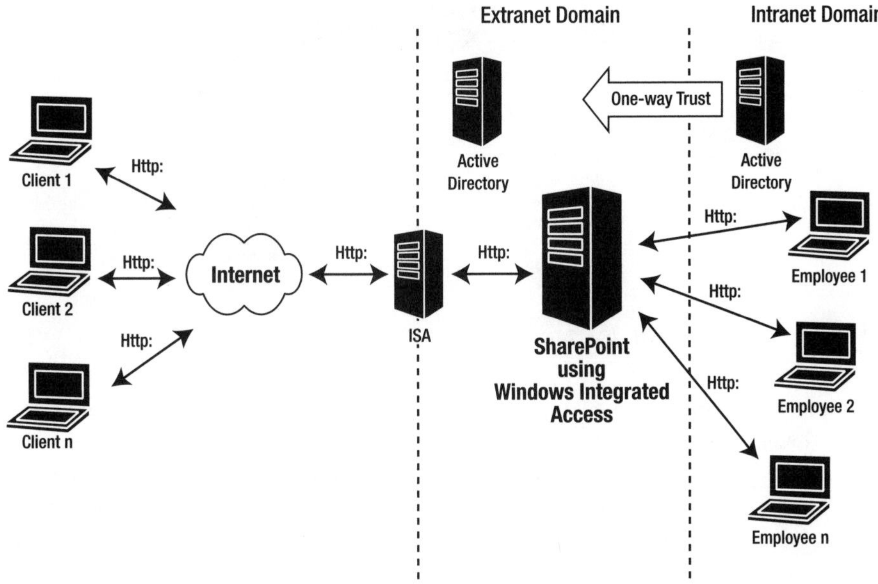

Figure 1-4. *SharePoint extranet with ISA Server 2004*

The trust relationship is termed *one way* because users authenticated in the INTRANET domain (that is, employees) are trusted by the EXTRANET domain, but the reverse is not true; users authenticated in the EXTRANET domain cannot access resources in the INTRANET domain without logging in again with a valid INTRANET domain username and password.

Scenario 5: Windows Authentication with ISA Server 2004 and SSL

Putting the preceding approaches together, we have an architecture that meets all our requirements, as shown in Figure 1-5. Windows Integrated Security ensures that all users are uniquely authenticated in the EXTRANET domain. SSL ensures that information is encrypted while traveling over the Internet. ISA Server prevents external users from having direct access to the SharePoint server or even knowing its address. Finally, the one-way trust allows internal users (or systems) access to resources in the extranet without logging in a second time.

In the remainder of this chapter, I'll show you how to install the various components that make up Scenario 5. Two aspects of the configuration that will differ in a production environment are the choice of CA and the creation of a public DNS.

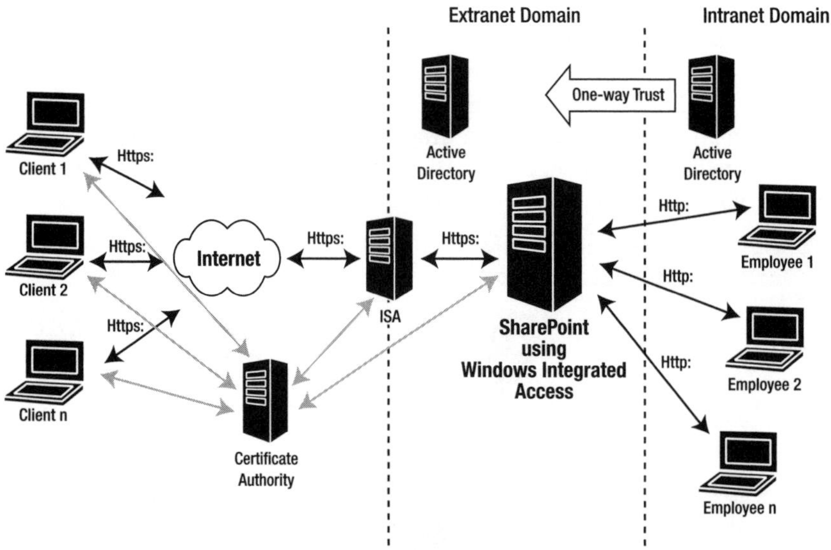

Figure 1-5. *SharePoint extranet with ISA Server 2004 and SSL*

First, in our test environment, we'll use Microsoft Certificate Services to create and validate our SSL certificates. Although this choice is fine for internal use, most external users will expect you to use a certificate verified by a third party such as VeriSign. Because the process of using an external CA is almost identical to using one created with Microsoft Certificate Services, you'll have the information you need to install your production extranet after following the procedure outlined here.

Second, we won't go through the process of creating a public domain name (for example, `extranet.mycompany.com`). Given that the DNS entry is simply a synonym for the IP address of the ISA Server, this omission is not material. If you want, you can use a domain name that points either to the ISA Server or to its external IP address.

In the next chapter, I will show you how to configure ISA Server 2004 to work with Windows SharePoint Services (WSS) and SSL.

Installing SharePoint As an Extranet

Configuring WSS as a secure extranet requires several components that are probably new to most application developers, meaning that on top of all of the complexity of SharePoint itself, additional layers of complexity must be added. Even in large IT organizations, in which setting up these components might be someone else's responsibility, it's important for you to understand the overall architecture so you can effectively troubleshoot problems and communicate with developers and administrators regarding your SharePoint deployment.

■ **Note** You can skip some or all of the following installations, with the exception of WSS, which is required to run the examples throughout this book. However, skipping any of the following steps will result in an extranet environment that fails to meet one or more of our previously stated requirements.

Installing an Extranet Domain Controller

The first step to a functioning SharePoint extranet environment is to install an EXTRANET domain controller. The EXTRANET domain controller is a Windows 2003 server on which you have installed and configured Active Directory Services. This server will authenticate external users and control access to SharePoint resources.

There are many ways to configure domains in an organization. For the purposes of this book, we assume that we will be creating a brand new EXTRANET domain with one domain controller. In a production environment, you would likely have at least one backup domain controller as well to provide fault tolerance and load balancing.

To create our new EXTRANET domain, we will start with a Windows 2003 server named EXTRANET-DC. We will convert this server into our primary EXTRANET domain controller by the following steps:

Caution Be sure to log in with an account that has Administrator privileges on the EXTRANET-DC server before beginning this process.

---

1. Open the Active Directory Installation Wizard by executing the command `dcpromo.exe`. The wizard will guide you through the steps of configuring the EXTRANET-DC server as a domain controller.

2. Because our EXTRANET domain will be independent of any existing internal domains, on the Domain Controller Type dialog box, I choose Domain Controller For A New Domain and then click Next (see Figure 1-6).

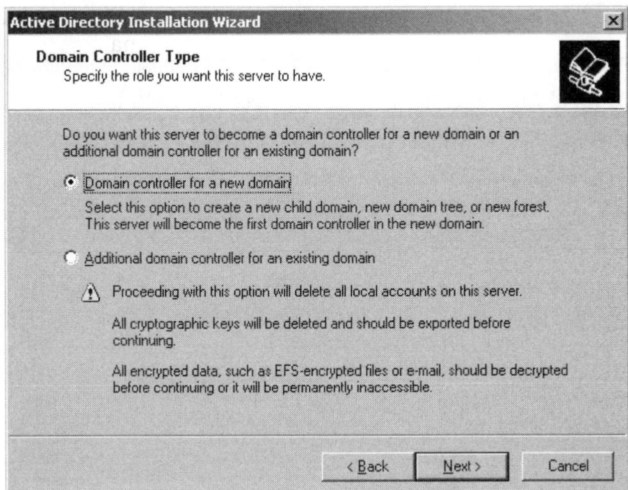

Figure 1-6. *Domain Controller Type dialog box*

3. On the Create New Domain dialog box, choose Domain In A New Forest and then click Next (see Figure 1-7). This will create a completely independent domain.

■**Note** In your production extranet environment you will probably want at least one backup domain controller to provide recovery in case the primary domain controller becomes unavailable. To do so, you will select the second option to add an Additional Domain Controller For An Existing Domain.

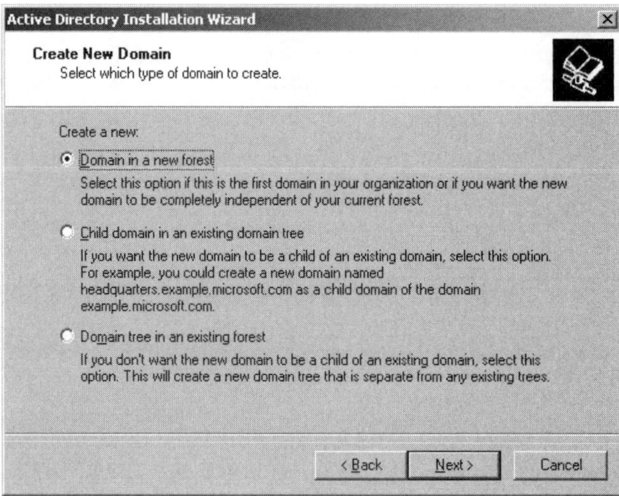

Figure 1-7. *Create New Domain dialog box*

4. On the New Domain Name dialog box, type the DNS name **`extranet.mycompany.com`** and then click Next (see Figure 1-8).

■**Note** We'll configure this server as a DNS server as well. The DNS entries for other computers in the EXTRANET domain should include the IP address of the EXTRANET-DC server.

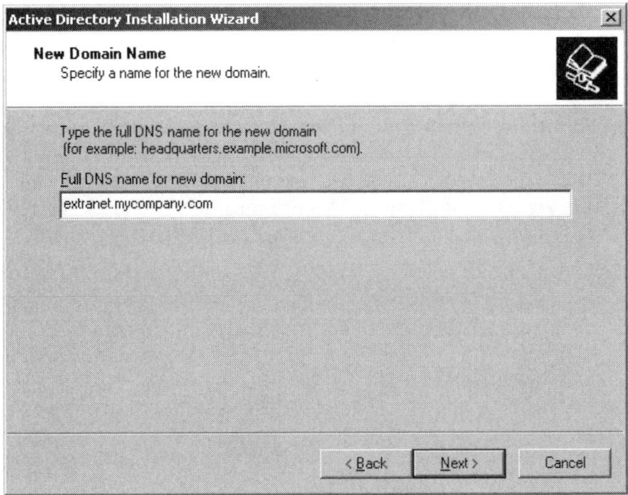

Figure 1-8. *New Domain Name dialog box*

5. On the NetBIOS Domain Name dialog box, type **EXTRANET** and then click Next (see Figure 1-9).

Note The domain name `extranet.mycompany.com` and the NetBIOS name EXTRANET are synonyms and for internal use can be used interchangeably.

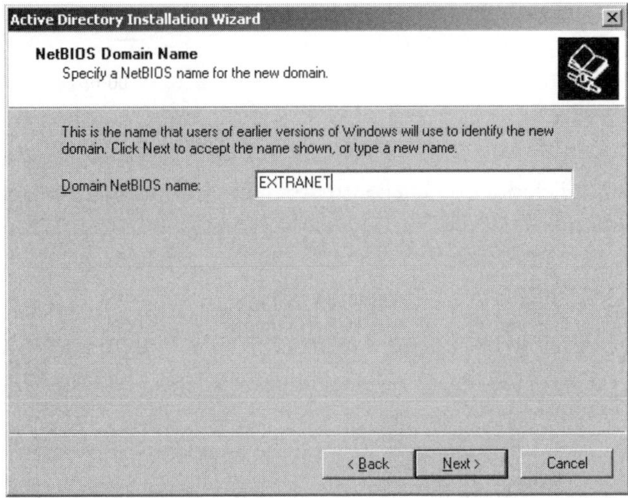

Figure 1-9. *NetBIOS Domain Name dialog box*

6. On the Database And Log Folders dialog box, we'll retain the defaults. In a production environment, you would typically place the Active Directory database and logs on separate volumes, but we'll keep things simple here. Click Next.

7. On the Shared System Volume dialog box, click Next to accept the default location.

8. Choose Install And Configure The DNS Server On This Computer, And Set This Computer To Use This DNS Server As Its Preferred DNS Server and then click Next, as shown in Figure 1-10. As noted previously, this will make the EXTRANET-DC server a DNS server as well. Other computers in the EXTRANET domain should include a reference to EXTRANET-DC's IP address in their Network DNS Server lists.

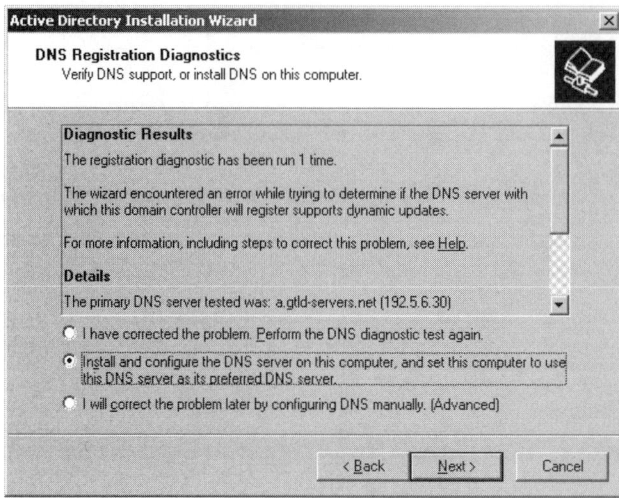

Figure 1-10. *DNS Registration Diagnostics dialog box*

9. Select Permissions Compatible Only With Windows 2000 Or Windows Server 2003 Operating Systems on the Permissions dialog box and then click Next.

Reboot the computer and voila! Your domain controller is ready for use. This server will handle all login authentications for the EXTRANET domain.

Configuring a One-Way Trust Relationship

A one-way trust from the INTRANET to EXTRANET domains will allow users in the INTRANET domain to access resources in the EXTRANET domain without the need to log in a second time.

■ **Note** A trust does not eliminate the need to grant permissions to INTRANET users in the EXTRANET domain; whether at the file system, IIS, or SharePoint levels, you must still grant permissions to resources as you would for EXTRANET users. The trust simply tells the EXTRANET domain to accept that INTRANET domain users are who they say they are without forcing them to log in again.

Caution To create a one-way trust you must have Administrator privileges in both domains.

To create the trust, follow these steps:

1. On the EXTRANET-DC server, open the Active Directory Domains And Trusts application from the Administrative Tools menu.

   The Active Directory Domains And Trusts dialog box displays, as shown in Figure 1-11.

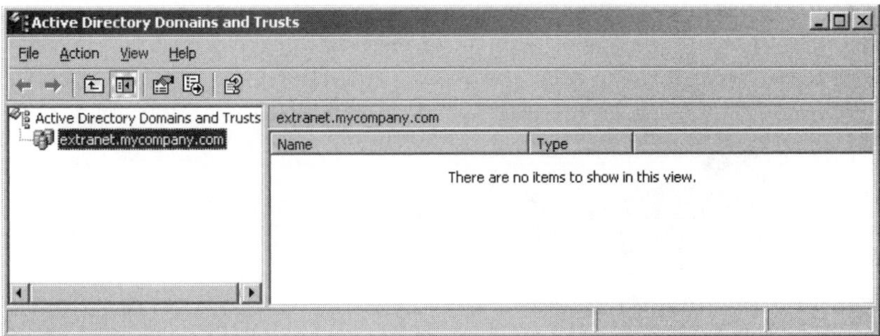

Figure 1-11. *Active Directory Domains And Trusts dialog box*

2. Right-click the domain `extranet.mycompany.com` (or whatever your domain name may be), select the Trusts tab, and then click the New Trust button (see Figure 1-12).

   The New Trust Wizard launches.

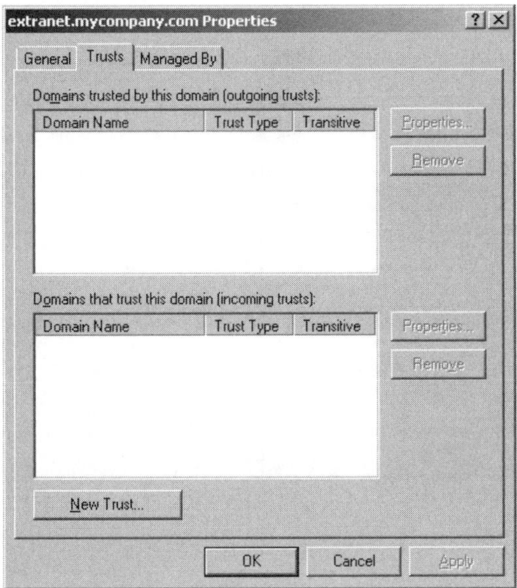

Figure 1-12. *Trusts tab*

3. On the Trust Name dialog box, enter the name of the INTRANET domain and then click Next (see Figure 1-13).

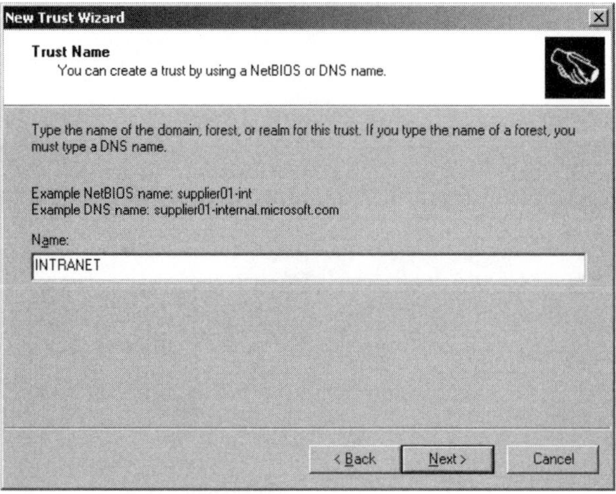

Figure 1-13. *Trust Name dialog box*

4. Select a One-Way: Outgoing trust and click Next (see Figure 1-14).

■ **Note** If you have a different NetBIOS name for your intranet, enter it here.

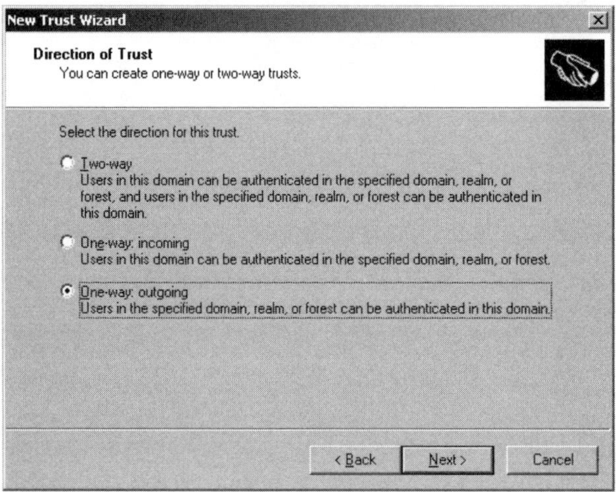

Figure 1-14. *Direction Of Trust dialog box*

5. On the Sides Of Trust dialog box, select Both This Domain And The Specified Domain to create the trust entries on both the EXTRANET and INTRANET domains; then click Next (see Figure 1-15).

■ **Note** If you choose This Domain Only, you will need to log in to the INTRANET-DC server and repeat this process using a one-way incoming trust.

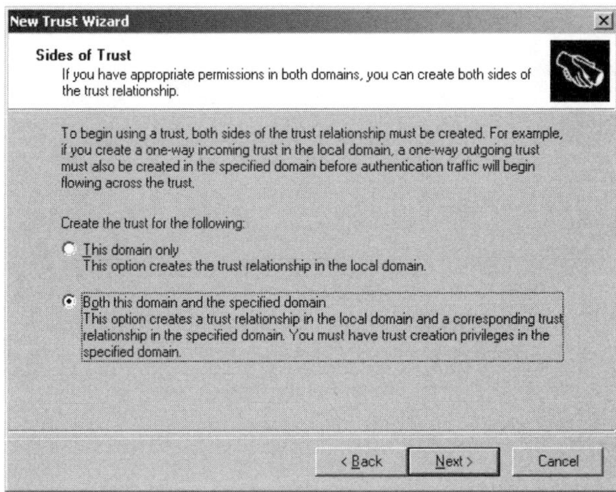

Figure 1-15. *Sides Of Trust dialog box*

6. Enter the Administrator username and password for the INTRANET domain and click Next (see Figure 1-16).

Figure 1-16. *User Name And Password dialog box*

7. Click Next twice, acknowledging the trust configuration. Select Yes, confirm the outgoing trust, and click Next.
8. Click Finish.
9. Acknowledge the dialog box regarding SID filtering.
10. To verify that the trust has been configured, open the domain Properties dialog box again, select the Trusts tab, and confirm that the INTRANET domain is listed in the Domains Trusted By This Domain list (see Figure 1-17).

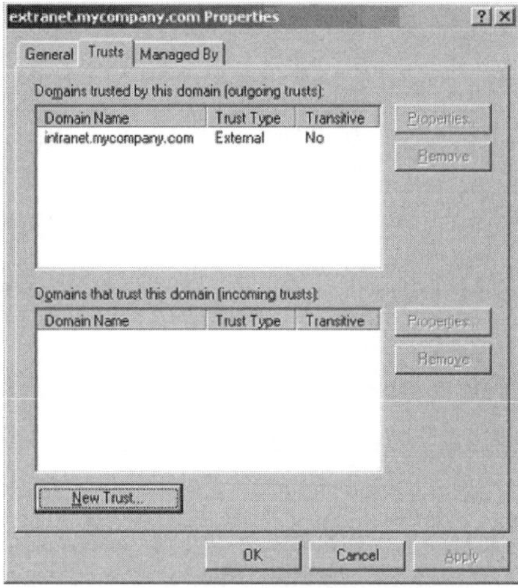

Figure 1-17. *Trusts tab displaying completed trust relationship*

You can repeat the previous step on the INTRANET-DC server, and you will see the `extranet.mycompany.com` in the Domains That Trust This Domain list.

Installing Microsoft Certificate Services

Microsoft Certificate Services (MCS) can be used to issue and establish the authenticity of SSL certificates, both within and between organizations. MCS is used here to allow us to test SSL without purchasing a commercial certificate from an independent CA such as VeriSign.

■ **Note** If you have a certificate from an independent CA, such as VeriSign, you might use it rather than installing MCS. If you choose not to install MCS, you can skip this section.

To install MCS, follow these steps:

1. Open the Add Or Remove Programs application from the Windows Control Panel dialog box. Then select Add/Remove Windows Components.
2. From the Windows Components dialog box, check Certificate Services and then click Next (see Figure 1-18). A dialog box informs you that you cannot change the machine name or the domain membership of the machine while it acts as a certificate server. Click Yes.

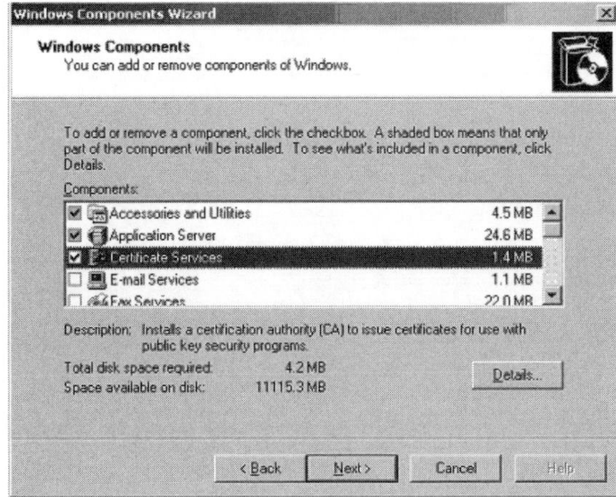

Figure 1-18. *Windows Components dialog box showing Certificate Services selection*

3. Choose Enterprise Root CA and click Next (see Figure 1-19).

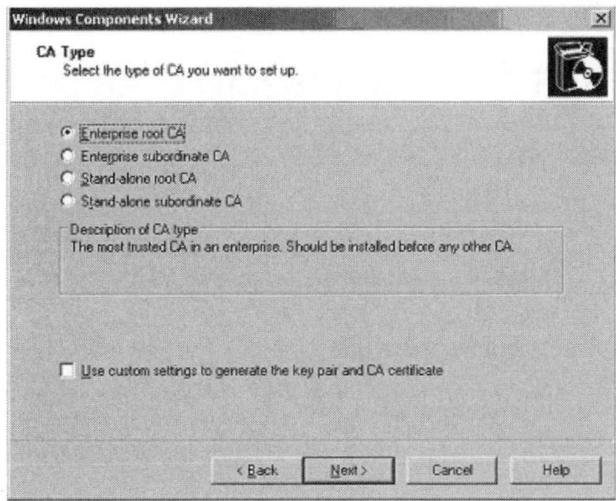

Figure 1-19. *CA Type dialog box*

4. On the CA Identifying Information dialog box, enter a Common Name For This CA. The common name of the CA is either the DNS host name or the NetBIOS name of the machine running Certificate Services. Click Next (see Figure 1-20).

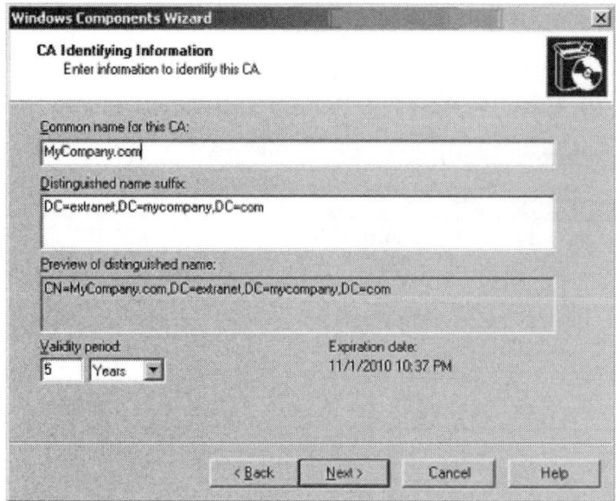

Figure 1-20. *CA Identifying Information dialog box*

5. Accept the default locations for Certificate Database and Certificate Database Log and then click Next.

6. The installation wizard will stop and restart IIS during the installation process. You will also be warned about the potential security risks of enabling Active Server Pages (ASP) in IIS, which is required to support the Web Enrollment feature. You should allow ASP support to be activated.

MCS is now installed.

Installing Internet Security and Acceleration Server 2004

ISA Server 2004 will serve as a reverse proxy, accepting requests from outside users and passing those requests to our SharePoint server. This will prevent external users from having direct access to any other servers in our EXTRANET domain. To install ISA Server 2004, follow these steps:

1. Run the `setup.exe` program in the root folder of the ISA Server 2004 installation CD.

2. On the main screen, click on Install ISA Server 2004.

3. Click Next twice to acknowledge the license agreement.

4. Select both Install ISA Server Services and Install Configuration Storage Server on the Setup Scenarios dialog box and click Next (see Figure 1-21).

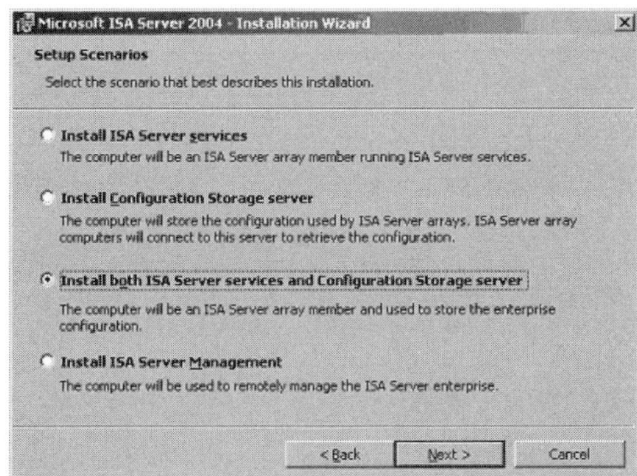

Figure 1-21. *ISA Server 2004 Setup Scenarios dialog box*

5. Click Next to accept the default install options on the Component Selections dialog box.

6. Select Create A New ISA Server Enterprise and click Next on the Enterprise Installation Options dialog box (see Figure 1-22).

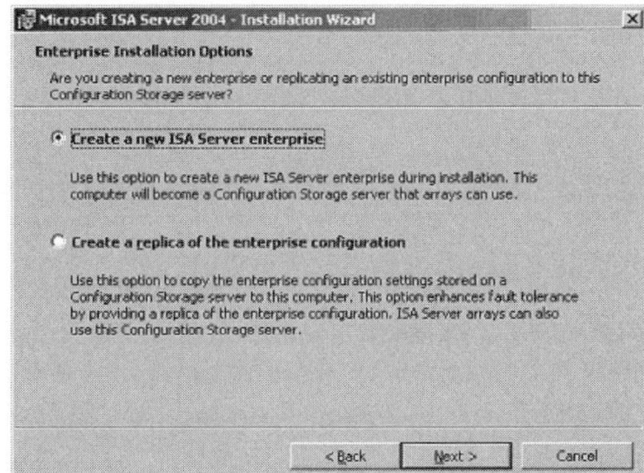

Figure 1-22. *Enterprise Installation Options dialog box*

7. Acknowledge the new enterprise warning by clicking Next.

8. Add an internal network IP range that includes all IP addresses that will be served by ISA Server 2004 (see Figure 1-23).

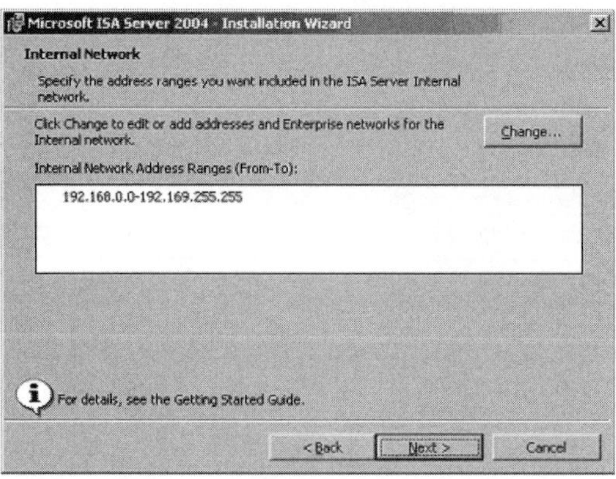

Figure 1-23. *Internal Network dialog box*

9. Click Next to acknowledge the Firewall Client Connection settings.
10. Click Next to acknowledge the Services Warning.
11. Click Next to acknowledge the Ready To Install dialog box.
12. Click Finish on the Installation Completed dialog box.
13. Click Yes to reboot the server.

ISA Server 2004 is now installed.

Installing Windows SharePoint Services

Now that all the supporting services are installed, it's time to install WSS.

■ **Note** I am assuming that SQL Server 2000 or greater is running and available on a computer in the domain. If this is not the case, you might choose to install WSS with the Microsoft Database Engine (MSDE); however, if you do so, the full-text search feature will not be available in WSS.

To install and configure WSS, follow these steps:

1. To install WSS, you must first obtain a copy of the file `STSV2.exe` from the Microsoft website. As of this writing, the download page can be found at: `http://www.microsoft.com/downloads/details.aspx?FamilyId=E084D5CB-1161-46F2-A363-8E0C2250D990&displaylang=en` (see Figure 1-24).

■ **Note** A bit of SharePoint trivia: the *STS* in the download file refers to *SharePoint Team Services*, which was the name used by WSS in version 1.0, which was released in 2001.

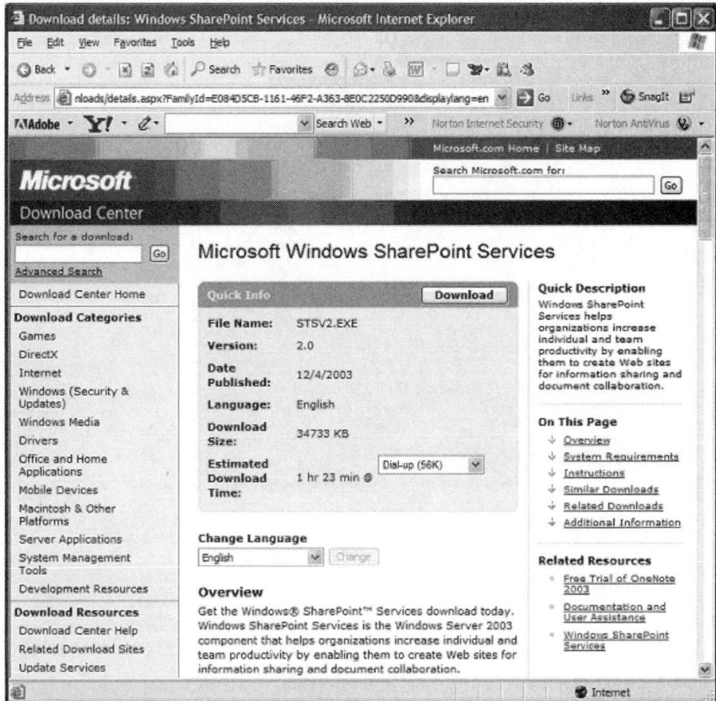

Figure 1-24. *Microsoft Windows SharePoint Services download page*

2. After the `stsv2.exe` file has downloaded to your computer, double-click the icon to begin the install. The icon is shown as follows.

■ **Note** You must have already installed IIS 6.0 on the server prior to installing WSS. It can be installed by selecting Windows Control Panel ➤ Add Or Remove Programs ➤ Add/Remove Windows Components ➤ Application Server (refer to Figure 1-18).

3. Click Next to accept the Windows SharePoint Services license agreement terms.
4. Select Server Farm as the installation type (see Figure 1-25).

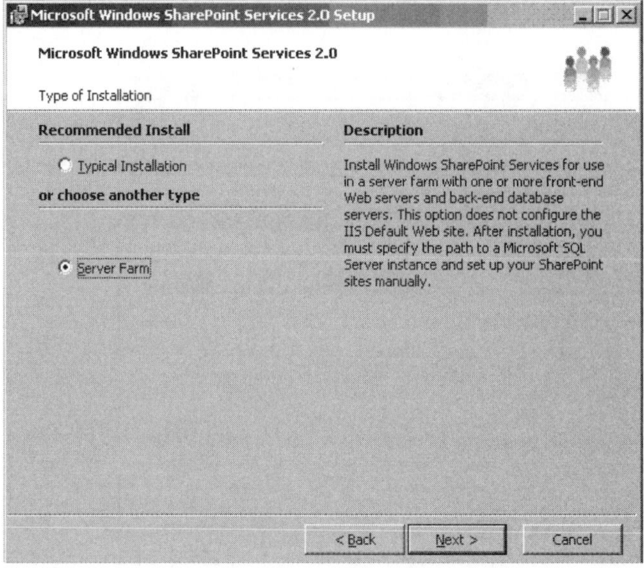

Figure 1-25. *Selecting the Windows SharePoint Services installation type*

Caution If you choose the Typical Installation option, full-text search will not be available in WSS because the MSDE, which is installed as part of the Typical Installation, does not include full-text indexing capabilities found in a full SQL Server installation.

---

5. Select the default StsAdminAppPool Application Pool and click OK.
6. Click OK to acknowledge the Application Pool Changed message.
7. On the Set Configuration Database Server page, enter the name of the SQL database server that will be hosting the WSS databases and provide a unique name for the Windows SharePoint Services database name, such as EXTRANET (see Figure 1-26).

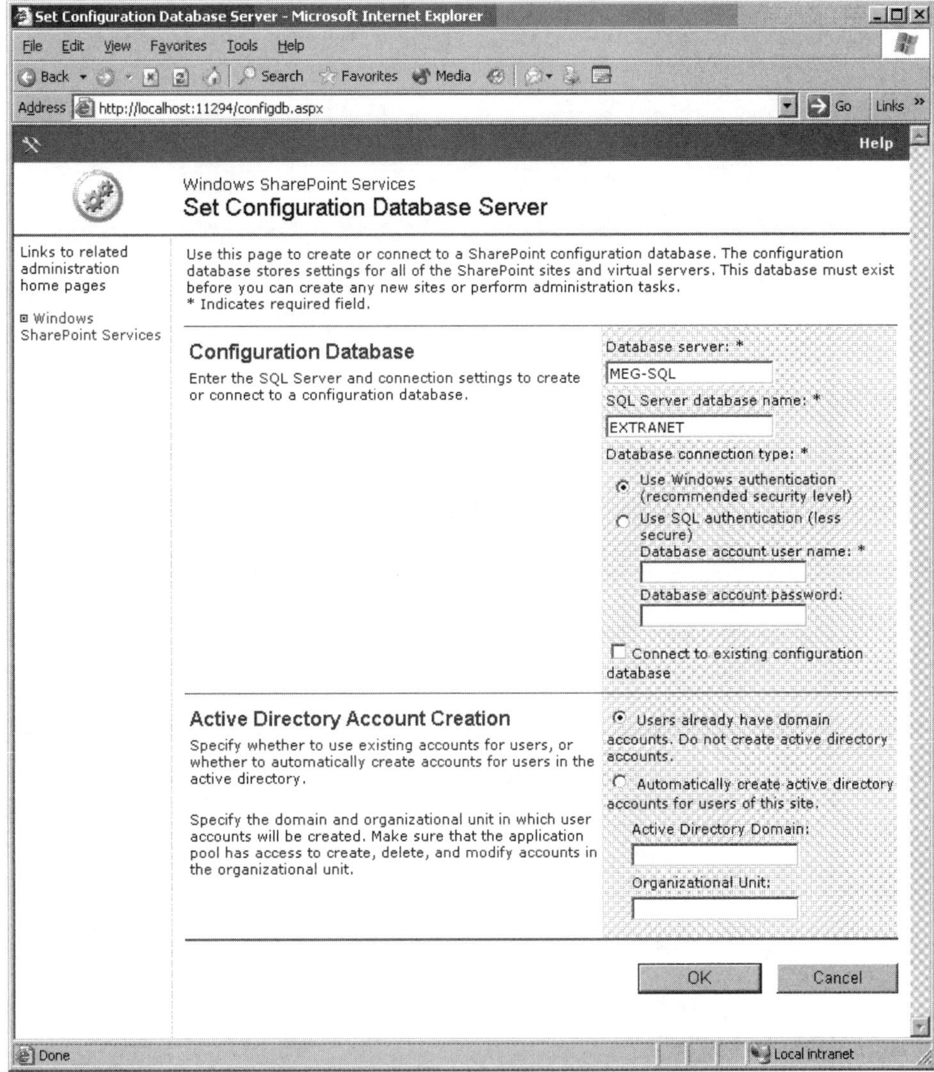

Figure 1-26. *Selecting a Windows SharePoint Services configuration SQL server and database*

8. Click the Extend Or Upgrade Virtual Server link on the WSS Central Administration page.

9. Click the Default Web Site link on the Virtual Server List page to display the Extend And Create Content Database page (see Figures 1-27 and 1-28, respectively).

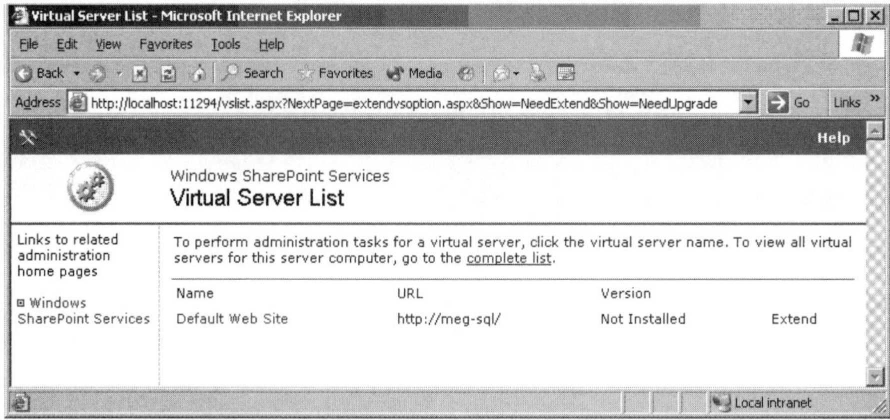

Figure 1-27. *Extending the Default Web Site*

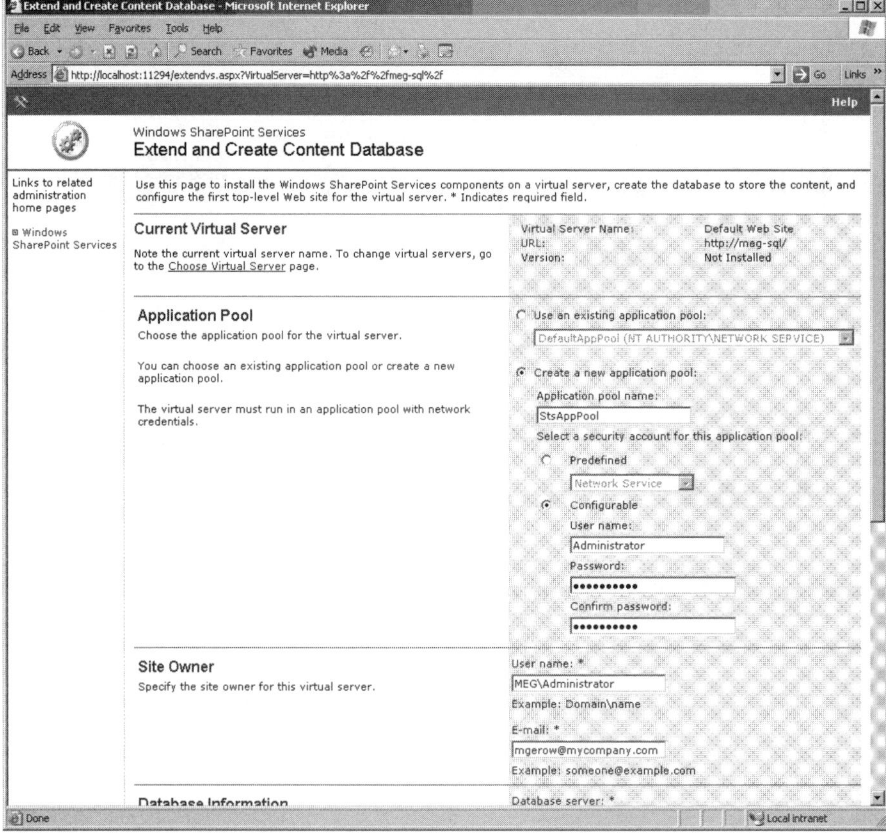

Figure 1-28. *Configuring the Windows SharePoint Services Application Pool*

10. In the Application Pool section of the Extend And Create Content Database page, enter **StsAppPool** in the Application Pool Name field, choose Create A New Application Pool and enter **Administrator** in the User Name field; then enter and confirm the Password (see Figure 1-28).

■ **Note** WSS runs in an IIS 6.0 Application Pool, which determines the Windows account that SharePoint will use and thus the privileges SharePoint will have on the server.

---

11. Enter a valid email address in the Site Owner section; then click OK to extend WSS to the default website.
12. On the Virtual Server Successfully Extended page, click the link following the text New Top-Level Web Site URL: To Display The Top-Level WSS Site For The Virtual Server Just Created.
13. You will see the Template Selection page, asking you to select a SharePoint template for the top-level site. Select a template and click OK.

WSS is now installed and ready for use on your server.

Summary

This chapter covered the installation of additional server components necessary to support a secure and robust SharePoint extranet. Now, even if you are not primarily responsible for installing the production versions of Active Directory, DNS, Certificate Services, or ISA Server 2004 at your firm, you understand how they are configured and the roles they play in providing a complete SharePoint solution. In the next chapter, I'll show you how to configure IIS, WSS, and ISA 2004 to use SSL-to-SSL bridging to provide secure access to WSS.

CHAPTER 2

Configuring ISA Server, WSS, and IIS with SSL

In the previous chapter, I covered the most common SharePoint extranet deployment scenarios, including a discussion of why one in particular was best suited to provide a robust and secure extranet environment. In addition, I provided you with step-by-step instructions for installing a Domain Controller, Certificate Server, Internet Security and Acceleration (ISA) Server, and Windows SharePoint Services (WSS). With those architectural components in place, we're now ready to tackle the configuration of ISA, WSS, Internet Information Server (IIS), and Secure Sockets Layer (SSL).

Before we get started, some review of what we're trying to accomplish is in order. The key technologies that enable our secure extranet are as follows:

- ISA provides a secure firewall that will receive requests for the externally published domain name (for example, `extranet.mycompany.com`), decrypt the requests and examine them for any suspicious content, encrypt the requests again using SSL and pass them on to the WSS server, and receive the responses from WSS and pass them back to the original external requestor.
- SSL provides end-to-end encryption that makes it virtually impossible for a third party to read data transferred between our SharePoint extranet and external users.
- Windows Integrated Security provides encrypted user name/password login, unambiguously identifying the extranet user to SharePoint.

Caution Because the process outlined here involves several servers (Domain Controller, IIS/WSS, ISA) as well as numerous services on each of those servers, the potential for error is great if each step is not completed correctly. Patience is definitely a virtue when configuring your extranet environment, so proceed carefully and be prepared to backtrack if necessary to correct configuration mistakes.

■ **Tip** When first experimenting with ISA, WSS, and SSL configurations, the ability to quickly create/re-create server configurations can prove invaluable. Two products are very helpful here: Microsoft's Virtual PC and VMWare's VMWare Workstation. Both of these products allow you to create multiple virtual machines and save those machines in various states. For example, I created three virtual machines; one serving as a domain controller and certificate authority (CA), one as an IIS/WSS/SQL server, and one running ISA. I then saved a "snapshot" of each of these virtual machines so that I could revert to a known-good-state within a minute or two if a particular configuration didn't work as expected. At the time this book was written, VMWare provided the most options for creating and managing virtual machines.

■ **Tip** For the benefit of those who might not have access to a certificate from a commercial certificate authority such as VeriSign, this chapter includes steps for requesting and generating a certificate with Microsoft Certificate Services (MCS). These steps can be skipped by those who have a commercial certificate without change to the remainder of the steps.

■ **Tip** As long as SSL is employed, Windows Integrated Security is not strictly required. Even though Basic security passes user name and password information between the end user's browser and IIS "in the clear" (that is, in plain text), SSL provides a layer of encryption around the text, making it unreadable by eavesdroppers.

The configuration process has three main parts: 1) configuring IIS and SSL so that WSS will use SSL to receive requests and send responses; 2) configuring ISA 2004 to receive, inspect, forward requests to, and return responses from WSS; and 3) configuring the root WSS `Web.Config` file to use ISA Server as a proxy for outbound Internet traffic. Figure 2-1 shows the overall flow of the ISA/WSS/IIS/SSL configuration process.

The following sections provide detailed instructions for completing all these tasks.

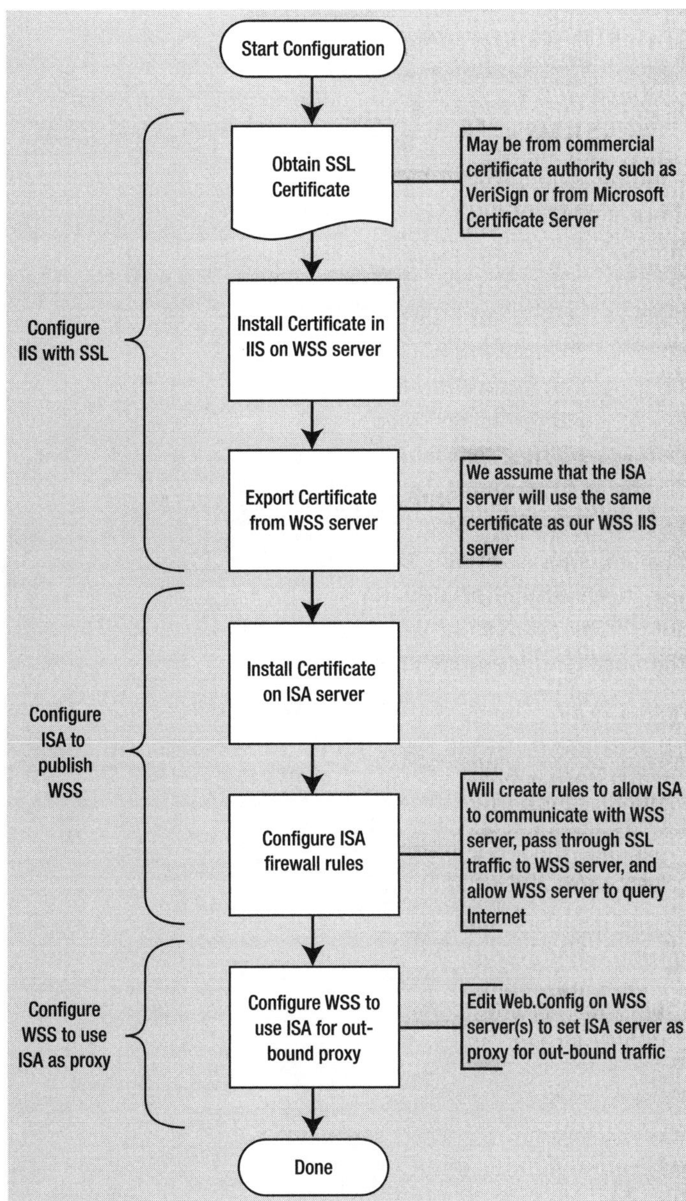

Figure 2-1. *Overall ISA configuration process flow*

Configuring IIS and SSL

The first step is to configure IIS to use an SSL certificate to encrypt information sent between the WSS server and the extranet user's browser. There is nothing in the process that is unique to SharePoint; the same steps are used to secure any IIS website with SSL.

Creating a Certificate Request

First, we use IIS to create a certificate request, which is simply a text file containing some encrypted text that is unique to our server, containing information about our firm and the website we want to secure. This request is then sent to a commercial CA, such as VeriSign or Thawte, or uploaded to an in-house Certificate Server.

■ **Caution** Although you can use a Certificate Server to issue certificates for testing or internal SSL use, for production extranets the use of a commercial certificate authority is preferred because your clients will expect certificates issued by a known and trusted third party.

To create a certificate request, follow these steps:

1. Open the Internet Information Services (IIS) Manager application.
2. Expand the current computer node.
3. Expand the Web Sites node.
4. Right-click on Default Web Site and choose Properties.
5. Select the Directory Security tab, and then click the Server Certificate button, as shown in Figure 2-2.

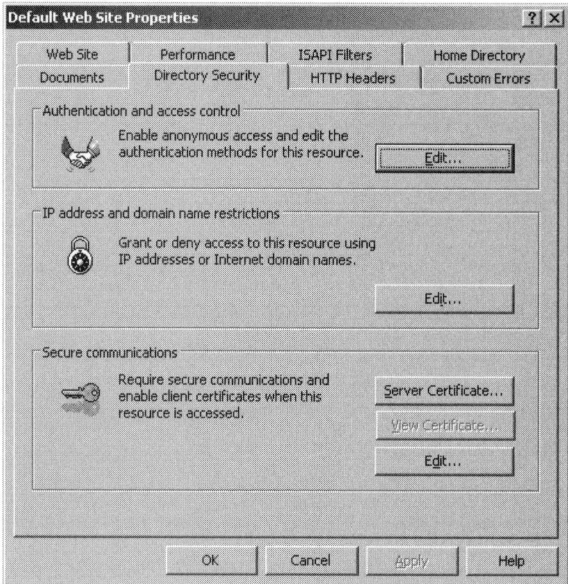

Figure 2-2. *IIS Directory Security dialog box*

6. Click Next to start the IIS Certificate Wizard.

7. Select the Create A New Certificate option and click Next.

8. Select Prepare The Request Now, But Send It Later and click Next.

9. Enter a friendly name for the new certificate, as shown in Figure 2-3. This name should be descriptive enough to help you identify the purpose of this certificate. Click Next.

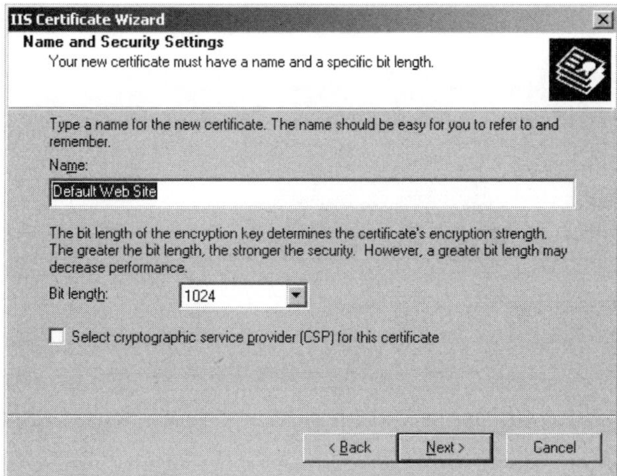

Figure 2-3. *Name And Security Settings dialog box*

10. Enter values for Organization and Organizational Unit in the Organization Information dialog box and then click Next (see Figure 2-4).

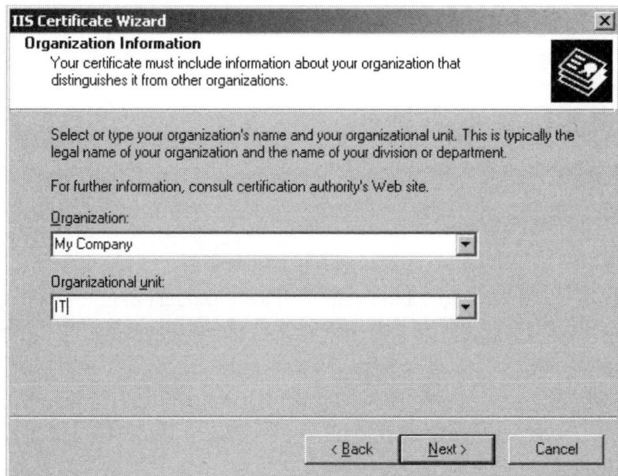

Figure 2-4. *Organization Information dialog box*

11. Enter the Domain Name Service (DNS) name by which external users will know your site into the Common Name field, and click Next (see Figure 2-5).

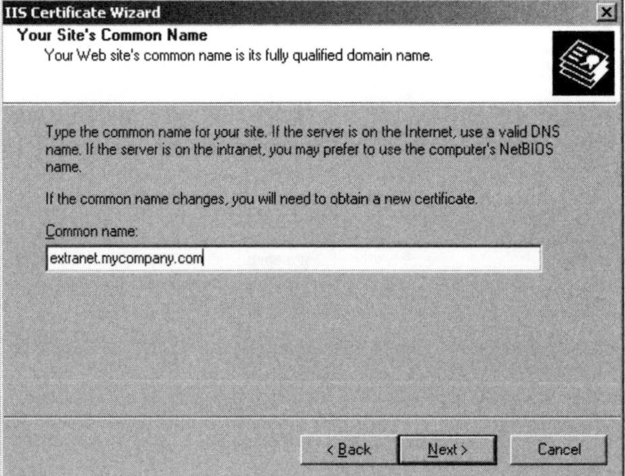

Figure 2-5. *Common Name dialog box*

■ **Caution** The value you enter for Common Name must match the name that external users will enter into their browsers to access your site.

---

12. Enter a Country, State, and City; then click Next.
13. Click Next to accept the default request filename: `c:\certreq.txt`.
14. Review the information on the Request File Summary dialog box, and then click Next.
15. Click Finish to save the request to disk.

Submitting the Certificate Request to Microsoft Certificate Server

---

■ **Note** If you are using a commercial CA you should submit your certificate request to that CA using its instructions. After you receive the certificate from the CA you can proceed to the "Installing the Certificate on IIS" section.

After the certificate request file is created, it must be submitted to a CA, which will then issue an SSL certificate. In the following example, you will use MCS, but for production purposes, you would typically submit the request to a commercial CA such as VeriSign. To submit the request to MCS, follow these steps:

1. When you installed MCS in the previous chapter, you selected the option to include a web form for submitting certificate requests. You will use this form to submit the request you created in the preceding section. To do so, open a browser window on the WSS server and enter the URL `http://extranet-dc/certsrv/`, as shown in Figure 2-6, and press Enter. Click the Request A Certificate link.

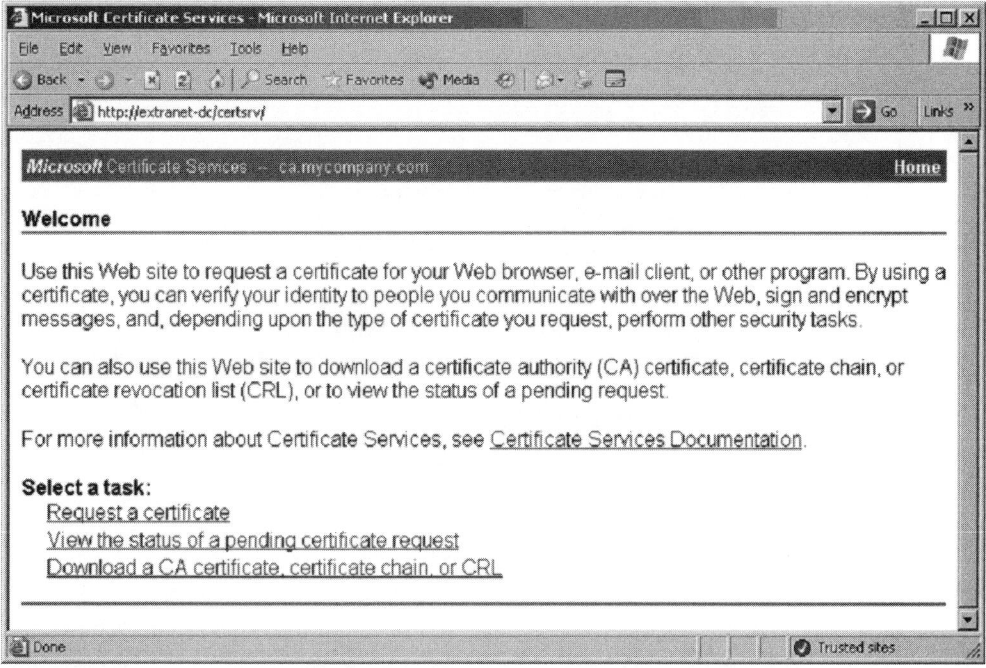

Figure 2-6. *Certificate Server Request page*

2. On the Request A Certificate page, click Advanced Certificate Request.

3. On the Advanced Certificate Request page, click Submit A Certificate Request by using a Base-64-encoded CMC or PKCS #10 file, or submit a renewal request by using a Base-64-encoded PKCS #7 file.

4. Open the file `certreq.txt`, which you created in the preceding section using Windows Notepad, select all the text in the file, and copy it to the clipboard using Ctrl-A+Ctrl-C.

5. Paste the selected text into the Saved Request text box on the Submit A Certificate Request Or Renewal Request page.

6. Select Web Server from the Certificate Template drop-down list and then click Submit, as shown in Figure 2-7.

7. On the Certificate Issued page, select DER Encoded and click the Download Certificate link, accept the default certificate name, and click Save.

The certificate is now ready to install on the IIS server.

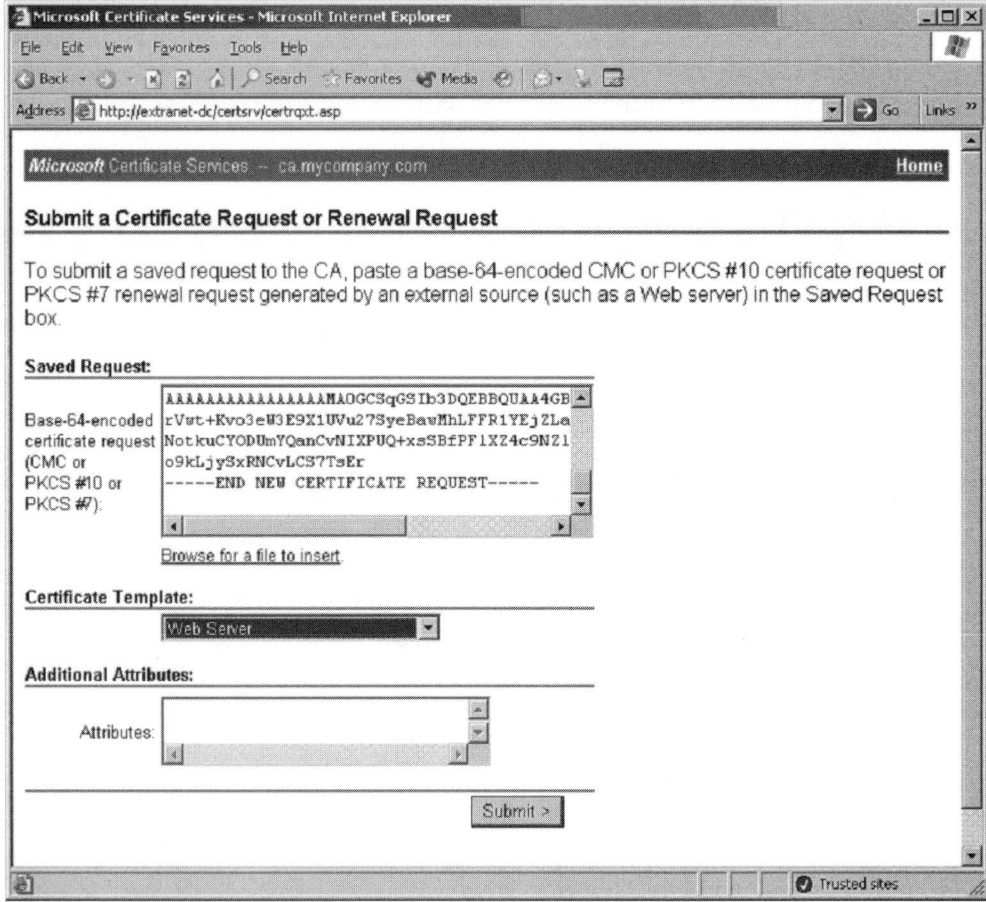

Figure 2-7. *Completed Certificate Request page on Certificate Server*

Installing the Certificate on IIS

Now that you have a valid SSL certificate, you can go back to IIS to complete the installation process. At the end of the following steps, IIS will be configured to send and receive information securely using SSL. To install the SSL certificate follow these steps:

1. Open the Internet Information Services (IIS) Manager application.
2. Expand the Current Computer node.
3. Expand the Web Sites node.
4. Right-click Default Web Site and choose Properties.

5. Select the Directory Security tab and then click the Server Certificate button.
6. Select Process The Pending Request, install the Certification option, and then click Next.
7. Enter or browse to the certificate file path and name that you created in the previous section and then click Next.
8. Accept port 443 (the default SSL port) and click Next.
9. Click Next after reviewing the Certificate Summary.
10. Click Finish.
11. To ensure that the certificate was correctly installed, click the View Certificate button. The General tab, as shown in Figure 2-8, should appear as follows:

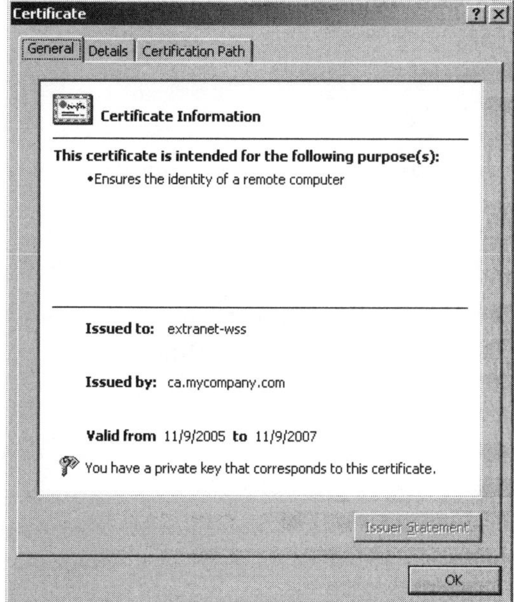

Figure 2-8. *Certificate Information for correctly installed certificate*

12. Click the Certification Path tab and confirm that the phrase This Certificate Is OK. appears in the Certificate Status box (see Figure 2-9).

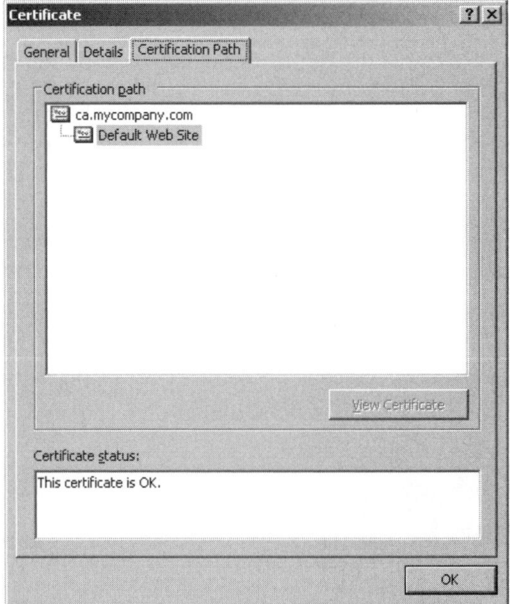

Figure 2-9. *Certificate Path information for correctly installed certificate*

13. Return to the Properties page for the Default Web Site, click the Directory Security tab, and then click the Edit button to view the Secure Communications dialog box.
14. Select Require Secure Channel (SSL) and Require 128-Bit Encryption, and then click OK. This will tell IIS to accept only `https:` requests for this website.
15. Select Accept Client Certificates.

■ **Note** As of this writing, the version of Microsoft Internet Explorer that supports 128-Bit encryption is available only in the United States (including territories, possessions, and dependencies) or Canada. If some or all of your users will access the extranet from outside these locations, you should not check the Require 128-Bit Encryption box.

Testing WSS and SSL

We should now be able to access our WSS site over a secure https connection. To do so, open a browser window and enter the address `https://extranet-wss/default.aspx`. If you chose to use MCS rather than a commercial CA to provide the SSL certificate, you might see a Security Alert dialog box, as shown in Figure 2-10.

Figure 2-10. *Browser security alert for untrusted certificate authority*

■ **Note** You can eliminate the previous security alert by importing the Trusted Root Certificate Authorities certificate from the MCS (extranet-dc in our example) into the certificate store of the computer from which you are browsing. You should not see this message if you use a certificate from a commercial CA because your local certificate store already has a certificate for that entity.

After acknowledging any security alerts, you should see the page shown in Figure 2-11.

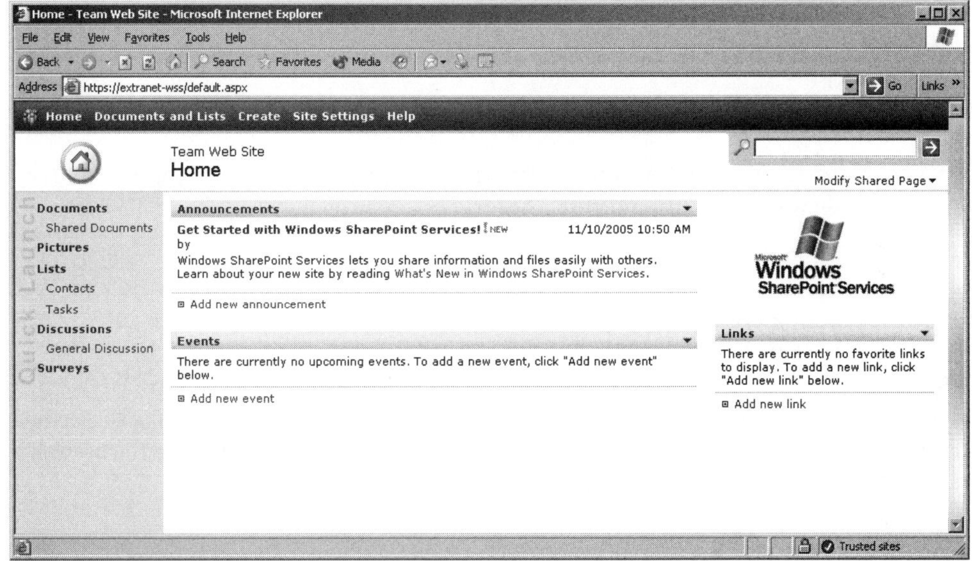

Figure 2-11. *WSS top-level site displayed using https:*

To verify that only secure connections will be permitted to the WSS site, change the address in the browser to `http://extranet-wss/default.aspx` and press Enter. You should see an error page similar to the one shown in Figure 2-12, indicating that the page must be viewed over a secure channel.

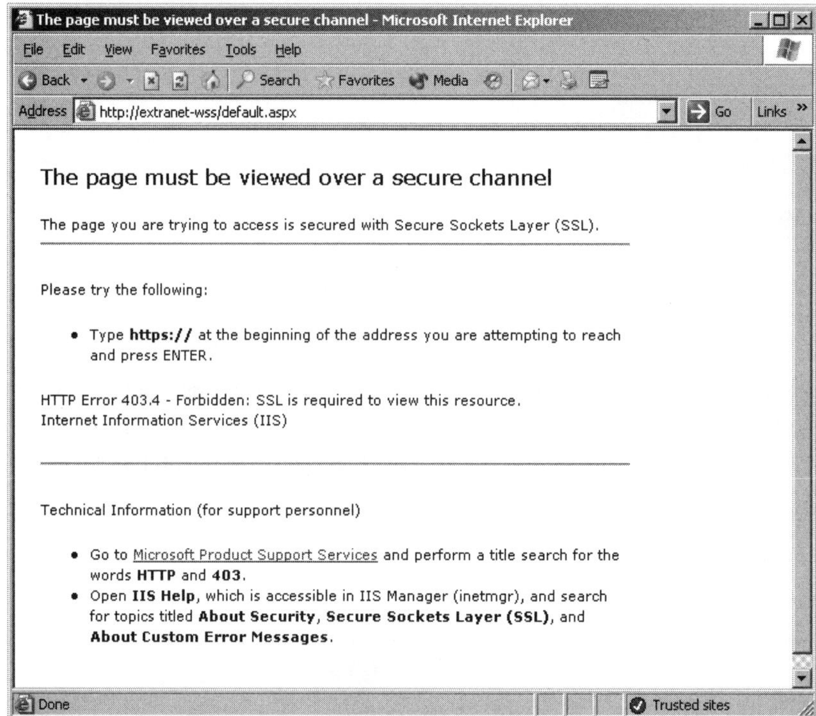

Figure 2-12. *Error page when attempting to display top-level site using http:*

We have now secured our WSS site so that extranet users must access it using a secure session. Next, I'll show you how to configure ISA Server as a firewall between external users and the WSS server.

Configuring ISA and WSS

ISA Server 2004 has two primary functions: 1) it serves as a firewall between internal systems and the Internet and 2) it caches content at the ISA Server to offload work from the IIS server, thus improving performance, scalability, and end user experience. We'll focus on the firewall aspect of ISA and specifically how to configure ISA to publish a WSS site.

Exporting the Certificate from IIS

Although we could use an SSL certificate on the ISA Server different than that on the WSS server, for simplicity I will use the same certificate on both. Therefore, we need to export a copy of the certificate we just installed on the IIS/WSS server so that it can be imported into the ISA Server's certificate store.

■ **Caution** Although you can install a different certificate on the ISA Server than on the WSS server(s), if there will be multiple WSS servers in a server farm, all must have the same SSL certificate installed.

To export the SSL certificate, follow these steps:

1. On the IIS/WSS server (extranet-wss) choose Start ➤ Run and enter **MMC** to open the Microsoft Management Console (MMC).
2. In the MMC, choose Add/Remove Snap-in from the File menu.
3. In the Add/Remove Snap-in dialog box, choose the Standalone tab, and then click the Add button.
4. Select Certificates from the list of available snap-ins and click Add.
5. Choose Computer Account and click Next.
6. Click Finish.
7. In the Console tree, navigate to Console Root ➤ Certificates (Local Computer) ➤ Personal ➤ Certificates and right-click extranet-wss (partially obscured by the pop-up menus in the following figure), as shown in Figure 2-13.
8. Choose All Tasks ➤ Export.

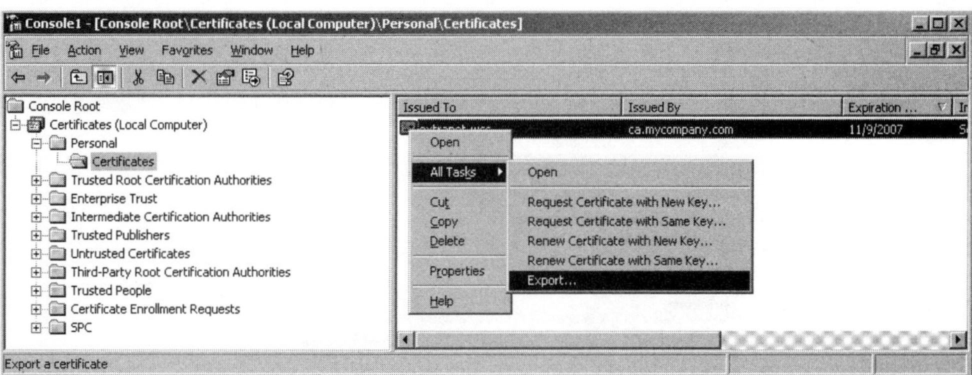

Figure 2-13. *Exporting a certificate from the WSS server*

9. Click Next in the Certificate Export Wizard dialog box.
10. Select Yes, Export The Private Key and click Next.
11. Select Personal Information Exchange – PKCS #12 (.PFX) and click Next.
12. Enter and confirm a password for the exported certificate file and click Next.

13. Provide a name for the export file and click Next.

14. Click Finish to complete the export; you should receive a confirmation that the certificate was successfully exported.

A copy of the SSL certificate is now ready to be imported by the extranet-ISA Server.

Importing the Certificate into ISA

The next step is to install the certificate on the server running ISA Server 2004, which in our example is extranet-isa. Once it's installed in the certificate store on that computer, ISA will use it to publish the WSS site. To import the certificate, we follow these steps on the extranet-isa server:

1. On the IIS/WSS server (extranet-isa) choose Start ➤ Run and enter **MMC** to open the MMC.

2. In the MMC, choose Add/Remove Snap-in from the File menu.

3. In the Add/Remove Snap-in dialog box, choose the Standalone tab and then click the Add button.

4. Select Certificates from the list of available snap-ins and click Add.

5. Choose Computer Account and click Next.

6. Click Finish.

7. In the Console tree navigate to Console Root ➤ Certificates (Local Computer) ➤ Personal and then right-click Certificates.

8. Choose All Tasks ➤ Import, as shown in Figure 2-14.

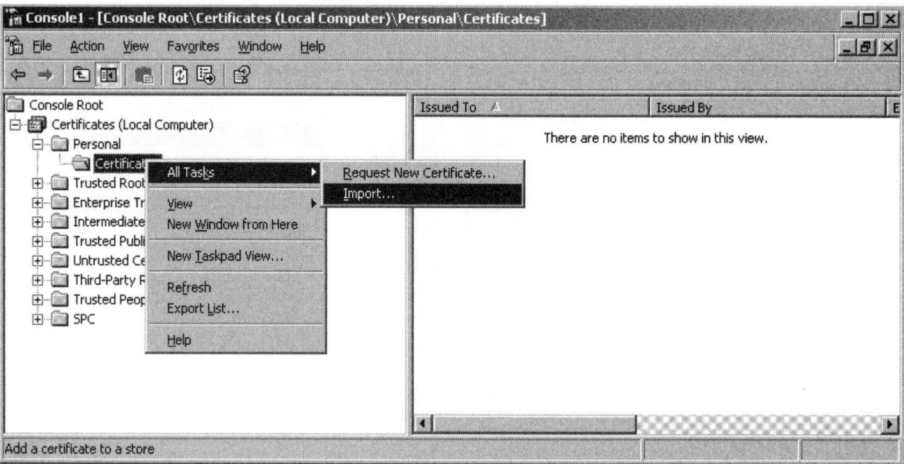

Figure 2-14. *Importing the certificate into the ISA Server's certificate store*

9. Click Next in the Certificate Import Wizard dialog box.
10. In the File To Import dialog box, enter the path and name of the certificate file exported in the preceding section (in our example: `\\extranet-wss\c$\cert.pfx`) and click Next.
11. In the Password dialog box, enter the password assigned to the certificate export file, select the option Mark This Key As Exportable, and click Next.
12. In the Certificate Store dialog box, leave the defaults of Place All Certificates In The Following Store and Personal and then click Next.
13. Click Finish to import the certificate. You should receive confirmation that the import was successful.

    The certificate should now appear in the Console tree in the Console Root/Certificates/Personal/Certificates folder, as shown in Figure 2-15.

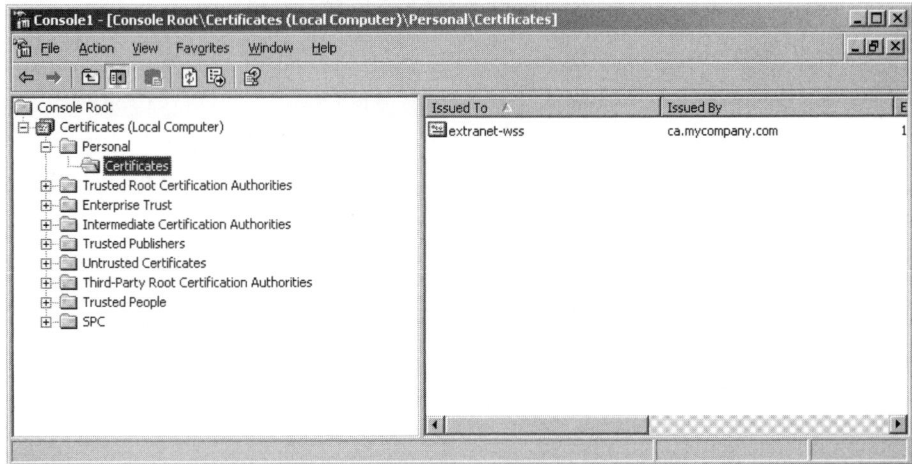

Figure 2-15. *Imported certificate shown in ISA Server certificate store*

14. Right-click the certificate extranet-wss, select the Properties, go to the Certificate Path tab, and confirm that the phrase This Certificate Is OK. appears at the bottom of the dialog box.

The certificate is now correctly installed and ready for use by ISA Server 2004.

Publishing a Secure WSS Site

We're now ready to create firewall rules in ISA 2004. We will create rules to allow ISA to respond to external requests for pages hosted on the WSS server and to allow ISA to communicate with the WSS server. To create these rules, follow these steps:

1. Open the ISA Server Management application.
2. Navigate to Arrays ➤ EXTRANET-ISA ➤ Firewall Policy (EXTRANET-ISA) in the left object tree.

3. Right-click the Firewall Policy node and choose New ➤ Secure Web Server Publishing Rule, as shown in Figure 2-16.

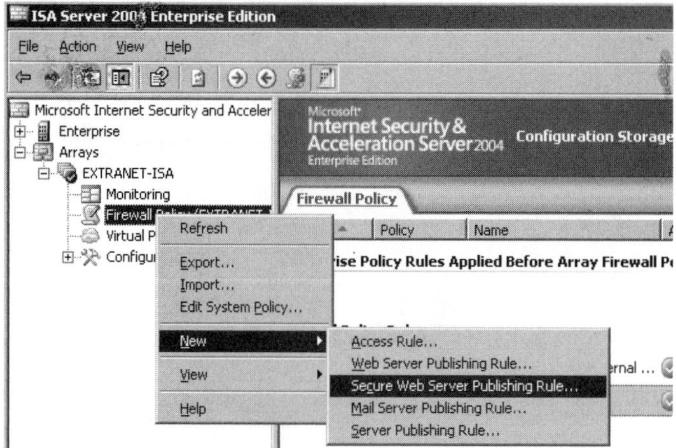

Figure 2-16. *Creating a new Secure Web Server Publishing rule in ISA 2004*

4. Enter Publish Extranet Sites (or some other descriptive name) for the new rule and click Next.

5. In the Publishing Mode dialog box select SSL Bridging and click Next.

6. Select Allow and click Next.

7. In the Bridging Mode dialog box, be sure to select Secure Connection To Clients And Web Server.

■ **Caution** The only option supported by SharePoint is Secure Connection To Clients And Web server, which is also known as SSL-to-SSL bridging. The reason is that SharePoint uses absolute URLs on many pages, and thus both the page requested by the end user and the page rendered by SharePoint must have the same URL. Either of the other two options would result in some pages or page components failing to render.

---

8. Enter the name or IP address of the WSS server (or DNS or cluster IP address if a multi-server web farm is being used).

9. Enter /* for the Path to ensure that all paths under the root on the WSS server will be available and then click Next.

10. In the Public Name Details dialog box, select Any Domain Name from the Accept Requests For field and click Next.
11. In the Select Web Listener dialog box, click New to create a new web listener.
12. Enter a descriptive name for the new web listener and click Next.
13. In the IP Addresses dialog box, select External, Internal and Local Host; then click Next.
14. In the Port Specification dialog box, de-select Enable HTTP and select Enable SSL (retaining the default port 443) so that ISA listens only for `https` requests for the WSS server (see Figure 2-17).

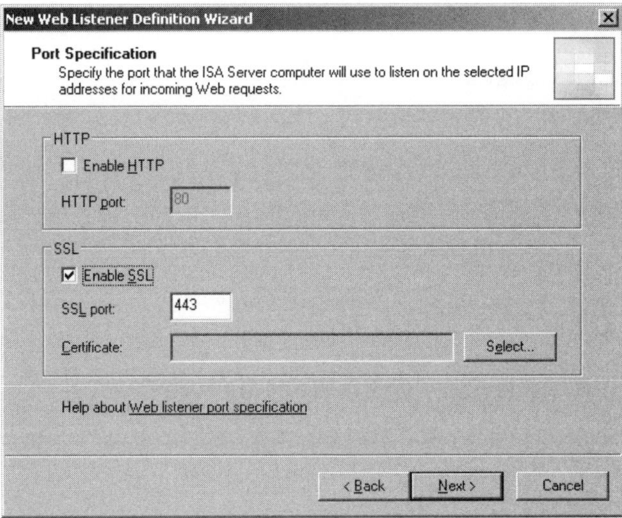

Figure 2-17. *Setting the port specification*

15. Click the Select button to select the certificate that was installed on this server earlier.
16. Highlight the extranet-wss certificate and click OK.
17. Click Next and Finish to complete the web listener configuration.
18. In the User Sets dialog box, accept the default of All Users and click Next.
19. Click Finish to complete the SSL web-publishing rule.

20. Click the Apply button at the top of the Firewall Policy window to save the new rule, as shown in Figure 2-18.

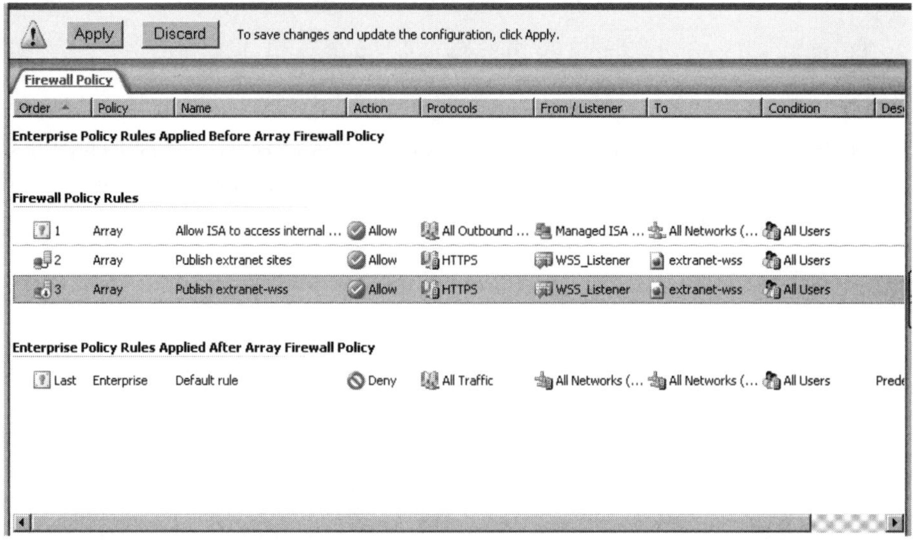

Figure 2-18. *Applying the new firewall policy*

Providing an Access Rule from ISA to WSS Server

Next, we need to allow the ISA Server to communicate with the WSS server. We do this with an access rule as follows:

1. Navigate to Arrays ➤ EXTRANET-ISA ➤ Firewall Policy (EXTRANET-ISA) in the left object tree.
2. Right-click the Firewall Policy node and choose New ➤ Access Rule.
3. Provide a descriptive name such as Allow ISA To Access Internal Servers and click Next.
4. Select Allow and click Next.
5. In the Protocols dialog box, select All Outbound Traffic from the This Rule Applies To List and click Next.
6. In the Access Rule Sources dialog box, click Add and select Computer Sets/Managed ISA Server Computers; then click Add, Close, and Next.
7. In the Access Rule Destinations dialog box, click Add and select Network Sets/All Networks (and Local Host); then click Add, Close, and Next.
8. In the User Sets dialog box, select the default of All Users and click Next; then click Finish.

Enabling WSS to Access the Internet

In some instances, WSS will need to access the Internet. For example, a web part that needs to query an external Really Simple Syndication (RSS) source for news, or the Microsoft stock quote web part, will attempt to execute a query against external URLs. Unless ISA Server is configured to allow WSS to access the Internet, these web parts will fail. To enable WSS to access the Internet, follow these steps:

1. Navigate to Arrays ➤ EXTRANET-ISA ➤ Firewall Policy (EXTRANET-ISA) in the left object tree.
2. Right-click the Firewall Policy node and choose New ➤ Access Rule.
3. Provide a descriptive name such as **Allow WSS To Access Internet** and click Next.
4. Select Allow and click Next.
5. In the Protocols dialog box, select Selected Protocols from the This Rule Applies To list, click the Add button, open the Common Protocols node, add HTTP and HTTPS to the list of selected protocols, and then click Next.
6. In the Access Rule Sources dialog box, click Add and select New ➤ Computer Set.
7. Type a descriptive name such as **WSS Servers Set**, click Add to add an IP range, enter **WSS Servers** for the name, and type the start and end range for the WSS extranet server(s) (for example, 192.168.1.151 – 192.168.1.152), and click OK twice.
8. Open the Computer Sets node; highlight the set you just added (for example, WSS Servers Set) and click Add, Close, and then Next.
9. In the Access Rule Destinations dialog box, click Add and select Network Sets/All Networks (and Local Host); then click Add, Close, and Next.
10. In the User Sets dialog box, select the default of All Users and click Next; then click Finish.

We also need to modify the `Web.Config` file in the root WSS folder (typically `c:\inetpub\wwwroot`) on each WSS server. This tells WSS what proxy server to use for outbound traffic. To accomplish this, open the `Web.Config` file, and immediately after the `</SharePoint>` tag place the following text:

```
<system.net>
  <defaultProxy>
    <proxy proxyaddress="http://extranet-isa:8080" bypassonlocal="true" />
  </defaultProxy>
</system.net>
```

■ **Caution** Be sure to make this change on *all* WSS servers in a server farm.

Testing ISA Server and Our WSS Site

If we completed all steps correctly, you should be able to open a browser window, type `https://extranet-isa/default.aspx`, and see the WSS site appear.

■ **Tip** If `http://extranet-isa/default.aspx` does not resolve to the WSS site, open a command prompt window on the extranet-isa server and enter the command **ping extranet-wss** to verify that the ISA Server can access the WSS server. If ISA cannot ping the WSS server, the most common cause is that the rule to allow ISA to access other computers on the network might be faulty. Go back and verify all steps for that rule.

Summary

In this chapter, you learned to navigate the myriad steps to configure IIS, ISA, WSS, and SSL to provide secure access to Windows SharePoint Services for your extranet users. Although no single step of the process is complex, the large number of steps leaves plenty of room for errors. The best defense against these errors is to follow the preceding directions carefully and to verify the configuration at key milestones, such as when the certificate is installed on IIS or ISA.

Architecting your SharePoint extranet solution using ISA Server with SSL-to-SSL bridging provides the security that both you and your clients need and expect to protect the documents and data that will be hosted on the extranet.

CHAPTER 3

Windows SharePoint Services Backup and Recovery Techniques

The last thing you want to be doing after a systems failure is scrambling to recover without a well-thought-out and reliable backup and recovery plan. This is especially important when clients are involved because how quickly service is restored will reflect on all aspects of your business's reputation.

Unfortunately, configuring database and file backups is like planning for retirement or exercising; it's easy to put off until later, but doing so can have dire consequences! In this chapter, I'll discuss four complementary backup/recovery techniques, each one providing insurance against some, but not all, risks to your SharePoint installation. Because no single technique covers all cases, you will most likely use each of them at different times to provide a robust backup and recovery strategy. The techniques I'll cover are:

- SQL Server Backup/Restore to recover an entire server
- STSADM Backup/Restore to recover a site collection or part of site collection
- SMIGRATE Backup/Restore to transfer a site to another location
- VSS/File System Backup/Restore to recover or roll back changes to configuration files

Having these backup/recovery strategies in place won't eliminate the possibility of systems failure or human error, but will enable you to recover as quickly as possible should an outage occur.

Configuring SQL Server Backup

Creating regular SQL Server backups of your SharePoint databases will allow you to quickly recover in case of a systems failure; that is, if you need to rebuild the SharePoint database server from the ground up. In this section, we'll cover the steps required to configure SQL Server backups for your SharePoint databases and how to restore those databases. This technique is composed of the following tasks:

1. Identify the names of the configuration and all content databases in your Windows SharePoint Services installation.
2. Use the SQL Server Enterprise Manager to schedule periodic backups to another volume or file server.
3. Periodically back up the SQL Server backup files to tape or other long-term storage medium.

Identify the Names of Configuration and Content Databases

In a default Windows SharePoint Services (WSS) installation, the configuration database will be named sts_config.mdf. The content databases will be named STS_servername_1.mdf, STS_servername_<n>.mdf, and so on.

■Note You can change the names of the configuration and content databases during WSS installation, so your database names may differ.

Figure 3-1 shows SQL Server Enterprise Manager for a WSS installation with a configuration database called EXTRANET and one content database called `STS_extwss01_1`.

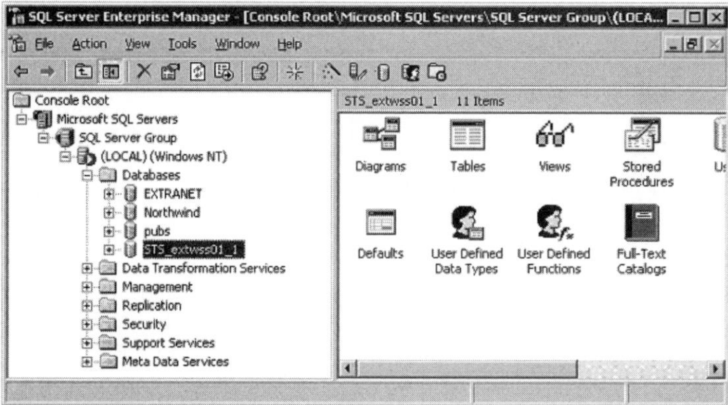

Figure 3-1. *SQL Enterprise Manager displaying databases to back up*

■Note The term (Windows NT) can be misleading to those unfamiliar with SQL Server Enterprise Manager. This text will appear next to *any* Windows SQL Server instance, regardless of the version. In all examples in this book, Windows 2003 Server was used.

Schedule Periodic Backups Using SQL Server Enterprise Manager

To schedule periodic backups of the WSS configuration and content databases you use the SQL Server Enterprise Manager backup feature. To access this feature, follow these steps:

1. Right-click one of the databases to be backed up, choose All Tasks and then Backup Database.

2. In the SQL Server Backup dialog box's Destination section, click the Add button to specify the location and filename of the backup file. Figure 3-2 shows the completed SQL Server Backup dialog box.

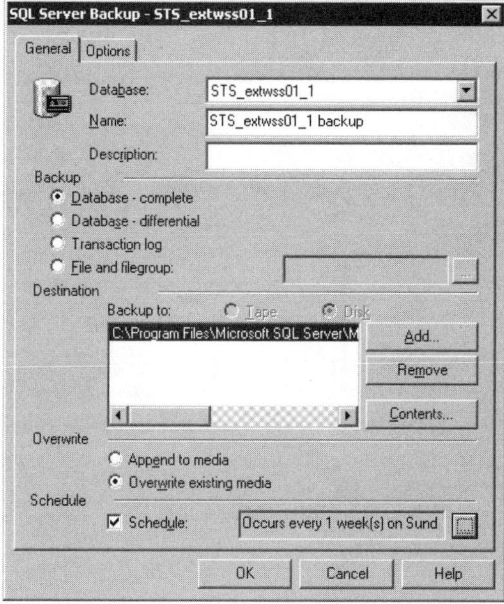

Figure 3-2. *Completed SQL Server Backup dialog box*

■ **Caution** You should specify a backup location that is on a different physical drive and ideally on a different server than your WSS databases. Such a location will ensure against the risk of the physical disk drive containing the WSS databases being unrecoverable due to a hardware malfunction and eliminate the need to move the backup drive to a functioning server in the case of a failed WSS server.

---

3. In the Select Backup Destination dialog box, enter the location and filename; then click OK.

4. In the SQL Server Backup dialog box's Overwrite section, choose Overwrite Existing Media.

5. In the Schedule section of that dialog box, check the Schedule option box and then click the ... button to specify the backup schedule. Click OK in the Edit Schedule dialog box when you're done with schedule modifications.

■ **Note** If a warning message appears telling you that the SQL Server Agent Is Stopped On Target Server, you need to configure the server to automatically start it when the server boots up; otherwise, SQL Server backup will not run, and your backup files will not be created. Figure 3-3 shows the SQL Server Properties dialog box with the Autostart SQL Server Agent option selected.

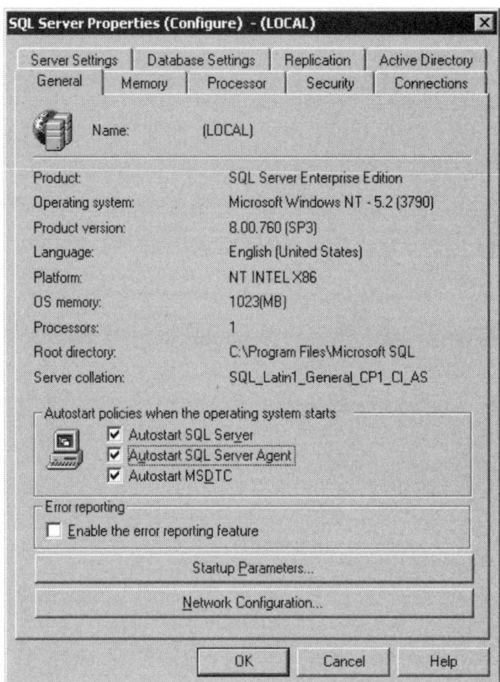

Figure 3-3. *Setting SQL Server Agent to Autostart*

6. Verify that the backup jobs have been successfully scheduled by opening the Management ➤ SQL Server Agent ➤ Jobs window for the SQL Server hosting your WSS databases. Figure 3-4 shows the backup jobs for my EXTRANET and STS_extwss01 databases.

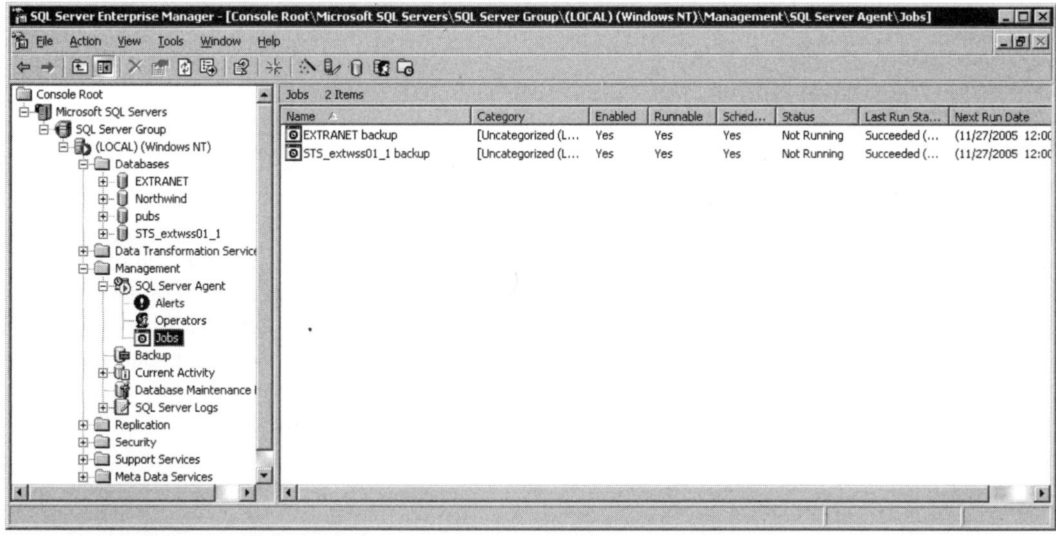

Figure 3-4. *Scheduled backup jobs in SQL Server Enterprise Manager*

Back Up SQL Server Backup Files to Tape

The final task is to periodically transfer the SQL Server backup files to tape or other offsite storage media. This will protect against a catastrophic disaster such as a building fire, flood, earthquake (. . . fill in your favorite disaster here) that might destroy your datacenter or otherwise make your online backups and servers unavailable.

Restoring from a SQL Backup

To restore a server or server farm from a database backup, do the following:

1. Create a virtual server on IIS, which will be used to host WSS.
2. Restore the backups to a SQL Server instance.
3. On IIS, create an application pool under which WSS will run.

Caution The domain account you use for the application pool should be a member of the Security Administrators, Process Administrators, and Database Creators roles on the SQL Server that will host the restored databases.

---

4. Install WSS on a server and then connect to the restored configuration database.

5. Set the default content database server to the restored database server.
6. Extend the Internet Information Server (IIS) virtual server using the Extend And Map To Another Virtual Server option on the Extend Virtual Server page.

Using STSADM Backup

Sometimes you need to restore a single site rather than the entire database, which might be the case if, for example, a user accidentally deleted a critical document library or list. In this section, we'll cover how to create individual site backups so that you can recover a single site quickly. Although only top-level websites can be backed up using the `STSADM Backup` command, the backup file will include any subsites of that site. If you need to back up or restore a single subsite, you can use the SMIGRATE utility, covered later in this chapter.

■ **Caution** You must be a member of the server computer's administrators group or a member of the SharePoint administrators group to be able to back up or restore a site using the STSADM utility.

To perform a backup of a site using STSADM, you would use syntax similar to the following:

```
Stsadm.exe -o backup -url http://extwss01/clients/acme -filename acme.dat
```

■ **Note** The `STSADM` command can be found in the `C:\Program Files\Common Files\Microsoft Shared\web server extensions\60\BIN` folder in a typical WSS installation.

It's often convenient to place all sites of a particular type under a given path. For example, all client sites might be created under the path `http://extwss01/clients/`, as in the previous example. Placing them together makes it easy to find and back up all sites of that type. To enable this, you use the Define Managed Paths page that can be accessed from the SharePoint Central Administration application. This page can be a bit difficult to find because it's buried three levels down in the menu structure. To get there, select Configure Virtual Server Settings from the main page of the SharePoint Central Administration application, then select Default Web Site (or whichever virtual server for which you wish to add a managed path), and finally select Define Managed Paths from the Virtual Server Settings page. Figure 3-5 shows the Define Managed Paths page.

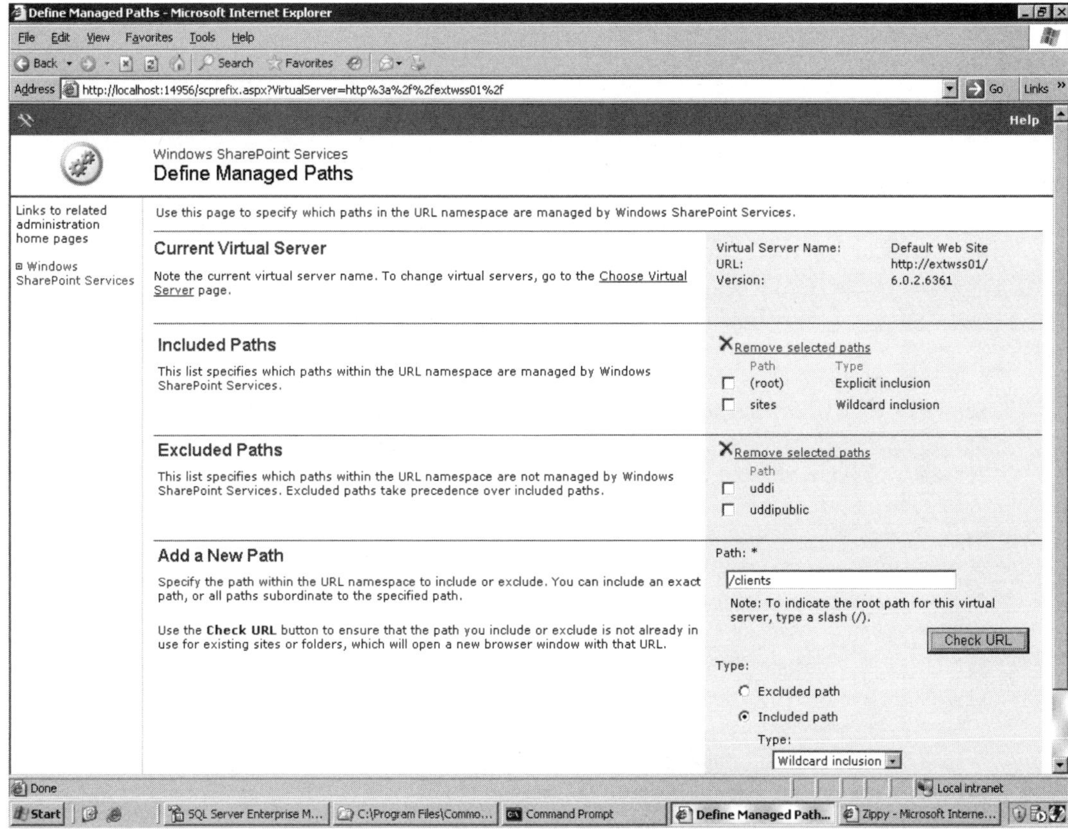

Figure 3-5. *Define Managed Paths page*

Automating STSADM Backup

One of the advantages of placing all sites you want to back up under a specific managed path is that it makes automating the process of backing up a collection of sites possible. In this section, we'll cover the use of a simple Windows script to create backup files for all sites in a given path. The script, shown in Listing 3-1, does the following:

1. Defines the location of the `STSADM` command.
2. Defines the location in which the backup files will be written.
3. Deletes any previous backup files.
4. Gets a list of all top-level sites on the specified WSS server.
5. Iterates through the list of top-level sites, creating a backup of each one.

Listing 3-1. *Windows Script to Automate WSS Site Backups*

```
' Back up the WSS sites...
' -----------------
Const STSADM_PATH =   _
  "C:\Program Files\Common Files\Microsoft Shared\" & _
  "web server extensions\60\BIN\stsadm"
Dim objFso, objFolder, objFiles, objFile, objShell, objExec
Dim strResult, objXml, objSc, objUrl, strUrl
Dim strFileName, strCmd
Set objFso = CreateObject("Scripting.FileSystemObject")

' Delete all backup files currently present in the backup folder.
Set objFolder = objFso.GetFolder("\\extwss01\WSSBackups\")
Set objFiles = objFolder.Files
For Each objFile in objFiles
  objFile.Delete(True)
Next

' Retrieve all site collections in XML format.
Set objShell = CreateObject("WScript.Shell")
Set objExec = objShell.Exec(STSADM_PATH & " -o enumsites -url http://extwss01/")
strResult = objExec.StdOut.ReadAll

' Load XML in DOM document so it can be processed.
Set objXml = CreateObject("MSXML2.DOMDocument")
objXml.LoadXML(strResult)

' Loop through each site collection and call stsadm.exe to make a backup.
For Each objSc in objXml.DocumentElement.ChildNodes
    strUrl = objSc.Attributes.GetNamedItem("Url").Text
    strFileName = "\\extwss01\WSSBackups\" & _
       Replace(Replace(strUrl, "http://", ""), "/", "_") & _
       ".bak"
    strCmd = STSADM_PATH & " -o backup -url """ + strUrl & _
       + """ -filename """ + strFileName + """"
    objShell.Exec(strCmd)
Next

WScript.Echo "WSS Backup complete."
```

Note As with your SQL Server backup, these backup files should be copied to tape periodically for disaster-recovery purposes.

Restoring from an STSADM Backup

There are three options for restoring sites from an STSADM backup file:

- *Option 1.* Restore over an existing site. For example, to restore a site named smithco, you might use the following command:

```
stsadm -o restore -url http://extwss01/clients/smithco -filename ➥
\\extwss01\WSSBackups\extwss01_clients_smithco.bak -overwrite
```

■ **Caution** When you restore over an existing site, all data for the original site is destroyed and cannot be recovered.

- *Option 2.* Restore a site to a new site on the same server. This is the option recommended by Microsoft because it allows you to restore the backup to a second site, copy just the needed content back to the original site. The following command can be used to restore the smithco client site to a new site named smithco2:

```
stsadm -o restore -url http://extwss01/clients/smithco2 ➥
    -filename \\extwss01\WSSBackups\extwss01_clients_smithco.bak
```

- *Option 3.* Restore a site to a separate server, with a separate installation of WSS that uses a copy of the original server's configuration database. This option, which is a variation of Option 1, is appropriate if the original server is unavailable, or if you don't want to restore to the same WSS installation for some other reason.

Using the SPBackup Utility to Automate STSADM Backups

One useful utility that can be found on Microsoft's SharePoint Products and Technologies Resource Kit CD is `SPBackup.exe`. This utility wraps the `STSADM Backup` command, providing the ability to create backups of sites that have been modified in the past day or week. This ability can dramatically reduce the time needed to run regular backups of large WSS installations.

■ **Note** The SharePoint Products and Technologies Resource Kit can be obtained from Microsoft Press or from various other book resellers.

The SPBackup utility writes a batch file containing one `STSADM Backup` command for each site to be backed up. That batch file can then be executed to produce the actual backup files. To combine these two operations, a batch file similar to the following (`Daily.bat`) can be used:

Listing 3-2. *Contents of* `Daily.bat`

```
REM ———————————————————————————————
REM - Back up all sites on the current server that have been changed
REM - in the past day.
REM ———————————————————————————————
spbackup -d -f bkup.bat
CALL bkup.bat
MOVE /Y *.spb \\extwss01\WSSBackups
```

Unfortunately, the SPBackup utility has no option to place the backup files anywhere other than the `C:\Program Files\Common Files\Microsoft Shared\web server extensions\60\BIN` folder, so the third line of the batch file shown in Listing 3-2 copies all the backups to the desired backup folder.

SMIGRATE Backup/Restore

The SharePoint Migration (SMIGRATE) utility can be used to back up and restore an individual site or subsite. FrontPage 2003 uses this same utility when it copies a site from one location to another.

■ **Caution** Unlike SQL Server backups of the content and configuration databases or the STSADM Backup utility, SMIGRATE is not *full fidelity*. That is, some customizations or settings will not be written to the backup and thus will not be restored. Specifically, security, personalization, and global administration settings will not be retained. For many uses, such as creating a copy of an existing site as a starting point for further customizations or to recover a single document that a user has inadvertently deleted, this may not be a problem. However, SQL Server and STSADM Backup are better options for creating backups to be used to recover from a system failure.

One advantage of SMIGRATE over STSADM Backup is that it can be run from any computer that has access to the WSS site, whereas STSADM Backup can be run from the server hosting the WSS site being backed up. The following command creates a backup of the acme client site to the file `acme.fwp` using the SMIGRATE utility:

```
smigrate -w http://extwss01/clients/acme -f acme.fwp -y -u extranet\mgerow -pw *
```

The SMIGRATE utility's parameters are shown in Table 3-1.

Table 3-1. *SMIGRATE Utility Parameters*

Parameter	Purpose	Example
-w	URL of website to be backed up.	http://extwss01/clients/acme
-f	Name of file to write backup to.	acme.fwp
-r	Flag indicating that this is a restore of a previously created backup.	none
-e	Flag indicating that subsites should not be backed up.	none
-y	Flag indicating that previous backup file (if any) can be overwritten.	none
-u	User name of domain user with sufficient rights to back up this site.	extranet\mgerow
-pw	Password of domain user with sufficient rights to back up this site. An "*" will cause SMIGRATE to prompt for the password at execution time.	*

The following command could be used to restore the acme site using the backup file `acme.fwp`:

```
smigrate -r -w http://extwss01/clients/acme -f acme.fwp -u extranet\mgerow -pw *
```

■ **Note** If you want to restore your backup to a new site, you must first create a new blank site using the `STSADM Createsite` command. You should not assign a site template to the new site because SMIGRATE can only restore to existing sites that have either the same template as the site originally backed up or no template at all. The following two commands will create a new blank site and restores the acme site content to it:

```
stsadm -o createsite -url http://extwss01/clients/acme_new
    -ownerlogin extranet\mgerow -owneremail mgerow@fenwick.com
smigrate -r -w http://extwss01/clients/acme_new -f acme.fwp -u extranet\mgerow -pw *
```

Backing Up SharePoint's Configuration Files

Many of the customizations you'll make to SharePoint will be stored in its configuration files on disk rather than in the configuration or content databases. Site templates, `.aspx` files, style sheets, and many other components of SharePoint are contained in subfolders of the `C:\Program Files\Common Files\Microsoft shared\web server extensions\60\templates` folder. If you make changes or additions to any of these configuration files you'll want to back them up as well.

■ **Caution** Recovered sites that are based on custom site templates or other customizations will fail to open unless the custom template and configuration files are also restored.

Using Visual SourceSafe (VSS) for Backup

Although a file system backup of the `C:\Program Files\Common Files\Microsoft Shared\web server extensions\60\templates` folder and all its subfolders is sufficient to allow recovery of a WSS configuration, you will gain many advantages by using some form of source control to manage your customizations and additions to the SharePoint configuration files. Specifically, a tool such as Microsoft's Visual SourceSafe (VSS) provides many benefits over a simple file system backup (see Table 3-2).

Table 3-2. *VSS Benefits*

Feature	Benefit
Versioning	Allows you to track each change made to a file. You can then restore any previous version, back to and including the original, out-of-the-box version that shipped with WSS.
Rollback	Allows you to easily revert to a previous known-good-version of a configuration file in case you introduce a bug through one of your modifications.
Diff	Allows you compare any two versions of a file. This is particularly useful in tracking down subtle bugs.

I typically add the original `C:\Program Files\Common Files\Microsoft Shared\web server extensions\60\templates` folder to the VSS database I'm using to track changes and enhancements to a WSS installation, which provides an audit trail of all changes back to the original out-of-the-box configuration. With this in place, I can make edits to the configuration files with the confidence of knowing that if I introduce an error that causes a site, or even the entire server, to fail, I can back that change out and return to a known-good-state.

■ **Note** As of this writing, VSS 2005 has just been released. With the exception of UNICODE support and support for remote web client access, there are few significant differences between VSS 6 and VSS 2005. VSS 2005 Team System has also been released. VSS 2005 Team System provides many more features than VSS 2005 and is designed for complex projects and large teams. Any of these products can be used to implement a versioned backup of WSS configuration files.

■ **Caution** The VSS database should be backed up regularly. The backup should be stored on a separate physical hard drive, preferably on a separate Windows server to ensure against the risk of WSS server disk failure. VSS 6 also provides an integrity check utility called `Analyze.exe` that should be run regularly to ensure that the VSS database has not become corrupted.

Summary

In this chapter, you learned the key components of a WSS extranet that need to be backed up and specific strategies to do so. You also saw how to restore those backups. Taken together, these techniques can form the foundation for a comprehensive backup and recovery strategy. They can also be used to build backup or STAGE servers, or to move subsections of your WSS installation to other computers.

Armed with this knowledge you'll be able to respond quickly and with a minimal amount of stress (it wouldn't be any fun if there were none!) in the case of a systems failure or human error.

CHAPTER 4

Creating the Custom Building Blocks

Up to this point, I have focused on installing and configuring the SharePoint extranet environment. In this chapter, you'll learn how to create several customized components that take SharePoint beyond its out-of-the-box capabilities to create a robust extranet solution. Specifically, I will show you how to create custom web parts that will provide extensive control over targeting and formatting of content.

Before I delve in to the details, however, let's address the question of why you would want to build these components in the first place. There are two primary reasons why the components in this chapter are required to build a robust extranet:

- Windows SharePoint Services (WSS) doesn't support targeting of content displayed in web parts.
- Creating these components will give you a level of mastery of the `SharePoint` object model that will enable you to solve many other SharePoint development problems using its object model.

To address the first point, you'll create a framework for determining whether a given web part should be displayed on the page when viewed by a particular user. Figure 4-1 shows the Base, SQL, and XML web parts in action. It also gives you a preview of the TreeView web part that I will discuss in the next chapter.

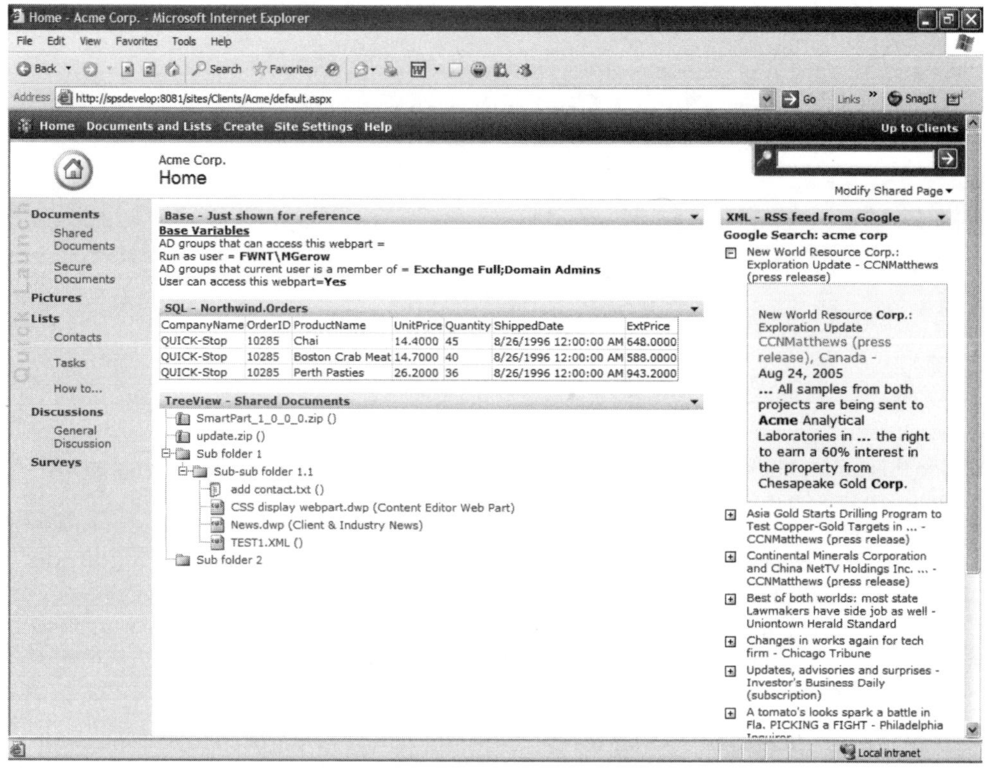

Figure 4-1. *Sample page showing Base, SQL, and XML web parts*

■ **Caution** All the discussion that follows assumes that you are coding and compiling on a server running Windows SharePoint Services. It is possible to do the programming on a machine that is not running WSS, but the applications must be executed on a WSS server.

Authorization Class and Web Service

The Authorization class will provide the business logic to determine what content a given user can see on a site. In conjunction with the Base class described in the next section, this class will give you full control of content targeting, a feature not present in WSS out of the box. The Authorization class, which will be wrapped in a web service when complete, provides the following methods:

- `GetGroups()` returns a list of Active Directory (AD) groups to which the current user belongs.
- `IsUserInAD()` returns a simple true/false value indicating whether the current web part should be displayed for the current user.

The Base web part class we create later will use this web service to determine whether to show or hide a given web part. With the base class in place, you can create a virtually unlimited number of targeted web parts and thus render the same web part page differently, depending on the needs and permissions of each visitor to that page.

Returning a List of Active Directory Groups to Which the Current User Belongs

AD is used to manage domain user accounts by Microsoft Windows Server and integrates closely with WSS. I assume that it is used to identify groups of users with like privileges or roles within your organization (for example, all "Executive Committee" members, or all "Widget Division Customers"). Using AD in this way not only makes administering permissions in WSS easier, but also facilitates the targeting of custom web parts, as you'll see shortly. Figure 4-2 illustrates the various components of the authorization process that you will create.

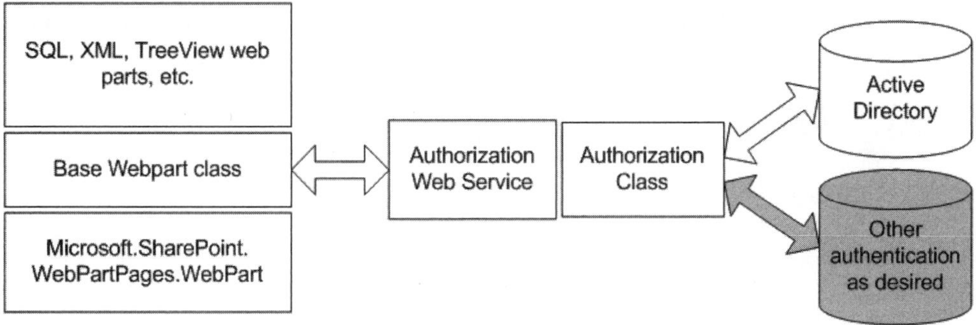

Figure 4-2. *Authorization process flow*

The Base class will call the Authorization web service to obtain a list of AD groups to which the current user belongs. Then this web service will call the Authorization class, which in turn queries AD using the DirectoryServices .NET namespace to obtain a list of AD groups for the specified user, returning that list to the Base web part. This list will be returned as a DataSet to the Authorization class, service, and ultimately to the Base class. The Base class will then compare the list returned by the Authorization service against its own list to determine whether to display itself. If the web part should be displayed for the current user, the Base class will continue to execute; otherwise, it will hide itself. The custom web part, which inherits from Base, will check the `CanAccess` property exposed by the Base class; if the property is set to True, the web part will write the content to the page. Otherwise, the custom web part will simply skip writing itself to the page. The end result of this process is that when a web part's `CanAccess` property is False for a given user, the web part's content will not appear on the page.

Note As Figure 4-2 indicates, you can insert other authentication processes as desired. Some examples could be to query a SQL Server database of user names and permissions, run a query against one of the SharePoint web services or objects, access an external accounting system, or execute any other process that would help you determine whether a particular web part should be viewable by a given user.

Creating the Authorization Web Service

To create the Authorization service, we will complete the following steps:

1. Create a web service project.
2. Create a class to query AD.
3. Modify the web service to use the Authorization class.
4. Test the service.

Create a Web Service Project

To start, you need to create a web service that accesses AD to return a list of AD groups for the current user. To do this, you will create a new Visual Studio ASP.NET Web Service project (see Figure 4-3). The figure shows the standard New Project dialog box with the ASP.NET Web Service template highlighted. This template provides a good starting point for developing a new web service.

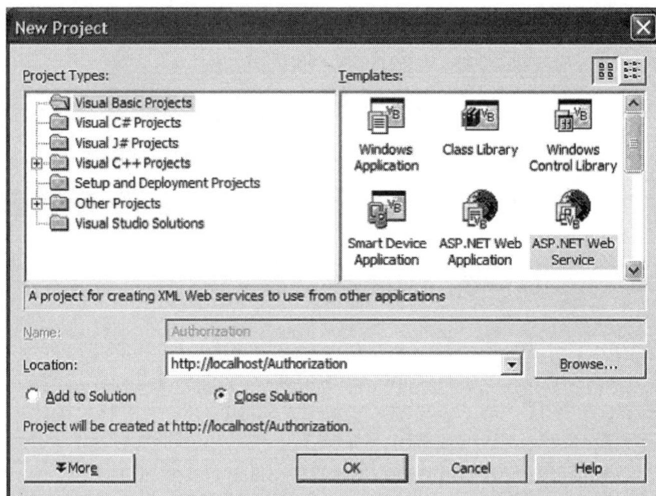

Figure 4-3. *Creating a web service project*

When you have successfully created the project in the Authorization solution, the Visual Studio Solution Explorer should appear, as shown in Figure 4-4.

Figure 4-4. *Solution Explorer window after adding projects*

■Note It is a best practice, when creating web services (such as the Authorization service), to place the bulk of the logic in a separate class and retain only the code to expose the methods and properties of the class in the web service. This has the advantages of keeping the web service code straightforward and making the logic placed in the class library available for other web services in the library.

Create a Class to Query Active Directory

The following listings show selected excerpts of the code that you will find in the online source code. Each code fragment is described before the listing.

The `IsUserInAD()` function does the bulk of the work. It sets up a `DirectoryServices.DirectorySearcher` to query the AD database, based on the SAMAcountName AD field. If the user is found, a memberOf collection returns a list of AD groups. (See Listing 4-1.)

Listing 4-1. `IsUserInAD()` *Function*

```
Public Function IsUserInAD(ByVal loginName As String, _

      ByVal ds As DataSet) As Boolean
  Dim userName As String = GetUserAlias(loginName)
  Dim search As DirectorySearcher = New DirectorySearcher
  search.Filter = String.Format("(SAMAccountName={0})", userName)
  search.PropertiesToLoad.Add("cn")
  search.PropertiesToLoad.Add("memberOf")
  Dim result As SearchResult = search.FindOne()
```

```
    If result Is Nothing Then
      Return False
    Else
      getGroups(result, ds)
      Return True
    End If
  End Function
```

The getGroups() function fills a DataSet.DataTable object with the AD groups for the specified user (see Listing 4-2).

Listing 4-2. getGroups() *Function*

```
Private Function getGroups(ByVal result As SearchResult, ByVal ds As DataSet) As _
          String
  Dim i As Integer
  Dim s As String = ""
  Dim delimStr As String = ",.:="
  Dim delimiter() As Char = delimStr.ToCharArray()
  Dim dr As DataRow

  For i = 0 To result.Properties("memberOf").Count - 1
    dr = ds.Tables(0).NewRow()
    dr(0) = result.Properties("memberOf")(i).ToString().Split(delimiter)(1)
    ds.Tables(0).Rows.Add(dr)
    s += ";" & dr(0)
  Next
  Return s.Substring(1)

End Function
```

This last small function simply returns the user alias component of a domain\useralias string.

```
Private Function GetUserAlias(ByVal loginName As String) As String
  Dim arrUserLogin() As String = loginName.Split("\")
  Return arrUserLogin(arrUserLogin.Length - 1)
End Function
```

Modify the Web Service to Use the Authorization Class

Now it's time to modify the web service to call the Authorization class. Listing 4-3 appears in the Authorization.asmx.vb file, which is part of the project. Notice the <WebMethod()> decoration that precedes the GetUserADGroups() function. This tells .NET to expose this as a public method through the SOAP web service interface, making it accessible by external routines, such as the Base web part I'll cover shortly.

Listing 4-3. `GetUserADGroups()` *Function*

```
<WebMethod()> _
Public Function GetUserADGroups(ByVal loginName As String) As DataSet
  Dim oAuthorization As New Authorization
  Dim ds As DataSet = New DataSet
  Dim dr As DataRow
  ds.DataSetName = "GetUserADGroups"
  ds.Clear()

  ' The table 'ADGroups' is the primary output of this service.  It
  ' contains a list of the AD groups the loginName is a member of.
  Dim dt As DataTable = New DataTable
  dt.TableName = "ADGroups"
  dt.Columns.Add("ADGroup")
  ds.Tables.Add(dt)

  ' The 'RetCode' table contains information indicating whether an
  ' error occurred, or if the user was found or not.  This data is for
  ' use by the calling web part so appropriate processing or error
  ' handling can take place.
  Dim dt2 As DataTable = New DataTable
  dt2.TableName = "RetCode"
  dt2.Columns.Add("RetCode")
  dt2.Columns.Add("RetMsg")
  ds.Tables.Add(dt2)

  If oAuthorization.IsUserInAD(loginName, ds) Then
    dr = dt2.NewRow()
    dr(0) = "0"
    dr(1) = "User found."
    dt2.Rows.Add(dr)

  Else
    dr = dt2.NewRow()
    dr(0) = "1"
    dr(1) = "User not found."
    dt2.Rows.Add(dr)

  End If

  Return ds

End Function
```

The second method in our service will return a logical value of either True or False, indicating whether the user belongs to one or more of the specified AD groups (see Listing 4-4).

Listing 4-4. `IsUserInGroupList()` *Function*

```
<WebMethod()> _
Public Function IsUserInGroupList(ByVal loginName As String, ByVal wpADGroups As _
          String) As Boolean
  Dim delimStr As String = ",.:=;"
  Dim delimiter() As Char = delimStr.ToCharArray()
  Dim arrWpADGroups() As String = wpADGroups.Split(delimiter)
  Dim ds As New DataSet
  Dim dr As DataRow
  Dim i As Integer

  ds = GetUserADGroups(loginName)
  For Each dr In ds.Tables(0).Rows
    For i = 0 To arrWpADGroups.Length - 1
      If dr(0).ToString.ToLower.Trim = arrWpADGroups(i).ToLower.Trim Then
        Return True
      End If
    Next
  Next
  Return False

End Function
```

Test the Web Service

To test out your work, set the AuthorizationService as the Start Page for the project and click the Run button. You should see a page similar to that shown in Figure 4-5. It is a built-in (and very handy) feature of web services created with Visual Studio.

Figure 4-5. *Authorization service test page*

When you click the GetUserADGroups link, you will see the page shown in Figure 4-6.

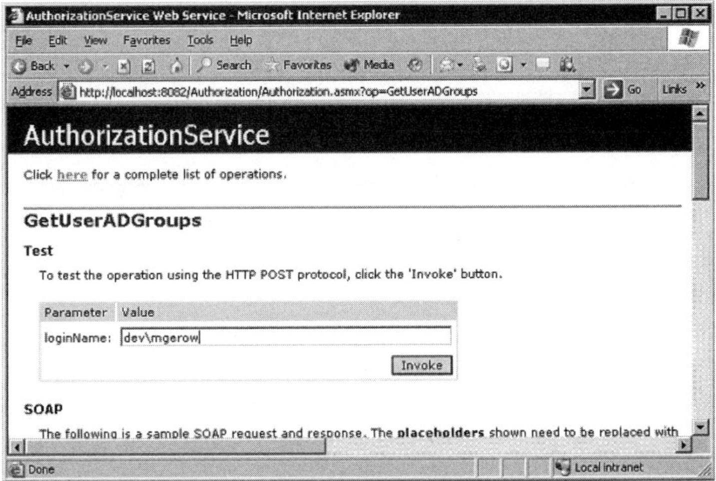

Figure 4-6. *GetUserADGroups invocation page*

Enter a valid AD domain\useralias and click the Invoke button. A new page showing the AD groups as an XML representation of a .NET DataSet will display (see Figure 4-7).

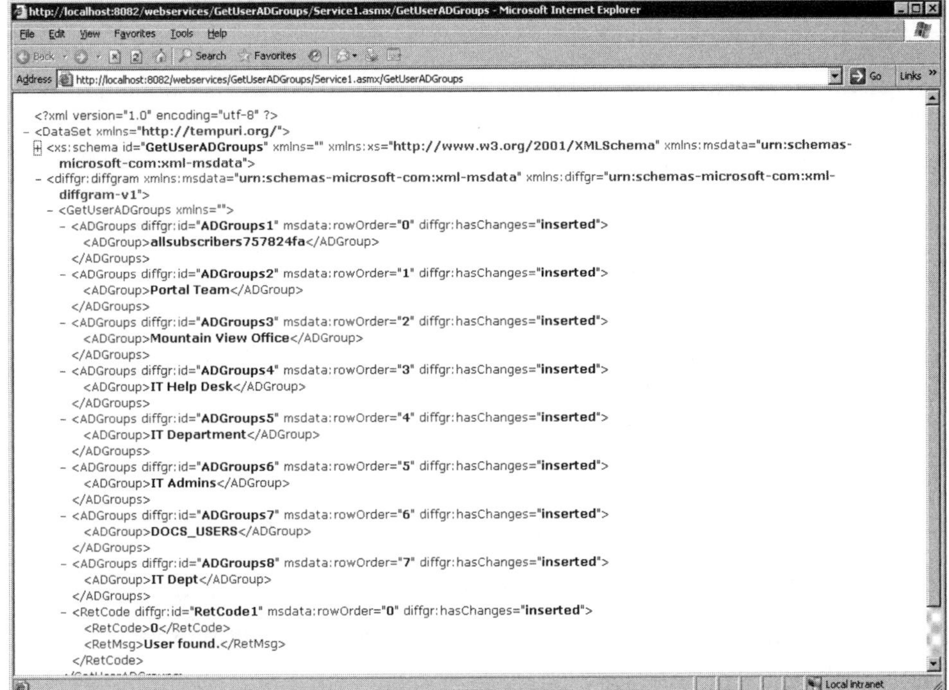

Figure 4-7. *XML DataSet returned by* `GetUserADGroups` *web method call*

The `IsUserInADGroupList()` method can be tested in a similar fashion.

■Note Testing a web service this way works only on the computer on which the web service is running. If you try this technique on a computer other than the one hosting the service, you will get a page similar to that shown in Figure 4-6, but without any fields in which to provide parameters. You can, of course, create a test harness application to call a remote web service and display any of the data returned by its methods.

Base Web Part

The Authorization class and Base web part are at the heart of the targeting architecture. These two components, working together, allow targeting of content to groups of users as you see fit, filling a major gap in the native WSS functionality.

The Base web part has to do two things (in addition to everything that the built-in WebPart class does):

- Check to see whether the current user is authorized to view the web part.
- Hide the web part if the user is not authorized to view it.

To create a Base web part class, do the following:

1. Create a new web part project called Base.
2. Add a reference to the Authorization web service created earlier.
3. Update the `PreRender()` method to hide the web part if the user is not authorized to view it.
4. Add the necessary web part properties.
5. Update the `RenderWebPart()` method to display optional debugging information.
6. Update the `AssemblyInfo.vb` file to include a strong key reference.
7. Update the `Webpart1.dwp` with name and title information.
8. Compile the .NET assembly .DLL created in the previous step into a CAB file.
9. Run the `STSADM.exe` tool to install the new web part.
10. Copy the `Base.dll` file to the website's `wwwroot\bin` folder.

I'll walk you through each step in turn, providing a detailed explanation of what's required.

■Note Many of the steps I'll cover in this section are common to creating any web part. Later sections will refer to those steps in this section rather than repeat the instructions.

Create a New Web Part Project Called Base

To create a web part project, you must have already installed the web part project template that can be downloaded from Microsoft at `http://www.microsoft.com/downloads/details.aspx?FamilyID=CAC3E0D2-BEC1-494C-A74E-75936B88E3B5&displaylang=en`. After you install the template, open Visual Studio and select the File ➤ New ➤ Project option; then select the web part template, as shown in Figure 4-8.

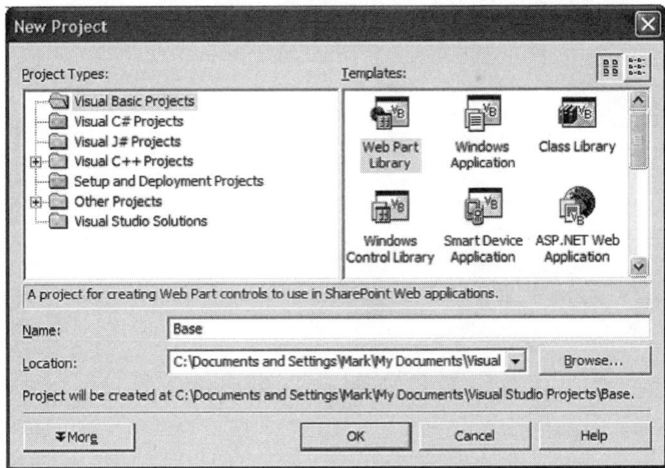

Figure 4-8. *Creating the Base web part project*

The web part template inserts the following line at the top of your class definition:

```
Public Class WebPart1
    Inherits Microsoft.SharePoint.WebPartPages.WebPart
```

This tells .NET that the custom web part will inherit from the standard web part class. What we need to do is to extend the behavior of the standard web part class to include the ability for a web part to hide itself from unauthorized users. The Base web part does just that. Any other web parts we create will then inherit from my new Base class instead of directly from the `Microsoft.SharePoint.WebPartPages.WebPart` class, and thus will have this show/hide capability. Subsequent web parts will then start with the following:

```
Public Class WebPart1
    Inherits MG.WebParts.Base
```

Add a Reference to the Authorization Web Service Created Earlier

Now I need a reference to the Authorization service we created in the preceding section. .NET makes using web services easy. After the appropriate reference has been created, a web service can be called in the same way as any other .NET class.

To add a reference to a web service, right-click the References node in the Project Explorer, and then choose Add Web Reference. When you see the Add Web Reference dialog box, click the Web services on the local machine link. After a few moments, a complete list of all web services running on the localhost will be displayed. Click the Authorization service. The dialog box should now appear as shown in Figure 4-9.

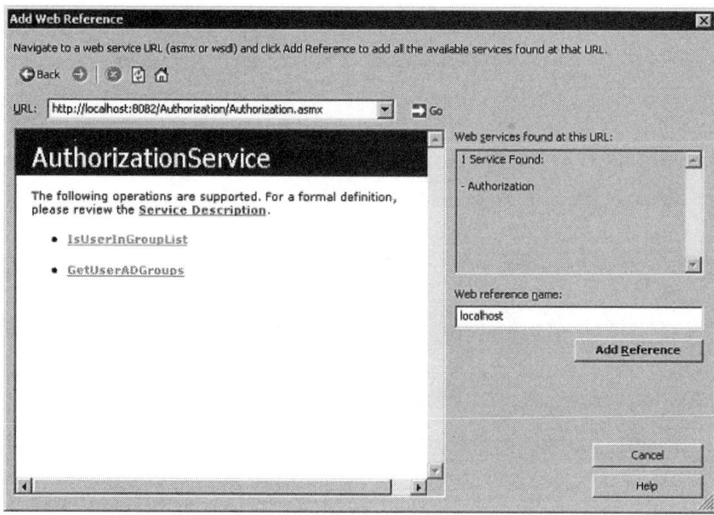

Figure 4-9. *Adding a web reference to the Authorization service*

Change the web reference name from localhost to **Authorization** and click Add Reference. The Authorization class is now available to invoke as you would any .NET class.

Update the PreRender() Method to Hide the Web Part If Necessary

One key piece of information that is not obvious by perusing the web part template is where you should place the code to render the web part invisible if the user does not have rights to view it. You might think, as I first did, that the `RenderWebPart()` method was the obvious choice. The problem with setting the visible property here is that the frame of the web part has already been rendered by this time. The correct location is in the method that handles the PreRender event, as shown in Listing 4-5.

Listing 4-5. `MyPreRender()` *Method*

```
Public Overridable Sub MyPreRender(ByVal sender As System.Object, _
      ByVal e As System.EventArgs) Handles MyBase.PreRender
  Dim oAuthorization As Authorization.AuthorizationService = New _
Authorization.AuthorizationService
  oAuthorization.Credentials = System.Net.CredentialCache.DefaultCredentials
  Dim usr As String = IIf(RunAsUser>"",RunAsUser, _
      context.Current.User.Identity.Name)
```

```
  ' If no AD groups have been specified, anyone can see this web part.
  If ADGroups > "" Then
    CanAccess = oAuthorization.IsUserInGroupList(usr, ADGroups)
  Else
    CanAccess = True
  End If

  'If user can't access, hide the web part unless Debug flag set to true.
  If Debug Or CanAccess Then
    FrameType = FrameType.Default
    PartOrder = BasePartOrder
  Else
    FrameType = FrameType.None
    PartOrder = 99
  End If
End Sub
```

Add the Necessary Properties

Next, we need some properties to allow the user to configure the Base web part. The following section introduces each of the properties of the Base web part.

- `ADGroups` gets or sets the list of groups that should have access to this web part.
- `CanAccess` indicates whether the current user can access this web part.

■ **Note** `CanAccess` is the only property that is not exposed to the end user, so the Browsable decoration field is set to False. This property will be used within the Base class, and within web parts derived from the Base class, to determine whether the inheriting web part should be rendered.

- `Debug` determines whether to display debugging information for this web part.
- `MyPartOrder` determines the order of this web part on the page.
- `RunAsUser` allows the web part to override the current user with a fixed user alias.

Let's look at the code for the first of these properties: `ADGroups`. (The remaining properties are defined in a similar fashion.) A bit of decoration code precedes each property.

```
<Browsable(True), Category("Base"), DefaultValue(_defaultText), _
WebPartStorage(Storage.Personal), FriendlyName("AD Groups"), _
Description("AD Groups with access to this webpart.")> _
```

The preceding clause modifies the property definition and defines which, if any, options the user has to modify this property from the web part property sheet. The following list gives the meaning of each clause.

- Browsable(True) indicates that this property appears on the property sheet.
- Category("Base") appears in the Base section of the sheet.
- DefaultValue(_defaultText) displays as a textbox with default value initialized to the value of the variable _defaultText.
- WebPartStorage(Storage.Personal) stores the value of this property on a per-user basis.
- FriendlyName("AD Groups") the text prompt displays on the property sheet next to the textbox.
- Description ("...") displays the tooltip text if the user moves the cursor over the property.

Next comes the property definition itself, which is simply a get/set routine that exposes a private variable: _AdGroups.

```
Property ADGroups() As String

  Get
    Return _AdGroups
  End Get

  Set(ByVal Value As String)
    _AdGroups = Value
  End Set

End Property
```

The rest of the properties are defined in a similar fashion.

Add the Optional Debugging Text to the RenderWebPart() Method

Web parts can be difficult to debug and troubleshoot when first deployed. That's why I find placing some key debugging text in the RenderWebPart() method invaluable. By placing this text in the Base web part class, all web parts that inherit from this class will also receive the benefit of this debugging text.

```
'Standard base variables.
If Debug Then
output.Write("<b><u>Standard base variables</u></b><br>")
output.Write("AD groups required to access this webpart = <b>" & _
SPEncode.HtmlEncode(ADGroups) & "</b><br>")
output.Write("Run as user = <b>" & usr & "</b><br>")
output.Write("AD groups of " & usr & " = <b>" & GetUserADGroups(usr) &_
"</b><br>")
output.Write("User can access this webpart = <b>" & _
IIf(boolCanAccess, "Yes", "No") & "</b><br>")
End If
```

This section of code displays text similar to Figure 4-10 if you set the `Debug` property to True.

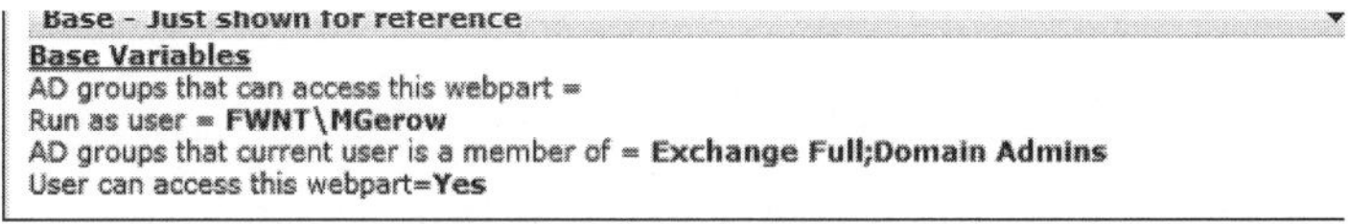

Base - Just shown for reference
Base Variables
AD groups that can access this webpart =
Run as user = FWNT\MGerow
AD groups that current user is a member of = Exchange Full;Domain Admins
User can access this webpart=Yes

Figure 4-10. *Base web part debug text*

Update the AssemblyInfo.vb File to Reference a Strong-Name Key File

Security is built into SharePoint from the ground up, and web parts are no exception. To successfully install a web part it must be "signed" with a strong-name key. This process is documented in detail in the SharePoint SDK, but the basics are included here for reference.

First, you need to create a strong-name key file. Although you can use a different key file for each web part for security if you want, we will use the same one for all web parts created throughout this chapter. To create the key file, open the Visual Studio.NET 2003 Command Prompt that can be found on the Visual Studio .NET Tools menu, which opens a command window in the directory in which the `SN.exe` program resides.

Run the `SN.exe` command in the command window using the following syntax:

```
SN.exe -k mykey.snk
```

After you press Enter, you should see the resulting output in the command window, as shown in Figure 4-11.

```
Visual Studio .NET 2003 Command Prompt
Setting environment for using Microsoft Visual Studio .NET 2003 tools.
(If you have another version of Visual Studio or Visual C++ installed and wish
to use its tools from the command line, run vcvars32.bat for that version.)

C:\Documents and Settings\Mark>SN.exe -k mykey.snk

Microsoft (R) .NET Framework Strong Name Utility  Version 1.1.4322.573
Copyright (C) Microsoft Corporation 1998-2002. All rights reserved.

Key pair written to mykey.snk

C:\Documents and Settings\Mark>dir mykey.snk
 Volume in drive C has no label.
 Volume Serial Number is 141B-C433

 Directory of C:\Documents and Settings\Mark

08/27/2005  12:52 PM               596 mykey.snk
               1 File(s)            596 bytes
               0 Dir(s)  25,076,244,480 bytes free

C:\Documents and Settings\Mark>_
```

Figure 4-11. *Creating a strong key file*

Now update the `AssemblyInfo.vb` file in the web part project to add a directive that will cause the key to be compiled into the `.dll` file. You should add the following line to the bottom of the `AssemblyInfo.vb` file:

```
<Assembly: AssemblyKeyFile("c:\Documents and Settings\Mark\mykey.snk")>
```

This effectively "signs" the web part with a unique key, thus preventing another web part from impersonating yours.

Update the Webpart1.dwp File to Set the Title and Description

By default, when a new web part project is created, the web part is named Webpart1, which is not a very descriptive name! To give the web part a more useful name we need to edit the `Webpart1.dwp` file to set the name and title properties. Following is the `Webpart1.dwp` file showing the edits made for the Base web part:

```
<?xml version="1.0" encoding="utf-8"?>
<WebPart xmlns="http://schemas.microsoft.com/WebPart/v2" >
      <Title>Base</Title>
      <Description>Base webpart</Description>
      <Assembly>MG.WebParts.Base</Assembly>
      <TypeName>MG.WebParts.Base.WebPart1</TypeName>
</WebPart>
```

Now that you have an understanding of what the Base web part does and how to build it, we'll walk through the steps to deploy it to the SharePoint server.

Compile the Web Part into a Cabinet (CAB) File

SharePoint provides a couple of ways to install a web part, but the simplest is to use the `STSADM.exe` utility. To use it, however, the web part must be compiled into a cabinet setup file first. To do so, add a setup project to your solution by selecting File ➤ New ➤ Project and then select a Cab project, as shown in Figure 4-12.

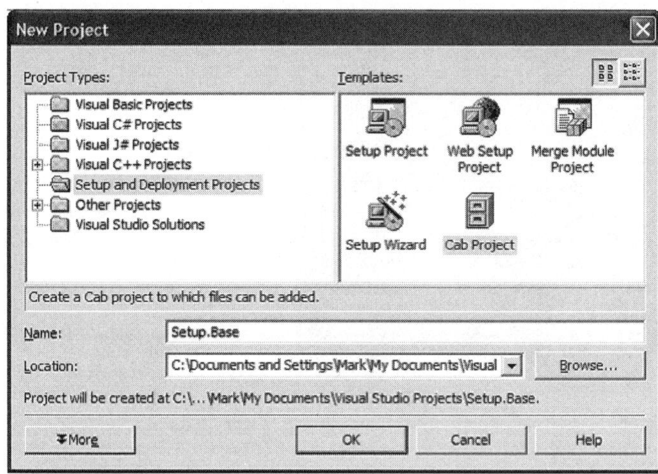

Figure 4-12. *Adding the Base web part setup project*

You must then add the output from the web part project to the Cab project for it to include all the necessary components. To do so, right-click `Setup.Base` in the Solution Explorer window and choose Add/Project Output (see Figure 4-13). Then build the solution.

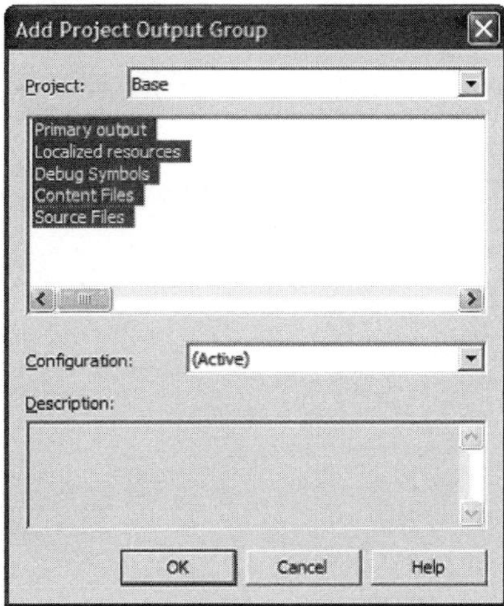

Figure 4-13. *Adding Base web part components to the CAB file*

Now we're ready to install the web part on the SharePoint server. To do so, we need to move to the `C:\Program Files\common files\Microsoft shared\web server extensions\60\bin` folder and run the `STSADM.exe` command using the following syntax:

```
Stsadm -o addwppack -filename <path to CAB file> -globalinstall -force
```

This command updates SharePoint's database to include a reference to the web part. Next, although not strictly required, I always run IISRESET to ensure that SharePoint reloads its application cache. Finally, we need to copy the web part's `.dll` file to the `wwwroot\bin` folder for this SharePoint virtual server. By placing a copy of the `.dll` file in this location, SharePoint recognizes it as a "trusted" executable.

■ **Caution** When SharePoint is installed, it doesn't automatically create a `bin` folder. Assuming that you install SharePoint on the default website, you might need to create the folder `C:\inetpub\wwwroot\bin`.

Testing the Base Web Part

Now you should be able to test the Base web part by placing a copy on a web part page. To do so, open any web part page and choose the Modify Shared Page ➤ Add WebPart ➤ Browse option from the drop-down menu in the upper-right corner of the page (see Figure 4-14).

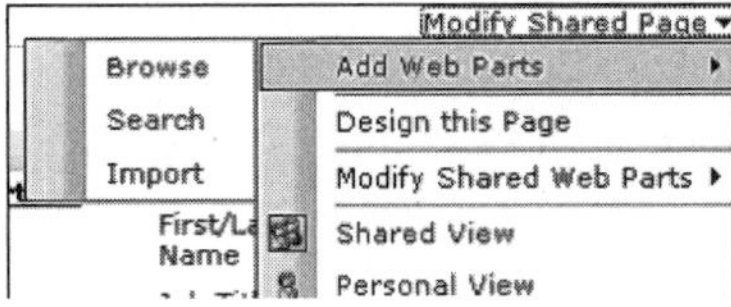

Figure 4-14. *Adding the Base web part to a page*

Select the Virtual Server Gallery option and then select Base (see Figure 4-15).

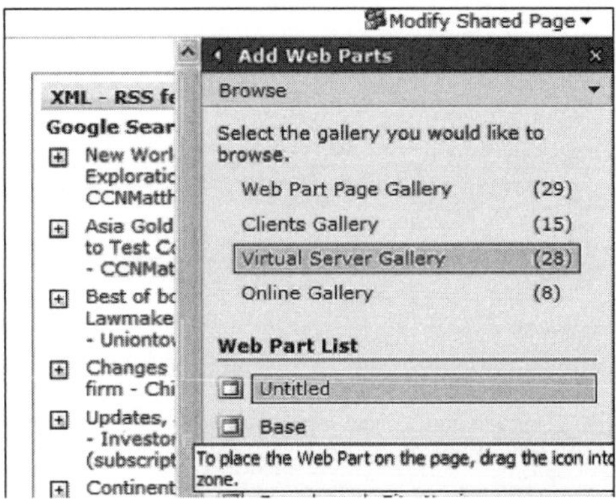

Figure 4-15. *Selecting the Base web part from the Virtual Server Gallery*

Drag the Base web part onto the page and then open its property sheet (see Figure 4-16). You will see each of the properties described previously (with the exception of `CanAccess`, for which the Browsable option was set to False).

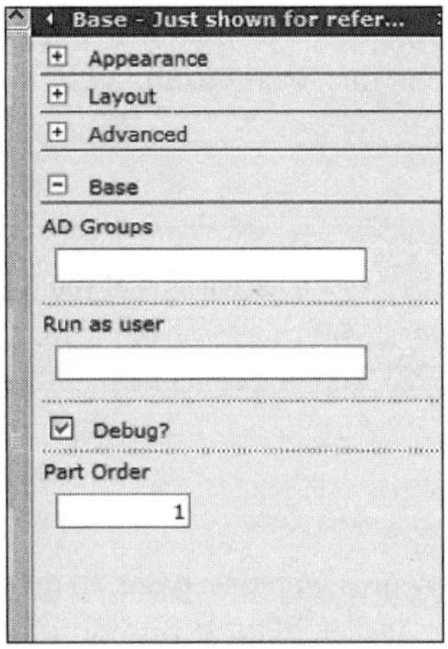

Figure 4-16. *Base web part property sheet*

To test the targeting function, type an AD group into the AD Groups field that you *are not* a member of. When you click OK, the web part disappears from the page (or if you select the Debug option, the text User Can Access This Webpart=No will display). Go back into the toolpart for the Base web part and enter an AD group that you *are* a member of (leaving the field blank is equivalent to Domain Users). When you click OK, you see the Base web part again.

To review, when the page refreshes, the Base web part does the following:

1. Compares the AD Groups assigned to the web part with those that the current user is a member of.

2. Sets the `CanAccess` property to False, the border to none, and the position to the bottom of the page, effectively hiding the web part if the user *is not* in any of the associated groups.

Now that I have my Base web part class working, I need a couple of additional web parts so I can display SQL and XML data.

SQL and XML Web Parts

The SQL and XML web parts are two of the workhorse components of the client extranet solution. With these web parts, you build on the capabilities of the Base web part to target content in any way needed, adding the ability to acquire both SQL and XML data and format it using either a data grid or XML Transform (XSLT). I have found these web parts so flexible that they serve 80–90 percent of my needs for displaying external content from sources such as databases, Really Simple Syndication (RSS) newsfeeds, financial systems, and the like. The SQL web part inherits from the Base web part created previously and adds the following functionality:

- Query a SQL database to return a result set of one or more tables

- Display the result as either as a DataGrid or format using XSLT

■ **Note** XSLT is an incredibly powerful tool for formatting data formatted as an XML document, and so is definitely a skill you'll want to acquire.

Creating the SQL Web Part

Do the following to create a SQL web part:

1. Create a new web part project called SQL (see Base).

2. Add a reference to the Base web part DLL created earlier.

3. Change the default inheritance to use the Base web part.

4. Add the necessary web part properties.

5. Update the `RenderWebPart()` method to display results and optional debugging information.

6. Create a couple of helper functions to read the source data and display the results.
7. Update the `AssemblyInfo.vb` file to include a strong key reference (see Base).
8. Update the `Webpart1.dwp` with name and title information (see Base).
9. Compile the SQL web part library (see Base).
10. Compile the DLL created in the previous step into a CAB file (see Base).
11. Run the `STSADM.exe` tool to install the new web part (see Base).
12. Copy the `SQL.dll` file to the website's `wwwroot\bin` folder (see Base).

I'll walk you through each step in turn, providing a detailed explanation of what's required.

■ Note The steps with the notation "(see Base)" have already been covered in the previous section, and so are not repeated here.

Add a Reference to Base Web Part DLL Created Earlier

After you create the project, you need to reference the Base class. If you added the SQL web part project to the same solution as the Base web part class, you can use a project reference, which is the preferred method. To do so, right-click the References section of the SQL Project Explorer and choose Add Reference. Click the Projects tab to add the Base web part class, as shown in Figure 4-17.

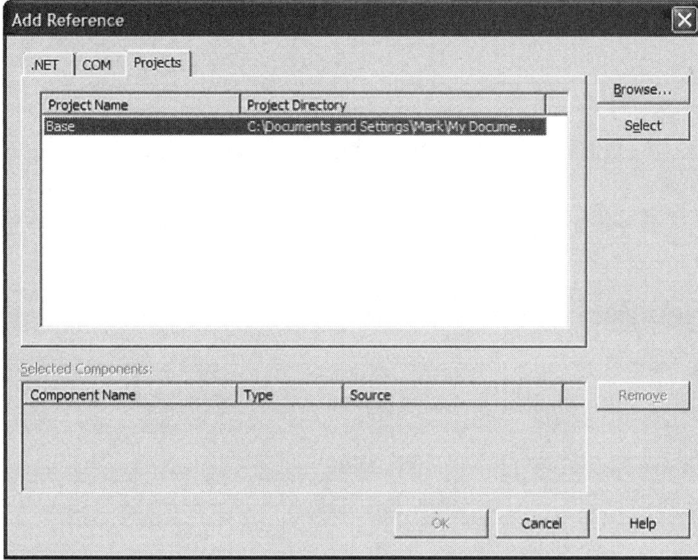

Figure 4-17. *Adding a reference to the Base web part class*

Inheriting from the Base Web Part Class

Because I want the SQL web part to inherit the authorization and hiding behavior of the Base web part, I need to change the default inheritance used in `Webpart1.vb`. The class header should be changed from the following:

```
Public Class WebPart1
    Inherits Microsoft.SharePoint.WebPartPages.WebPart
```

to the following:

```
Public Class WebPart1
    Inherits MG.Base.WebPart1
```

Add the Necessary Web Part Properties

The SQL web part needs to know which SQL source to connect to and which query to issue to return the desired result set. We also need to tell it whether to display its output using a DataGrid or format it using XSLT. Listing 4-6 shows you how to write the code that defines the necessary properties.

Listing 4-6. *Defining the SQL Web Part Properties*

```
' Create local variables to hold property data
Dim _connectionString As String = ""
Dim _connectionKey As String = ""
Dim _query As String = ""
Dim _formatUsing As enumFormatUsing = enumFormatUsing.DataGrid
Dim _xsltPath As String = ""

' Using an enum for a property type creates a drop-down list
Public Enum enumFormatUsing
  DataGrid = 1
  XSLT = 2
End Enum

<Browsable(True), Category("SQL"), DefaultValue(_defaultText), _
WebPartStorage(Storage.Personal), _
FriendlyName("Connection String"), _
Description("SQL connection string")> _
Property ConnectionString() As String
  Get
    Return _connectionString
  End Get
  Set(ByVal Value As String)
    _connectionString = Value
  End Set
End Property
```

```
<Browsable(True), Category("SQL"), DefaultValue(_defaultText), _
WebPartStorage(Storage.Personal), _
FriendlyName("Connection Key in Web.config"), _
Description("Refers to a web.config key for connection string")> _
Property ConnectionKey() As String
  Get
    Return _connectionKey
  End Get
  Set(ByVal Value As String)
    _connectionKey = Value
  End Set
End Property

<Browsable(True), Category("SQL"), DefaultValue(_defaultText), _
WebPartStorage(Storage.Personal), FriendlyName("SQL Query"), _
Description("Text Property")> _
Property Query() As String
  Get
    Return _query
  End Get
  Set(ByVal Value As String)
    _query = Value
  End Set
End Property

<Browsable(True), Category("SQL"), DefaultValue(enumFormatUsing.DataGrid), _
WebPartStorage(Storage.Personal), FriendlyName("Format output using"), _
Description("How to format the output from the data source.")> _
Property FormatUsing() As enumFormatUsing
  Get
    Return _formatUsing
  End Get
  Set(ByVal Value As enumFormatUsing)
    _formatUsing = Value
  End Set
End Property

<Browsable(True), Category("SQL"), DefaultValue(""), _
WebPartStorage(Storage.Personal), FriendlyName("XSLT path"), _
Description("Path to XSLT to format data with.")> _
Property XSLTPath() As String
  Get
    Return _xsltPath
  End Get
  Set(ByVal Value As String)
    _xsltPath = Value
  End Set
End Property
```

Update the RenderWebPart() Method to Display Results

The `RenderWebPart()` method is where the rubber meets the road for a web part; it's where the web part's HTML is written to the web part page. In addition to writing out the results of the SQL query, we need to display the debug information from the Base class if the Debug property has been set to True through the web part's tool part property sheet. Listing 4-7 shows the `RenderWebPart()` method code for the SQL web part.

■ **Note** To render the debug information supplied by the Base web part, we use the `MyBase.ShowDebugText()` method call. `MyBase` refers to the parent class of the current class, which in this case is the Base web part.

Listing 4-7. `RenderWebPart` *Method*

```
'Render this Web Part to the output parameter specified.
Protected Overrides Sub RenderWebPart(ByVal output As System.Web.UI.HtmlTextWriter)
  Try
    If Debug Then
      MyBase.ShowDebugText(output)
      output.Write("<hr>")
      output.Write("<b><u>SQL variables</u></b><br>")
      output.Write("Connection string = <b>" & ConnectionString & "</b><br>")
      output.Write("Connection key = <b>" & ConnectionKey & "</b><br>")
      output.Write("SQL query = <b>" & Query & "</b><br>")
      output.Write("Format output using = <b>" & FormatUsing.ToString & "</b><br>")
      output.Write("XSLT path = <b>" & XSLTPath & "</b><br>")
      output.Write("<hr>")
    End If
    If CanAccess() Then
      RenderSourceData(ReadSourceData(output), output)
    End If
  Catch ex As Exception
    output.Write("<font color=red>" & ex.Message & "</font><br>")
  End Try
End Sub
```

The function in Listing 4-8 checks to see whether the user has provided a full connection string in the `ConnectionString` property, or provided a `web.config` key where the full connection string can be found.

■ **Note** If the `ConnectionKey` property is used, a corresponding `appSettings` key must be added to SharePoint's `Web.Config` file. If you installed SharePoint on your C: drive `Web.Config` will be in `C:\Inetpub\wwwroot`. The key entry might look something like this: `<add key="MyDSN" value="user id=Northwind_test_user; data source=(local); persist security info=False; initial catalog=Northwind"/>`.

Listing 4-8. `ReadSourceData()` *Function*

```
Private Function ReadSourceData(ByVal output As System.Web.UI.HtmlTextWriter) _
As DataSet
  Try
    Dim conString As String
    If ConnectionKey > "" Then
      conString = _
        Configuration.ConfigurationSettings.AppSettings.Item(ConnectionKey)
    Else
      conString = ConnectionString
    End If
    Dim sa As New SqlClient.SqlDataAdapter(Query, conString)
    Dim ds As New DataSet
    sa.Fill(ds)
    Return ds
  Catch ex As Exception
    output.Write("<font color=red>" & ex.Message & "</font><br>")
  End Try
End Function
```

The function in Listing 4-9 does the actual writing of the HTML text to the web part page. It demonstrates how any web control's `RenderControl()` method can be used to generate HTML and write it to an HtmlTextWriter.

Listing 4-9. `RenderSourceData()` *Function*

```
Private Function RenderSourceData(ByVal ds As DataSet, _
ByVal output As System.Web.UI.HtmlTextWriter)
  Try
    If FormatUsing = enumFormatUsing.DataGrid Then
      Dim dg As New DataGrid
      dg.DataSource = ds
      dg.DataBind()
      dg.RenderControl(output)
    Else
      Dim xsl As New System.Web.UI.WebControls.Xml
      xsl.DocumentContent = ds.GetXml
      xsl.TransformSource = XSLTPath
      xsl.RenderControl(output)
    End If
```

```
  Catch ex As Exception
    output.Write("<font color=red>" & ex.Message & "</font><br>")
  End Try
End Function
```

The remaining steps are almost identical to those used to compile and deploy the Base web part and are not repeated here. After the web part is deployed, find it on the web part gallery menu, drag it onto a page, set the properties, and enjoy!

Note For now, I use the DataGrid output option to output the result of the SQL web part. Much more control of the output is possible using XSLT to display the result, and there are several examples later in this book that demonstrate the use of XSLT formatting. A full discussion of XSLT formatting is beyond the scope of this book, but it is well worth your study because it provides almost unlimited ways to format XML content.

Creating the XML Web Part

The XML web part also inherits from the Base web part class created previously and adds the following functionality:

- Query an XML source
- Display the returned XML using XSLT

Follow these steps to create an XML web part:

1. Create a new web part project called XML (see Base).
2. Add a reference to the Base web part DLL created earlier (see SQL).
3. Change the default inheritance to use the Base web part (see SQL).
4. Add the necessary web part properties.
5. Update the `RenderWebPart()` method to display results and optional debugging information.
6. Update the `AssemblyInfo.vb` file to include a strong key reference (see Base).
7. Update the `Webpart1.dwp` with name and title information (see Base).
8. Compile the XML web part library (see Base).
9. Compile the DLL created in the previous step into a CAB file (see Base).
10. Run the `STSADM.exe` tool to install the new web part (see Base).
11. Copy the `XML.dll` file to the website's `wwwroot\bin` folder (see Base).

■ **Note** The steps with the notation "(see Base)" have already been covered in the Base section; those with the notation "(see SQL)" have been covered in the SQL section and so are not repeated here.

I'll walk through each step not covered previously in turn, providing a detailed explanation of what's required.

Add the Necessary Web Part Properties

To create the XML web part, you need to define two required properties: XMLSource and XSLSource.

Listing 4-10. *Properties of XML Web Part*

```
Dim _XmlSource As String = ""
Dim _XslSource As String = "XSLT/companyinfo.xslt"

<Browsable(True), Category("XML"), DefaultValue(_defaultText), _
WebPartStorage(Storage.Personal), FriendlyName("XML Source Url"), _
Description("Url where XML document can be read")> _
Property XMLSource() As String
  Get
    Return _XmlSource
  End Get
  Set(ByVal Value As String)
    _XmlSource = Value
  End Set
End Property

<Browsable(True), Category("XML"), DefaultValue(_defaultText), _
WebPartStorage(Storage.Personal), FriendlyName("XSL Source Url"), _
Description("Must be relative to root of this site.")> _
Property XSLSource() As String
  Get
    Return _XslSource
  End Get
  Set(ByVal Value As String)
    _XslSource = Value
  End Set
End Property
```

Update the RenderWebPart() Method to Display Results and Optional Debug Text

The last programming step is to modify the default `RenderWebPart()` method and to add one helper function to read the XML and transform it using an XML web control, as shown in the following listing:

Listing 4-11. *XML Web Part's* `RenderWebPart()` *Method*

```
Protected Overrides Sub RenderWebPart(ByVal output As System.Web.UI.HtmlTextWriter)
  Try
    If Debug Then
      MyBase.ShowDebugText(output)
      output.Write("<hr>")
      output.Write("<br>XML Source=<b>" & XMLSource & "</b>")
      output.Write("<br>XML Source (tokens replaced)=<b>" & _
ReplaceMyTokens(XMLSource) & "</b>")
      output.Write("<br>XSL Source=<b>" & XSLSource & "</b>")
      output.Write("<br>XSL Source (tokens replaced)=<b>" & _
ReplaceMyTokens(XSLSource) & "</b>")
      output.Write("<hr>")
    End If
    If CanAccess() Then
      Dim xml As New System.Web.UI.WebControls.Xml
      xml.DocumentContent = GetUrlAsString(XMLSource)
      xml.TransformSource = ReplaceMyTokens(XSLSource)
      xml.RenderControl(output)
    End If
  Catch ex As Exception
    output.Write("<font color=red>" & ex.Message & "</font>")
  End Try
End Sub
```

The helper function `GetUrlAsString()` is used to make a web request to the specified URL of the XML source and convert the result into a string.

Listing 4-12. `GetUrlAsString()` *Function*

```
Private Function GetUrlAsString(ByVal strUrl As String) As String
  Dim wReq As System.Net.WebRequest
  wReq = System.Net.WebRequest.Create(strUrl)
  wReq.Credentials = Net.CredentialCache.DefaultCredentials

  ' Return the response.
  Dim wResp As System.Net.WebResponse = wReq.GetResponse()
  ' Read the response stream into a string
  Dim respStream As System.IO.Stream = wResp.GetResponseStream
  Dim respStreamReader As New System.IO.StreamReader(respStream, _
```

```
System.Text.Encoding.ASCII)
  Dim strXML As String = respStreamReader.ReadToEnd
  Return strXML
End Function
```

Testing the XML Web Part

Unlike the SQL web part created previously, the XML web part requires a little more work to test. Specifically, I need an XSLT document to format the XML returned. Before I can create an XSLT however, I need to know the structure of the XML to be formatted. Prevalent sources of XML today are RSS feeds from various news services. RSS is a simple standard that can be easily formatted. For the purposes of this example, I use the Google news service found at `http://news.google.com/news?hl=en&q=Acme+Corp&ie=UTF-8&output=rss`.

The XML returned (a fragment of which follows) is similar to any RSS source, and is shown in Listing 4-13.

Listing 4-13. *Google RSS Fragment*

```
<?xml version="1.0" encoding="UTF-8"?>
<rss version="2.0">
  <channel>
    <generator>NFE/0.8</generator>
    <title>Google Search: Acme Corp</title>
    <link>http://news.google.com/news?hl=en&amp;q=Acme+Corp&amp;ie=ISO-8859-1</link>
    <description>Google Search: Acme Corp</description>
    <language>en</language>
    <webMaster>news-feedback@google.com</webMaster>
    <copyright>&amp;copy;2005 Google</copyright>
    <pubDate>Sat, 27 Aug 2005 22:43:22 GMT</pubDate>
    <lastBuildDate>Sat, 27 Aug 2005 22:43:22 GMT</lastBuildDate>
    <image>
      <title>Google Search: Acme Corp</title>
      <url>http://news.google.com/images/news_res.gif</url>
      <link>http://news.google.com/</link>
    </image>
    <item>
      <title>New World Resource Corp.: Exploration Update - (press release)</title>
      <link>http://www.ccnmatthews.com/news/releases.Controller?Id=552993</link>
      <pubDate>Wed, 24 Aug 2005 16:43:00 GMT</pubDate>
      <description>Short description of article...</description>
    </item>
    <item>
        ...
    </item>
  </channel>
</rss>
```

The information between each <item>...</item> element represents a link to one article returned by the RSS service. There might be only one or many, but the XSLT to format the news feed is the same. The following is the XSLT that formats this (or any) RSS feed. I saved it to the file called newsfeed.xsl.

In most cases, any statement without an xsl: at the beginning is rendered verbatim in the output. The first part simply defines the document as an XSLT and describes the type of output to be produced: HTML.

```
<?xml version='1.0' encoding='utf-8'?>
<xsl:stylesheet version="1.0" xmlns:xsl="http://www.w3.org/1999/XSL/Transform">
<xsl:output method="html"/>
<xsl:template match="/">
```

The <script> block writes a JavaScript function into the body of the web part page to display the full description of the news item if the user clicks on the + next to the link in the list of items. (See Listing 4-14.)

Listing 4-14. toggleRssItem() *JavaScript Function*

```
<script language="javascript">
function toggleRssItem(theParentDiv, resourcePath)
{
  var parentId = theParentDiv.id;
  var childDiv = document.getElementById(parentId + "__child");
  if (theParentDiv.src.indexOf("collapsePlus.gif") > -1) {
    theParentDiv.src = resourcePath + "/collapseMinus.gif";
    childDiv.style.display = "";
  } else {
    theParentDiv.src = resourcePath + "/collapsePlus.gif";
    childDiv.style.display = "none";
  }
}
</script>
```

Listing 4-15 renders the HTML. Note the <xsl:for-each select="rss/channel/item"> directive, which tells the XSLT processor to loop through each <item> element in the XML document. The other key directive is <xsl:value-of select="...">, which tells the XSLT processor to insert an element value from the XML document at that location.

Listing 4-15. *XSLT to Render an RSS Feed*

```
<html>
  <table border="0">
    <tbody>
    <tr>
      <td colSpan="2">
        <a href="{rss/channel/link}" target="_news">
          <strong><xsl:value-of select="rss/channel/title"/></strong>
        </a>
         </td>
    </tr>
       <xsl:for-each select="rss/channel/item">
      <tr>
        <td align="center" width="3%" valign="top">
<img id="{link}"
  onclick="toggleRssItem(this,'http://svcspsstage01/_layouts/images');"
  alt="Click here to expand/collapse item detail"
  src="http://svcspsstage01/_layouts/images/collapsePlus.gif"
border="0"/> 
           </td>
           <td valign="middle">
             <a href="{link}" target="_news">
               <xsl:value-of select="title" disable-output-escaping="yes"/>
             </a>
             <br/>
             <div id="{link}__child" style="display:none;border:1px solid
               #cccccc;padding:2px;background-color:#FFFFCC">
               <xsl:value-of select="description" disable-output-escaping="yes"/>
             </div>
           </td>
         </tr>
       </xsl:for-each>
    <tr>
      <td colSpan="2">
        <hr/>last update on: <xsl:value-of select="rss/channel/lastBuildDate"/>
         </td>
       </tr>
     </tbody>
   </table>
</html>
</xsl:template>
</xsl:stylesheet>
```

■ **Tip** Although you can code XSLT documents by hand, and there are many excellent books on the subject of XSLT document construction, my recommendation is for you to acquire a WYSIWYG XSLT editor. There are several on the market—and several free ones as well. My favorite is Stylus Studio Professional from Progress Software. Another widely used product is XML Spy from Altova. Either product makes creating XSLT documents vastly simpler and more productive.

Summary

In this chapter, you learned how to create several components that allow content targeting based on a user's Active Directory group membership. Based on this foundation, you can build a virtually limitless variety of web part pages that display targeted content from any SQL or XML data source. Moreover, in the process, you learned the basic steps for creating any web part.

The next chapter covers several navigation tools that will enhance the user's experience on your extranet site..

CHAPTER 5

Creating a TreeView Web Part

SharePoint 2003 is an impressive platform for providing, among other things, document collaboration. Microsoft provided a robust foundation, but some user interface (UI) elements could be improved. One such UI improvement is the addition of a treeview for document libraries, a visual metaphor that users have come to expect based on their experience with Windows Explorer. It's a seemingly small feature that will make a large difference in how users perceive the quality of your SharePoint implementation.

In this section, I will take you through the steps of creating a document library treeview (TreeView) web part that will allow your users to view and navigate complex document libraries with ease.

To illustrate the benefits, let's look briefly at the differences between the native SharePoint document library web part and the TreeView described in this chapter. Figure 5-1 shows how two document libraries, Internal Documents and Shared Documents, might be displayed using out-of-the-box SharePoint document library web parts.

Internal Documents - standard view

Type	Name	Modified By
	Article2 ! NEW	VMWIN2003MEG\administrator

Shared Documents - standard view

Type	Name	Modified By
	Recent articles	VMWIN2003MEG\administrator
	General documents	VMWIN2003MEG\administrator

Figure 5-1. *Standard SharePoint doclib web part*

Note that there are no visual cues to indicate whether a given folder contains any documents or subfolders. The problem is compounded by the fact that if the user drills down into one of the folders contained in a document library, there is no indication at all that the user is viewing a subfolder (see Figure 5-2).

Shared Documents - standard view

Type	Name	Modified By
	ExampleA	VMWIN2003MEG\administrator
	Artilce1	VMWIN2003MEG\administrator

Figure 5-2. *Standard doclib web part when showing contents of General documents subfolder*

Figure 5-3 shows the same two document libraries displayed using the TreeView, which provides the folder/subfolder navigation metaphor with which users are familiar.

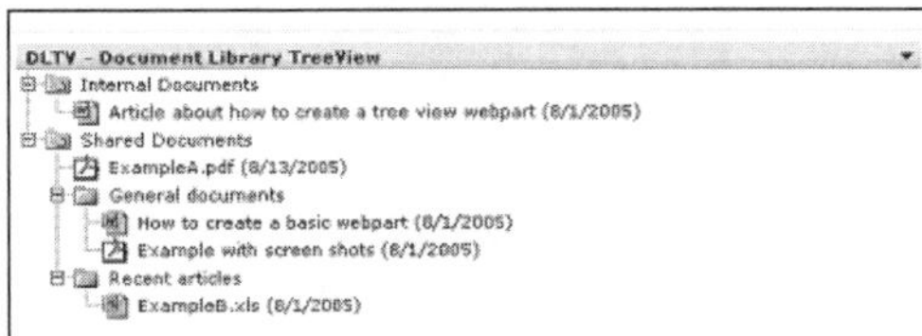

Figure 5-3. *Sample of TreeView web part in action*

The TreeView web part you will create also provides a number of properties that allow you or your end users to customize its appearance without programming. Figure 5-4 shows the TreeView web part property sheet.

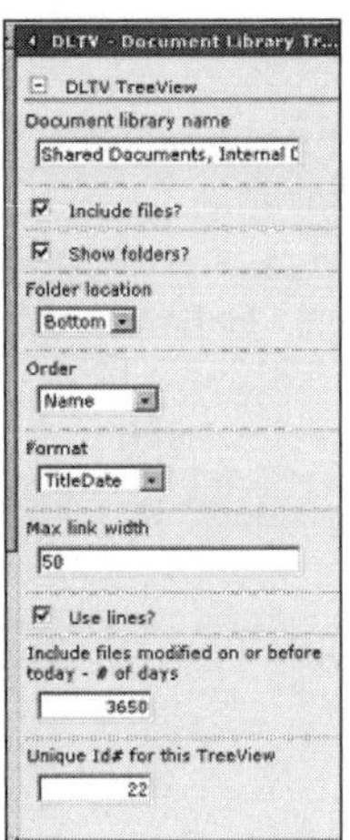

Figure 5-4. *Property sheet for TreeView*

Later in this chapter, I will describe each of these properties in more detail. Of course, these are just the properties I've found useful. After you have installed the code and become familiar with the TreeView, you might easily add other properties as needed.

Not only will your users appreciate the improved user interface; you will also gain invaluable insights into the SharePoint 2003 object model that will enable you to extend it as well as build many other document-centric web parts.

Jtree JavaScript Library

To create the TreeView as shown, you'll need to install the dtree treeview library under the SharePoint `C:\program files\common files\Microsoft shared\web server extensions\60\bin\templates\LAYOUTS` folder (you can find more information about dtree at `http://www.destroydrop.com/javascripts/tree/`). The dtree treeview library is a compact, reliable, and *free* library for rendering an interactive tree control in generic JavaScript.

■ **Note** A note about the dtree treeview script: This is a freeware program that renders a hierarchical tree using JavaScript. It can be used and distributed freely as long as the credit, which appears at the top of the `dtree.js` file, is retained in the code. I have used this routine to reliably display document libraries containing thousands of documents. You might be aware that Microsoft provides an IE-based treeview control, and wonder why that wasn't used. My reasons are that the MSIE control has some display "anomalies" that cause nodes to be displayed incorrectly and is designed only for IE, whereas the included script should work with any JavaScript-compatible browser. You might, however, substitute the MSIE control or another treeview of preference through minor modifications to the provided source code.

It would also be helpful if you've had some prior experience creating at least a simple web part. If you skipped over Chapter 3 and have not had prior experience creating web parts, I strongly recommend you go back and work through the examples in that chapter before continuing.

Installing and Compiling the Sample Code

The sample download for this chapter contains a VS.NET solution containing two projects: `MG.WebParts.TreeView` and `Setup.MG.WebParts.TreeView`. This solution builds the TreeView web part DLL and creates a CAB setup file that SharePoint needs to install the web part.

To install the sample, you should extract the two projects to the following locations on your hard drive:

- `C:\development\portal\MG.WebParts.TreeView`
- `C:\development\portal\Setup.MG.WebParts.TreeView`

If you prefer moving either of the projects to another location, that's fine but you need to edit the references in `Setup.MG.WebParts.TreeView` to point to the actual location for `MG.WebParts.TreeView`.

You also need to extract the following two files:

- `Add.TreeView.webpart.cmd`, which is used to add the web part to SharePoint. This file can be extracted anywhere on your hard drive.
- `TreeViewKey.snk`, the strong-name key used to build the project. This file should be extracted to `C:\` unless you change the reference in the `AssemblyInfo.vb` file in the `MG.WebParts.TreeView` project.

Finally, extract the dtree library to the `C:\program files\common files\Microsoft shared\web server extensions\60\template\layouts\Jtree` folder.

To install the web part, go to VS.NET and choose the Build Solution option; then open a command window and run the `add.TreeView.webpart.cmd` file.

You should then see the web part in the web part gallery menu in SharePoint, as shown in Figure 5-5.

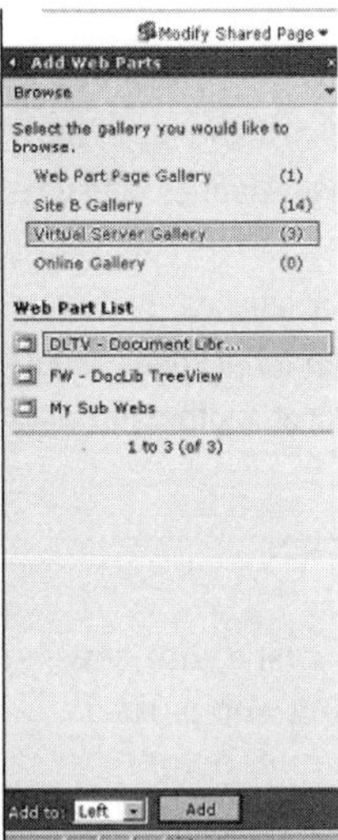

Figure 5-5. *Document library TreeView in web part gallery*

Building the TreeView

I'll discuss the task of building the TreeView web part in three stages:

1. How to iterate through the object library collection classes that represent doclibs, folders, and files
2. How to format the output that will produce the TreeView
3. How to create the web part properties that will be visible via the Modify Shared Web Part option

A Bit of Pseudo-Code

The following pseudo-code is included to help you visualize the flow of the code before we dig in to the details. One aspect that pseudo-code or flowcharts cannot capture, however, is the recursion necessary to "walk" the document library hierarchy.

```
For each list in site
      If list is a document library
            For each file in root folder
                  Add file node to treeview
            For each folder in root folder
                  Add folder node to treeview
                  Process contents of folder
```

As you can see, the program is very simple in concept. (Of course, you know it's the details that keep programmers up at night!)

Recursion occurs when the `Process contents of folder` line is executed and looks something like this:

```
For each file in folder
      Add a file node to treeview
For each subfolder in folder
      Process contents of subfolder
```

Document Libraries and the SharePoint Object Model

Before you can build a web part to navigate and display the contents of a document library, you need to know which classes, methods, and properties from the SharePoint object model you will be using.

As with any .NET development, half the battle is figuring out which classes to use to get the job done. The SharePoint classes you'll use to create the TreeView are as follows:

- `SPWeb`
- `SPListCollection`, `SPList`, and `SPListItem`
- `SPFolderCollection`, `SPFolder`, and `SPFile`

Iterating Through the Document Libraries, Folders, and Files

With the previously noted classes, you can navigate the list of document libraries, folders, documents, and document properties on the current site. I'll focus first on the steps to iterate through the list of document libraries, access their folders, files, and file properties. After that, I'll come back to the steps required to format this data as a treeview.

Step 1: Get the Current Site Context

Most SharePoint classes that you will use to create web parts need a *context*, which tells the class on which site it is operating. The following code fragment gets the context of the site on which the web part is placed:

```
Dim site As SPWeb = _

Microsoft.SharePoint.WebControls.SPControl.GetContextWeb(Context)
```

Because all other SharePoint objects used will be based on child classes of `site`, they will inherit its context.

■ **Note** One thing to remember is that all web parts run in the context of the site of the page on which they're placed. Although it's possible to create a web part that uses a context other than that of the current site, this is the exception rather than the rule. There are other uses for the SharePoint object model (such as to build administrative console applications or web services) in which a context cannot be derived from the environment in which the application runs, and so must be provided by the end user or via some other means. The context ultimately resolves to the URL of the site to which the methods and properties refer.

Step 2: Get a Collection of All Lists in the Site

The next step is to obtain a collection of lists in the site, which will provide a starting point for navigating through all the document libraries, folders, and files needed to display the TreeView.

```
dlCollection = site.Lists
```

Step 3: Extract the Document Library Lists

Of course, there are many types of lists, and the only ones you're interested in are document libraries. Use the following conditional statement to return only the document libraries:

```
For Each dl In dlCollection
  If IsInDoclibList(dl.Title, [DoclibName]) And dl.BaseType = _
        SPBaseType.DocumentLibrary Then
```

The `SPBaseType` enumeration allows you to select just the document libraries. Note the `IsInDoclibList()` method call. This is a helper function I wrote to determine whether the document library being examined is one of those named in the web part `Document library name property`.

Step 4: Display the Files in the Root Folder Level for a doclib

Now that I have a pointer (`dl`) to a document library, I want to include in the TreeView, I need a way to iterate through the files and folders of that library. To do so, I wrote a couple of helper functions that are executed recursively: `ShowSortedFiles()` and `ShowSortedFolders()`. Recursion is used to make it possible to process a tree structure of arbitrary depth without needing to know anything about the structure beforehand. If you've ever written code to navigate a file system directory structure, you've probably created similar code. I'll discuss `ShowSortedFiles()` in this step and `ShowSortedFolders()` in the next.

First, let's dissect the parameter list for the helper function:

```
ShowSortedFiles(site.GetFolder(dl.Title.Trim),thisNodeId,output,colOutput)
```

The parameters for the ShowSortedFiles() method are

- `site.GetFolder(dl.Title.Trim)` returns a folder object, in this case the document library's root folder.
- `thisNodeId` is a variable whose value uniquely identifies a node in the tree. If you are using a treeview other than dtree, this might or might not apply.
- `output` is a reference to the web part's `System.Web.UI.HtmlTextWriter` property. I need a handle to this to write out the client-side JavaScript that will display the tree.
- `colOutput` is a reference to a collection variable I use to buffer the output if the user has unchecked the `Show folders?` property. I'll come back to this later.

The skeleton of the `ShowSortedFiles()` method, shown as follows, is straightforward:

```
Private Function ShowSortedFiles(ByVal fldr As SPFolder, _
ByVal thisNodeId As Integer, _
ByVal output As System.Web.UI.HtmlTextWriter, _
```

```
ByVal colOutput As Collection)
  Dim arrFlSorted() As String
  Dim i As Integer
  Dim j As Integer

  If _includeFiles Then
    For i = 0 To fldr.Files.Count - 1

      If fldr.Files(i).TimeLastModified >= _
     Now.AddDays(-_daysBack2Include) Then

        ReDim Preserve arrFlSorted(i)
        If Order = EnumSortField.Name Then
          arrFlSorted(i) = fldr.Files(i).Name & CONST_SPLITCHAR & i
        ElseIf Order = EnumSortField.Title Then
          arrFlSorted(i) = fldr.Files(i).Title & CONST_SPLITCHAR & i
        ElseIf Order = EnumSortField.Sequence Then
            arrFlSorted(i) = fldr.Files(i).Item("Sequence") & _
               CONST_SPLITCHAR & i
        End If
      Next
    End If

    If _showFolders Then
            Array.Sort(arrFlSorted)
            For i = 0 To arrFlSorted.Length - 1
                j = arrFlSorted(i).Split(CONST_SPLITCHAR)(1)
                output.Write("d" & _treeViewId.ToString & ".add(" & _
                  IncrNodeId() & "," & thisNodeId & ",'" & _
                  FormatTreeNode(fldr.Files(j).Name, fldr.Files(j).Title, _
                  _maxLinkWidth, _
                  fldr.Files(j).TimeLastModified.ToShortDateString) & "','"_
                  & fldr.Files(j).Url & "','','_self','_layouts/images/" & _
                  fldr.Files(j).IconUrl & "');")
            Next
        Else
            'If not showing folders, delay writing out until all files
            'gathered, then sort all together.
        End If

    End Function
```

This code iterates through the files collection of the current folder and writes a list of sort keys and associated indices to an array (delimited by `CONST_SPLITCHAR` so they can later be broken apart). After I write data for all the files to the array, I sort it and write out the JavaScript to create the treeview nodes to the output stream. One twist occurs if I am not showing folders; the sort key and desired output are written to the `colOutput` collection to be sorted and written to the output stream later.

This same process is repeated (through recursion) for all subfolders of the root, as described in the following section.

Step 5: Display All Subfolders in the Root Folder

Any given folder, including the root, can have zero or more subfolders. I want to display them using a folder icon and allow the user to drill down to display any files or subfolders under that folder. The following code shows how the `ShowSortedFolders()` helper function is called from the root level:

```
flCollection = site.GetFolder(dl.Title.Trim).SubFolders
ShowSortedFolders(flCollection, 1, thisNodeId, output, colOutput)
```

The parameters for the `ShowSortedFolders()` method are the following:

- `site.GetFolder(dl.Title.Trim).SubFolders` that returns a collection of all subfolders of the root folder.
- `1` is level of the folder in the folder hierarchy, where 1=root.
- `thisNodeId` is simply the node id of the root in our treeview; in recursive calls to this function, this parameter will be replaced with the treeview node id of the folder in which the subfolders reside.
- `output` is a reference to the web part's `System.Web.UI.HtmlTextWriter` property.
- `colOutput` is a reference to a collection variable used to buffer the output.

Following is the code for this method with most comments removed:

```
Private Function ShowSortedFolders(ByVal fldrCol As SPFolderCollection, _
        ByVal lvl As Integer, ByVal thisNodeId As Integer, _
        ByVal output As System.Web.UI.HtmlTextWriter, _
        ByVal colOutput As Collection)

  Dim arrFldrSorted() As String
  Dim i As Integer
  Dim j As Integer

  For i = 0 To fldrCol.Count - 1
    ReDim Preserve arrFldrSorted(i)
    arrFldrSorted(i) = fldrCol(i).Name & CONST_SPLITCHAR & i
  Next

  Array.Sort(arrFldrSorted)

  For i = 0 To arrFldrSorted.Length - 1
    j = arrFldrSorted(i).Split(CONST_SPLITCHAR)(1)
    'Don't include forms library
```

```
    If fldrCol(j).Name.ToLower <> "forms" Or lvl <> 1 Then
      ShowFolderFiles(fldrCol(j), lvl, output, thisNodeId, colOutput)
    End If
  Next

End Function
```

Notice that most of the processing is delegated to the ShowFolderFiles() method, which handles all the logic to add the appropriate nodes to the treeview. This code could have been included in the ShowSortedFolders() method, but was extracted into a separate method for clarity.

One line of code you might be puzzled by is this one:

```
If fldrCol(j).Name.ToLower <> "forms" Or lvl <> 1 Then
```

SharePoint automatically adds a Forms folder when a doclib is created, so this folder needs to be explicitly excluded from the list of folders to process if we are at the root level (i.e., lvl = 1).

Now let's look at the ShowFolderFiles() method, which does the bulk of the work. For now, I want you to note the section that starts with the following:

```
If _folderLocation = EnumFolderLocation.Bottom Then
```

The two lines that follow this conditional add nodes for the files and folders, respectively, to the treeview. The call to the ShowSortedFolders() method is the recursive call that walks the hierarchy of folders. The conditional exists because the user can choose to display subfolders at the top of a folder (as in Windows Explorer) or at the bottom (as does SharePoint).

```
Private Sub ShowFolderFiles(ByVal fl As SPFolder, ByVal lvl As Integer, _
        ByVal output As System.Web.UI.HtmlTextWriter, _
        ByVal parentNodeId As Integer, ByVal colOutput As Collection)

  Dim sfl As SPFolder
  Dim fi As SPFile
  Dim thisNodeId As Integer = IIf(_showFolders, IncrNodeId(), parentNodeId)

  If _showFolders Then
    output.Write("d" & _treeViewId.ToString & ".add(" & thisNodeId & "," & _
          parentNodeId & ",'" & fl.Name & "','" & fl.Url & _
          "','','','_layouts/jtree/img/folder.gif'", _
          "'_layouts/jtree/img/folderopen.gif');")
  End If

  If _folderLocation = EnumFolderLocation.Bottom Then

    ShowSortedFiles(fl, thisNodeId, output, colOutput)
    ShowSortedFolders(fl.SubFolders, lvl + 1, thisNodeId, output, colOutput)
```

```
    Else

      ShowSortedFolders(fl.SubFolders, lvl + 1, thisNodeId, output, colOutput)
      ShowSortedFiles(fl, thisNodeId, output, colOutput)

    End If

End Sub
```

That's really all there is to iterating through the document libraries, folders, and files. Now let's turn to the problem of formatting the output using the dtree treeview routine.

Formatting the Output to Produce the TreeView

The TreeView is rendered in the user's browser via JavaScript. The following pseudo-code outlines the basic process:

```
Include the dtree .js and .css files
Initialize the tree object in JavaScript
Add node objects to the tree object
Write out the tree
```

■Note Because there is an excellent document covering the dtree API, I won't cover it in this chapter. To learn more about the parameters passed to the dtree constructor, please read `API.html` under the `Jtree` folder.

In any web part, the code to render contents to the web part page, whether HTML or JavaScript, occurs in the `RenderWebPart()` method, which overrides the method of the same name in the base `Microsoft.SharePoint.WebPartPages.WebPart` class. In effect, the TreeView web part is simply a JavaScript generator that inserts calls to the dtree.js library into the web part page.

Step 1: Include References to the dtree Library and .css Files

The first step is to make sure the dtree.js library and its associated components are included in the page:

```
output.Write("<link rel='StyleSheet' href='_layouts/jtree/dtree.css'
   type='text/css' />")
output.Write("<script type='text/javascript'
   src='_layouts/jtree/dtree.js'></script>")
output.Write("<script type='text/javascript'>")
```

■ **Note** During installation, you placed the `Jtree` folder under `[drive]:\program files\common files\Microsoft shared\web server extensions\60\TEMPLATE\LAYOUTS`. Any web application components under this folder will be available as relative URLs within a SharePoint site by prefacing the reference with `_layouts/`.

The `output.Write` statements appear throughout the code and are similar to the `Response.Write()` statements used in typical ASP.NET programming. `output` refers to the `System.Web.UI.HtmlTextWriter` output stream that is used to write contents to the web part page. Note that in the third output statement I am opening a JavaScript tag. All subsequent output will be JavaScript within this `<script>` tag and the `</script>` tag that will be written at the end of the `RenderWebPart()` method.

Step 2: Create an Instance of the TreeView Object

The next line of code instantiates the treeview object in JavaScript:

```
output.Write("d" & _treeViewId.ToString & " = new dTree('d" &
   _treeViewId.ToString & "');")
```

The `_treeViewId` returns the value of the user-settable TreeViewId property. The default for this is "0", but it can be set to any integer value. If there will be multiple TreeViews on a single page, each one must have a unique `_treeViewId`, or else the dtree routine will add its nodes to the wrong tree!

Step 3: Insert Document Library Node If Multiple Libraries Displayed

The next section of code, shown following, checks to see whether more than one document library will be displayed, and if so, adds a root node for each document library to the tree. If there is only one document library specified in the `DoclibName` property, we skip over this code:

```
If _showFolders And IsMultipleDocs([DoclibName]) Then
  thisNodeId = IncrNodeId()
  output.Write("d" & _treeViewId.ToString & ".add(" & thisNodeId & "," & _
             parentNodeId & ",'" & dl.Title.Trim & "','" & _
             GetDoclibDefaultViewUrl(dl) & "','','_self','" & _
             dl.ImageUrl & "','" & dl.ImageUrl & "');")
End If
```

The `IncrNodeId()` method simply returns the value of a global integer and increments it at the same time (a la i++). This is necessary because each node must have a unique id#.

The previous code also has references to several properties of a SharePoint list object. These are self-evident, but one of the more interesting ones is `ImageUrl()`, which returns the URL of the image .GIF for the type of list (in our case, a document library) referenced. By using this property, you can let SharePoint figure out which icon to use for this node of the tree.

Because I want the user to be able to click the document library link to go to the associated default (usually `allitems.aspx`) page for this library, I need a way to determine the URL to that view. The following code does just that.

```
Private Function GetDoclibDefaultViewUrl(ByVal dl As SPList) As String
  Dim i As Integer
  Dim vw As SPView
  For Each vw In dl.Views
    If vw.DefaultView Then
      Return vw.Url
    End If
  Next
  Return ""
End Function
```

Step 4: Insert Nodes for Each File in the Current Folder

As noted previously, the `ShowSortedFiles()` method writes treeview nodes for each file in the folder. The following code from that routine does the work:

```
Array.Sort(arrFlSorted)
For i = 0 To arrFlSorted.Length - 1
  j = arrFlSorted(i).Split(CONST_SPLITCHAR)(1)
  output.Write("d" & _treeViewId.ToString & ".add(" & IncrNodeId() & "," & _
              thisNodeId & ",'" & FormatTreeNode(fldr.Files(j).Name, _
              fldr.Files(j).Title, _maxLinkWidth, _
              fldr.Files(j).TimeLastModified.ToShortDateString) & "','" &_
              fldr.Files(j).Url & "','','_self','_layouts/images/" & _
              fldr.Files(j).IconUrl & "');")
Next
```

This is very similar to the statement to write a document library node. A few differences include the following:

- `FormatTreeNode()` helper function to format the node text based on the `NodeFormat` property
- `_maxLinkWidth` parameter, based on the `MaxLinkWidth` property
- `fldr.Files(j).IconUrl` property, which returns the appropriate icon .GIF URL for the current document

Step 5: Insert Nodes for Each Subfolder of the Current Folder

Finally, in the `ShowFolderFiles()` method, there is a variant of the previous output statement to display a folder:

```
If _showFolders Then
  output.Write("d" & _treeViewId.ToString & ".add(" & thisNodeId & "," & _
              parentNodeId & ",'" & fl.Name & "','" & fl.Url & _
              "','','','_layouts/jtree/img/folder.gif'," & _
              "'_layouts/jtree/img/folderopen.gif');")
End If
```

The only difference is that the folder icons are explicitly referenced as _layouts/jtree/img/folder.gif and _layouts/jtree/img/folderopen.gif.

If the ShowFolders property was set to False, the data for the file nodes was written to a global collection rather than directly to the output stream. This code appears at the bottom of the RenderWebPart() method:

```
If Not _showFolders Then
  Dim arrSortValue(colOutput.Count - 1) As String
  For i = 1 To colOutput.Count
    arrSortValue(i - 1) = CType(colOutput.Item(i), _
                          String).Split(CONST_SPLITCHAR)(0) & _
                          CONST_SPLITCHAR & CType(colOutput.Item(i), _
                          String).Split(CONST_SPLITCHAR)(1)
  Next
  Array.Sort(arrSortValue)
  For i = 0 To arrSortValue.Length - 1
    j = arrSortValue(i).Split(CONST_SPLITCHAR)(1)
    output.Write(CType(colOutput.Item(j + 1), _
                 String).Split(CONST_SPLITCHAR)(2))
  Next
End If
```

Finally, you write out the JavaScript to display the treeview and close the <script> tag:

```
output.Write("document. write(d" & _treeViewId.ToString & ");")
output.Write("</script>")
```

Creating the Web Part Properties

As you learned in the previous chapter, SharePoint web part properties are defined in much the same way that properties are defined for ASP.NET server controls. Each property has some special code "decoration" that tells SharePoint how to display the property on the web part's property sheet. (For reference, a screen shot of the property sheet is repeated here.)

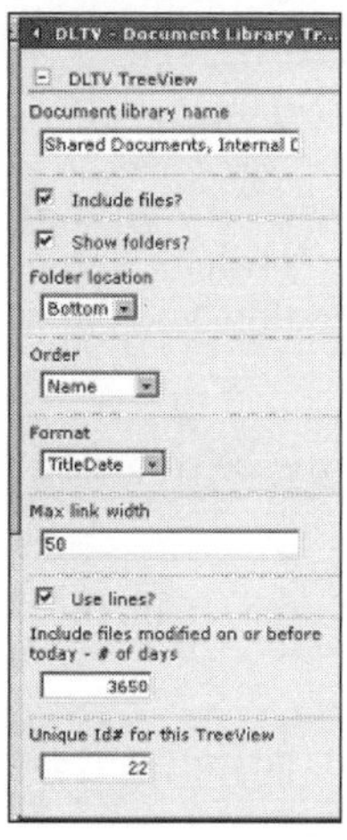

The purpose of each property is as follows:

- **Document Library Name:** A comma-separated list of document libraries to include in the TreeView.
- **Include Files?:** Indicates whether to show files or just folders.
- **Show Folders?:** Indicates whether to show folder structure or to "flatten" the hierarchy and show all files as a simple list.
- **Folder Location:** Either bottom (as in SharePoint) or top (as in Windows Explorer).
- **Order:** The sort order for documents.
- **Format:** Determines which document properties to use when creating a node.
- **Max Link Width:** If name/title length exceeds this length, it will be truncated.
- **Use Lines?:** Indicates whether the TreeView includes lines between nodes.
- **Include Files Modified On Or Before Today - # Of Days:** Documents older than this # of days will not be included in the TreeView.
- **Unique Id# For This TreeView:** Required if multiple TreeViews will appear on the same page.

In this section, I'll cover the code required to define the Folder location property in detail. Other property definitions were created in a similar fashion.

```
<Browsable(True), Category("TreeView"), _
        DefaultValue(EnumFolderLocation.Bottom), _
        WebPartStorage(Storage.Personal), _
        FriendlyName("Folder location"), _
        Description("Should folders be displayed before or after files")> _
```

The preceding code modifies the property definition and defines what, if any, options the user will have to modify this property from the web part property sheet. The clauses have the following meanings:

- **Browsable(True):** Indicates that this property will appear on the property sheet.
- **Category("TreeView"):** Indicates that this property will be in the TreeView section of the sheet.
- **DefaultValue(EnumFolderLocation.Bottom):** Indicates that the property will be a drop-down list made up of values from the `EnumFolderLocation` enumeration, and the default value will be Bottom.
- **WebPartStorage(Storage.Personal):** Indicates that values of this property are stored on a per-user basis.
- **FriendlyName("Folder Location"):** Indicates that the text that will be displayed on the property sheet next to the drop-down list.
- **Description("..."):** Indicates that the tooltip text that will be displayed if the user moves the cursor over the property.

The rest of the property definition simply gets or sets the value of _folderLocation:

```
Property FolderLocation() As EnumFolderLocation

  Get
    Return _folderLocation
  End Get
  Set(ByVal Value As EnumFolderLocation)
    _folderLocation = Value
  End Set

End Property
```

Notice that the property returns a value of type EnumFolderLocation, which is defined in the following code:

```
Public Enum EnumFolderLocation As Integer
  Bottom = 0
  Top = 1
End Enum
```

When you define a property as having an enumeration type, SharePoint displays the property as a drop-down list, with the enumeration item values as the list text. A Boolean property will be rendered as a checkbox, and any other type will be displayed as a textbox. (More information on creating custom properties can be found at http://msdn.microsoft.com/library/default.asp?url=/library/enus/spptsdk/html/CreateWPCustomProperties_SV01003710.asp.)

Summary

In this chapter, you learned how to create a TreeView web part to provide an enhanced user experience when navigating complex document libraries. The TreeView web part does for document libraries what the SQL and XML web parts do for structured data: It's a Swiss army knife for formatting and navigating document libraries. Although there are other TreeView web parts available on the market today, having the source code means you can add features as required. One useful enhancement that we haven't discussed here is the ability to connect this web part to a standard document library web part, thus using the TreeView for folder navigation. Another is to add context menus to each element, similar to those available from the document library list page.

I'll discuss additional navigational improvements in Chapter 7.

CHAPTER 6

Integrating with Non-SharePoint Data Sources

SharePoint provides all the tools you need to create and store documents and structured data such as contacts, events, and tasks in its own database. However, a robust SharePoint extranet needs to include non-SharePoint data from sources such as customer relationship management (CRM), financial, human resource, project management, or other enterprise-wide systems. The challenge addressed in this chapter is how to provide access to this data while you overcome several problems inherent in opening up internal systems to external users. The problems include the following:

- Internal systems need to be protected from unauthorized access.
- Adding accounts for external users to internal systems might be undesirable or even impossible.
- Taking an internal system down for maintenance might "break" portions of the extranet that rely on its data.
- Fluctuations in LAN/WAN traffic and other internal systems factors might make it difficult to predict performance of those web parts that access internal data.

This chapter explores ways to extract and format internal system data, using the XML web part created in Chapter 4. Before deciding on architecture, however, we need to answer the following questions:

- What is the source of the data?
- How current does the data need to be?
- What authentication is required by the source system?
- How should the data be presented to the end user?

Non-SharePoint data sources can include billing, client relationship, inventory, project management, or custom applications unique to your firm (to name just a few). The common denominator is that all these systems store their data in a repository, such as a SQL database, that can be queried by .NET.

■ **Note** Although I assume that the source system's data can be accessed via a SQL query, the XML cache loader can easily be extended to support XML as well as SQL data sources.

Another question is how frequently the data available to the SharePoint user needs to be refreshed from the source system. If a client's contact information changed in the last five minutes in the source system, does it matter that the extranet is showing yesterday's data? The question of how consistent the extranet needs to be with the underlying source systems must be asked for all data that will be displayed on the extranet. In most cases, daily updates are sufficient, although the approach described here will support any update schedule.

Ways to authenticate users against the internal systems are obviously critical, as well as the question of who can see the data extracted from that system. I assume that the permission to see the extracted data is an either-or proposition. In other words, I don't worry about the case in which a user could see orders placed for widgets, but not for gadgets—although I could use the following approach to meet such a requirement. Given this assumption, the targeting feature of the Base web part we created in Chapter 4, in combination with Active Directory (AD) groups, will meet our needs.

Finally, how to present the data to the end user needs to be addressed. Should the result be displayed in tabular form like a DataGrid, in a more structured format similar to a printed invoice, or in a largely free-form layout? Whatever the required layout, we'll enlist the capabilities of XSLT to format XML in just about any way imaginable.

Selecting an Architecture That Meets Our Security Needs

Few IT departments allow access to internal systems from outside the firm's wide area network (WAN), and with good reason, given the rising number of malicious attempts to breach network security. Firms of all sizes and in all industries need to guard their internal data, and that of their business partners, carefully. So, the question is how to expose that data to extranet users in a way that doesn't compromise the security of the source systems.

One approach is to copy well-defined subsets of data from the internal systems to a *demilitarized zone* (DMZ) that exists outside the firm's secure WAN environment. In this scenario, the SharePoint extranet also exists in the DMZ and reads this data cache to present content sourced from internal systems to the extranet user. Figure 6-1 depicts this architecture.

Notice that there is no access from the Extranet domain to the Internal domain. Rather, data from internal systems is copied to the external XML cache from the source systems in the Internal domain. This approach has the advantages that internal systems do not need to maintain user name/password information for extranet users, and that external access to internal systems is not required. A one-way trust from the Internal domain to the Extranet domain can be used to permit the Cache Loader Process to write the XML to an extranet file share.

When a web part page containing an XML web part is rendered, the web part finds its source data in the XML cache rather than reaching back to one of the internal systems.

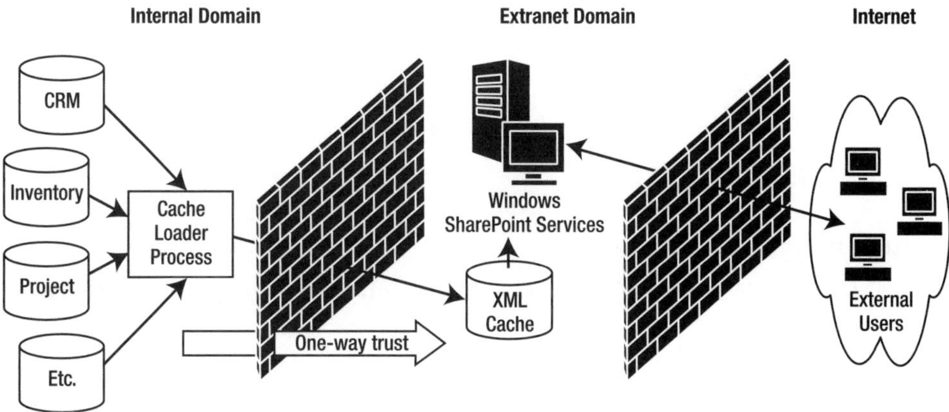

Figure 6-1. *Cache loader architecture*

■ **Note** This model can also be used to implement a cache using a SQL Server database, and indeed these two approaches are not mutually exclusive. One advantage of an XML cache is that response time at page-render is reduced because the XML cache loader executes the query ahead of time; the only work that the XML web part has to do is to read the XML document from disk and format it with the XSLT. A second advantage of XML is that although it's easy to represent SQL Server data as XML, there are non-SQL sources that can't be easily transformed into the row/column structure of a SQL Server table. Moreover, systems vendors are increasingly providing web service APIs that return XML and discouraging direct access to the underlying databases. XML fits the bill by providing a single syntax that can represent structured and semistructured data.

XML and XSLT

This section provides a more detailed discussion of XML and XSLT and how they can be used in the context of SharePoint and our client extranets.

As you learned in Chapter 4, XML is a commonly understood way to represent structured data (for example, a client record from a CRM system) as text. XML can also be easily manipulated by .NET using the DataSet class. XSLT is a variant of XML, which you can use to "transform" XML into a new document. For our purposes, we will use XSLT to transform XML into HTML for display on a web part page.

For a more thorough exploration of what you can do with XSLT technology you might want to pick up a copy of *Beginning XSLT* by Jeni Tennison (Apress) or browse to `http://www.w3.org/TR/1999/REC-xslt-19991116.html` for a formal discussion of the standard. Of course, there are any number of other fine books and articles available on the topic.

In my opinion, the best way to learn XSLT is to use a software tool that lets you be productive right away while teaching you the underlying syntax. See "Additional XSLT Resources" at the end of this chapter for a list of some of the many resources and tools that are available to help you become more proficient with XSLT technology.

■ **Note** Several of the figures in this section show XML and XSLT documents in Stylus Studio Professional from Progress Software. However, you can use another XML/XSLT editor such as XML Spy, Visual Studio, or even Notepad to work with any of these examples.

Just the Basics . . .

In principle, how the XML and XSLT documents work together is very simple, as depicted in Figure 6-2.

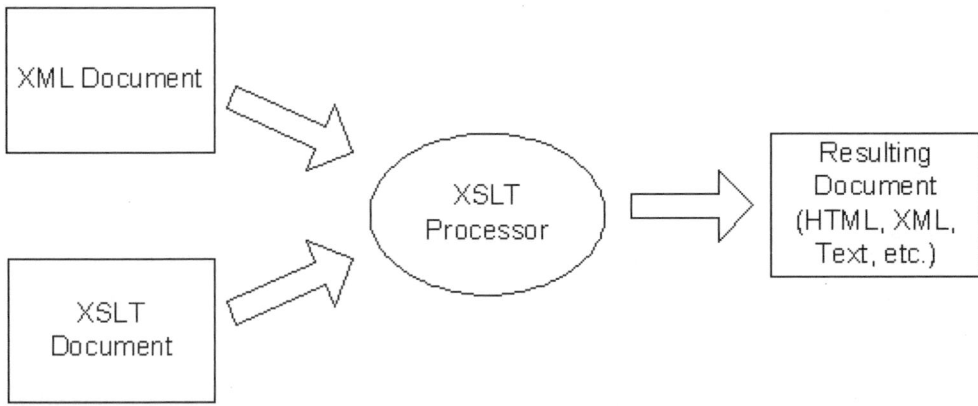

Figure 6-2. *XML/XSLT processing*

You provide the XML and XSLT documents, .NET provides the XSLT processor, and voila! Notice that the resulting document is not limited to any particular format. The XSLT processor renders its output as text, but the content of that output is up to you. In most cases, you will want the transformation to produce HTML for display in a web part; but you can also use XSLT to transform XML to make it easier to work with in .NET. Other possible uses include generating program code (that is, create your own code generator) or formatting the text of a book to include markup tags.

Northwind Orders Example Revisited

In Chapter 4, you used a query against the Northwind database (which is automatically installed with SQL Server 2000) as the source of data for the SQL web part. I'll use the same query here to generate XML for our cache loader. The underlying SQL, which should run on any SQL Server installation that has retained the Northwind sample database, looks like this:

```
SELECT Customers.CompanyName, Orders.OrderID, Products.ProductName,
[Order Details].UnitPrice, [Order Details].Quantity,
Orders.ShippedDate,
[Order Details].Quantity*[Order Details].UnitPrice AS ExtPrice
FROM   Customers INNER JOIN Orders
ON Customers.CustomerID = Orders.CustomerID
```

```
INNER JOIN [Order Details]
ON Orders.OrderID = [Order Details].OrderID
INNER JOIN Products
ON [Order Details].ProductID = Products.ProductID
WHERE  (Customers.CustomerID = N'QUICK') AND (Orders.OrderID = 10285)
```

If you type the preceding code into the SQL Query Analyzer, you will get the result shown in Figure 6-3.

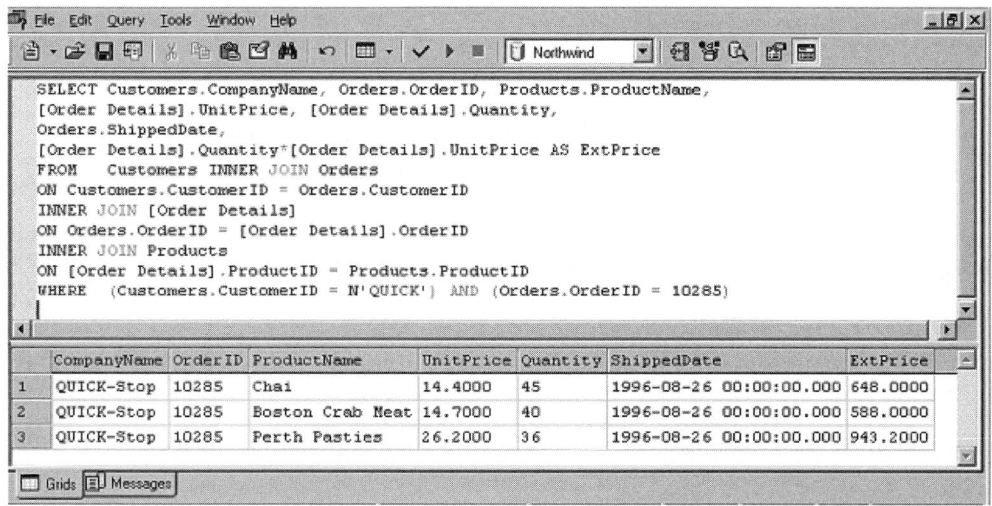

Figure 6-3. *Northwind query result*

What we need is to store the preceding result set in the form of an XML document in our XML cache, ready to be displayed by our custom XML web part. Converting the result into XML is easy. We use the .NET DataSet's WriteXML() method that (as the name implies) writes an XML representation of the data contained in a DataSet to disk. The code shown in Listing 6-1 is all that is required to accomplish this.

Listing 6-1. *The* `WriteDataSet2XML()` *Routine*

```
Private Sub WriteDataSet2XML()
  Dim strCon As String = "user id=Pubs_Test;data source=spsdev;initial" & _
"catalog=Northwind"
  Dim strQry As String
  strQry = "SELECT Customers.CompanyName, " & _
     "Orders.OrderID, Products.ProductName, " & _
     "[Order Details].UnitPrice, [Order Details].Quantity, " & _
     "Orders.ShippedDate, " & _
     "[Order Details].Quantity*[Order Details].UnitPrice AS ExtPrice " & _
     "FROM  Customers INNER JOIN Orders " & _
     "ON Customers.CustomerID = Orders.CustomerID " & _
     "INNER JOIN [Order Details] " & _
     "ON Orders.OrderID = [Order Details].OrderID " & _
```

```
        "INNER JOIN Products " & _
        "ON [Order Details].ProductID = Products.ProductID " & _
        "WHERE  (Customers.CustomerID = N'QUICK') AND (Orders.OrderID = 10285)"

    Dim sa As New SqlClient.SqlDataAdapter(strQry, strCon)
    Dim ds As New DataSet
    sa.Fill(ds)
    ds.DataSetName = "Northwind"
    ds.Tables(0).TableName = "Orders"
    ds.WriteXml("c:\Northwind.xml")

End Sub
```

The preceding code is no different from any that you would write to retrieve SQL data in .NET. The only addition is the `ds.WriteXml("c:\Northwind.xml")` statement, which writes an XML document file to disk (see Listing 6-2).

Listing 6-2. *Resulting Orders XML Document*

```
<?xml version="1.0" standalone="yes"?>
<Northwind>
  <Orders>
    <CompanyName>QUICK-Stop</CompanyName>
    <OrderID>10285</OrderID>
    <ProductName>Chai</ProductName>
    <UnitPrice>14.4000</UnitPrice>
    <Quantity>45</Quantity>
    <ShippedDate>1996-08-26T00:00:00.0000000-07:00</ShippedDate>
    <ExtPrice>648.0000</ExtPrice>
  </Orders>
  <Orders>
    <CompanyName>QUICK-Stop</CompanyName>
    <OrderID>10285</OrderID>
    <ProductName>Boston Crab Meat</ProductName>
    <UnitPrice>14.7000</UnitPrice>
    <Quantity>40</Quantity>
    <ShippedDate>1996-08-26T00:00:00.0000000-07:00</ShippedDate>
    <ExtPrice>588.0000</ExtPrice>
  </Orders>
  <Orders>
    <CompanyName>QUICK-Stop</CompanyName>
    <OrderID>10285</OrderID>
    <ProductName>Perth Pasties</ProductName>
    <UnitPrice>26.2000</UnitPrice>
    <Quantity>36</Quantity>
    <ShippedDate>1996-08-26T00:00:00.0000000-07:00</ShippedDate>
    <ExtPrice>943.2000</ExtPrice>
  </Orders>
</Northwind>
```

A quick look at the structure shows how it maps back to the source data. Each pair of `<Orders></Orders>` tags encloses the data for a single row of the result set. Each column's data is likewise enclosed in a pair of tags with the column name. Although our DataSet contained only one table, it is possible to export any DataSet to an XML file. Let's now turn to the question of how we should format our orders XML document.

Formatting the Northwind Orders Data Using XSLT

Although it is possible to write the XSLT to format the Northwind orders XML document by hand using Notepad or Visual Studio, you'll be much more productive if you use an XSLT editor. This is true for the same reasons that HTML editors make you more productive when creating web pages: the scripting language is very exacting, and simple mistakes can be hard to fine. Figure 6-4 shows Stylus Studio Professional with the `Northwind.xml` document loaded.

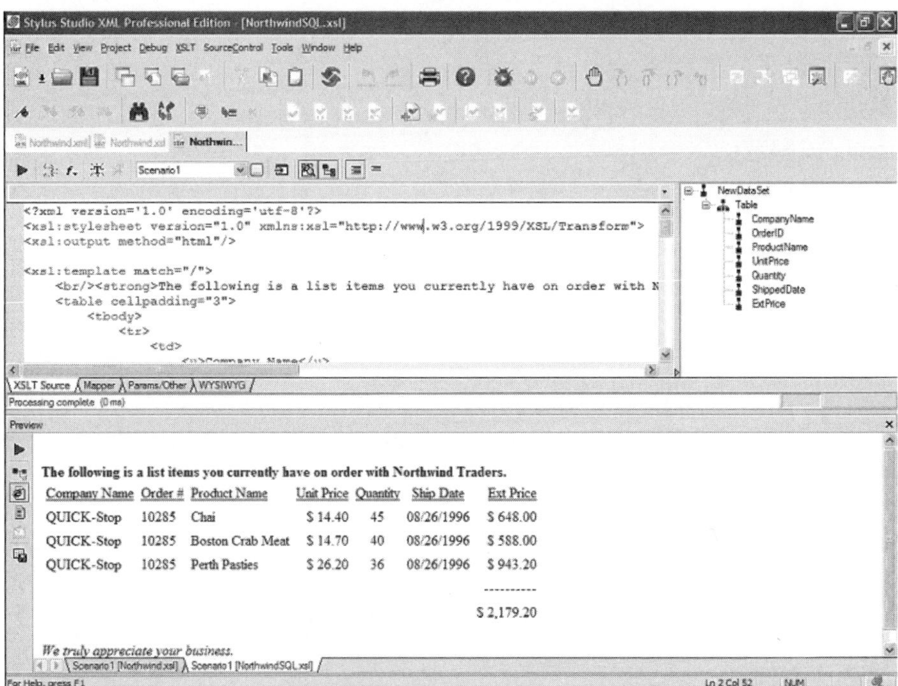

Figure 6-4. *Northwind.xml loaded in XSLT editor*

To produce the desired HTML, I need an XSLT document that performs the transformations on the source. Here are the steps that the XSLT processor needs to perform on the XML:

1. Create an HTML table.

2. Loop through each row of the result set.

3. Insert rows in an HTML table for each row of the result set.

4. Convert the date values to standard *MM/DD/YYYY* format.

5. Convert the price and extended price values to currency format.

6. Sum the extended price column.

The resulting XSLT (see Listing 6-3) does just that.

Listing 6-3. *XSLT to Format Orders XML*

```
<?xml version='1.0' encoding='utf-8'?>
<xsl:stylesheet version="1.0" xmlns:xsl="http://www.w3.org/1999/XSL/Transform">
<xsl:output method="html"/>
<xsl:template match="/">

  <table cellpadding="3">
    <tbody>
    <tr>
        <td><u>Company Name</u></td>
        <td><u>Order #</u></td>
        <td><u>Product Name</u></td>
        <td><u>Unit Price</u></td>
        <td><u>Quantity</u></td>
        <td><u>Ship Date</u></td>
        <td align="right"><u>Ext Price</u></td>
    </tr>
    <xsl:for-each select="Northwind/Orders">
    <tr>
        <td><xsl:value-of select="CompanyName"/></td>
        <td><xsl:value-of select="OrderID"/></td>
        <td><xsl:value-of select="ProductName"/></td>
        <td><xsl:value-of select="UnitPrice"/></td>
        <td><xsl:value-of select="Quantity"/></td>
        <td><xsl:value-of select="substring(ShippedDate,6,2)"/>/
<xsl:value-of select="substring(ShippedDate,9,2)"/>/
<xsl:value-of select="substring(ShippedDate,1,4)"/>
        </td>
        <td align="right">
            <xsl:value-of select="format-number(ExtPrice,'$ #,###.00')"/>
        </td>
    </tr>
    </xsl:for-each>
    <tr>
<td colspan="6"></td>
        <td align="right">----------</td>
    </tr>
    <tr>
        <td colspan="6"></td>
        <td align="right">
```

```
<xsl:value-of
select= "format-number(sum(Northwind/Orders/ExtPrice),
'$ #,###.00')"/>
</td>
    </tr>
    </tbody>
  </table>
</xsl:template>
</xsl:stylesheet>
```

The resulting HTML looks like Figure 6-5 when you view it in a browser.

Figure 6-5. *Resulting HTML output*

Although each XSLT document will differ depending on how you want to display the output on the screen, they all invariably contain many of the same elements. For example, each XSLT must have both an XML and XSL header declaration, and generally an `output` and `template` declaration as well. I'll now step you through these elements so you can see how they work together.

Because XSLTs are a special type of XML document, every XSLT document begins with the standard XML header:

```
<?xml version='1.0' encoding='utf-8'?>
```

Following this header is the standard XSLT header:

```
<xsl:stylesheet version="1.0" xmlns:xsl="http://www.w3.org/1999/XSL/Transform">
```

Next comes the XSL statement that tells the XSLT processor that its output will be HTML:

```
<xsl:output method="html"/>
```

Finally, there is a directive telling the processor where in the XML document tree to begin processing (`"/"` indicates that it should begin at the "root"):

```
<xsl:template match="/">
```

Most of the XSLTs you create for use with SharePoint need to process result sets with multiple rows. The `xsl:for-each` directive handles this:

```
<xsl:for-each select="Northwind/Orders">
```

Throw in a couple of formatting functions and one aggregate function and we're done:

```
<xsl:value-of select="substring(ShippedDate,6,2)"/>
<xsl:value-of select="format-number(ExtPrice,'$ #,###.00')"/>
<xsl:value-of select="format-number(sum(Northwind/Orders/ExtPrice),'$ #,###.00')"/>
```

As you can see, these functions are quite similar to their .NET or SQL counterparts.

Caution XSLT document processors are case-sensitive, which means that typing **<Northwind>** is not the same as typing **<northwind>** as far as the XSLT processor is concerned. This is generally not an issue if you use an XSLT editor, but it can result in hard-to-find bugs if you decide to use Notepad. You must also be sure to place all constant expressions in quotation marks. For example, although HTML allows `<td align="right">` to be written as `<td align=right>`, the omission of quotes will cause the XSLT processor to throw an exception and stop processing the XML document.

Displaying Northwind Orders with the XML Web Part

So far, you've seen how you can extract internal system data to an XML file and how you can format an XML document using an XSLT. Before I proceed to show you how to build an XML cache loader, I want to take a brief detour to show you how the XML web part we created in Chapter 4 will use these two documents.

Remember that the XML web part has two user-definable properties: the XML source and the XSLT source. In Chapter 4 we used the Google Really Simple Syndication (RSS) news service and a local XSLT document. In our current example, the XML source will also point to a local document; the result is shown in Figure 6-6.

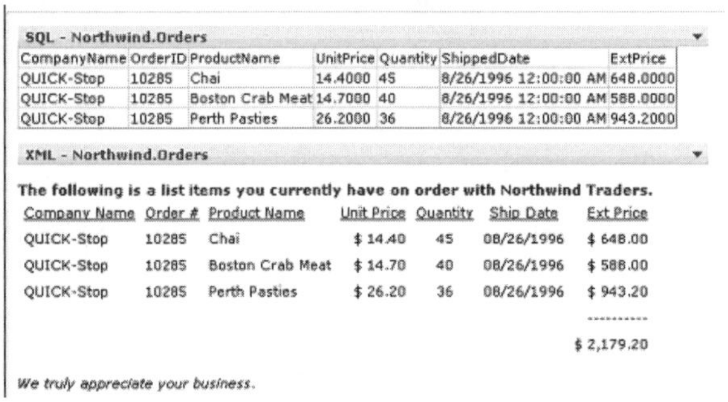

SQL - Northwind.Orders

CompanyName	OrderID	ProductName	UnitPrice	Quantity	ShippedDate	ExtPrice
QUICK-Stop	10285	Chai	14.4000	45	8/26/1996 12:00:00 AM	648.0000
QUICK-Stop	10285	Boston Crab Meat	14.7000	40	8/26/1996 12:00:00 AM	588.0000
QUICK-Stop	10285	Perth Pasties	26.2000	36	8/26/1996 12:00:00 AM	943.2000

XML - Northwind.Orders

The following is a list items you currently have on order with Northwind Traders.

Company Name	Order #	Product Name	Unit Price	Quantity	Ship Date	Ext Price
QUICK-Stop	10285	Chai	$ 14.40	45	08/26/1996	$ 648.00
QUICK-Stop	10285	Boston Crab Meat	$ 14.70	40	08/26/1996	$ 588.00
QUICK-Stop	10285	Perth Pasties	$ 26.20	36	08/26/1996	$ 943.20

						$ 2,179.20

We truly appreciate your business.

Figure 6-6. *Display of Northwind Orders using the custom XML web part*

You can see that using XSLT allowed me to present the data in a much more readable format than the format used for a simple DataGrid. You might remember that the custom SQL web part also has an option to format the result using an XSLT. In fact, I can produce the same output by changing the SQL web parts `Format output using` and `XSLT path` properties, as shown in Figure 6-7.

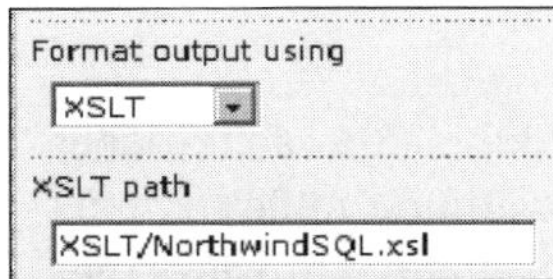

Figure 6-7. *Setting SQL web part properties to use an XSLT*

Figure 6-8 shows the results of these property changes.

SQL - Northwind.Orders

The following is a list items you currently have on order with Northwind Traders.

Company Name	Order #	Product Name	Unit Price	Quantity	Ship Date	Ext Price
QUICK-Stop	10285	Chai	$ 14.40	45	08/26/1996	$ 648.00
QUICK-Stop	10285	Boston Crab Meat	$ 14.70	40	08/26/1996	$ 588.00
QUICK-Stop	10285	Perth Pasties	$ 26.20	36	08/26/1996	$ 943.20

						$ 2,179.20

We truly appreciate your business.

XML - Northwind.Orders

The following is a list items you currently have on order with Northwind Traders.

Company Name	Order #	Product Name	Unit Price	Quantity	Ship Date	Ext Price
QUICK-Stop	10285	Chai	$ 14.40	45	08/26/1996	$ 648.00
QUICK-Stop	10285	Boston Crab Meat	$ 14.70	40	08/26/1996	$ 588.00
QUICK-Stop	10285	Perth Pasties	$ 26.20	36	08/26/1996	$ 943.20

						$ 2,179.20

We truly appreciate your business.

Figure 6-8. *SQL and XML web parts with XSLT formatting*

Given that both the SQL and XML web parts provide the same output, you might be wondering why bother to extract the data to an XML file; why not just query the database directly? Wouldn't it be better to provide end users with up-to-the-minute reports of their orders? The answer is that we could if we allow the extranet SharePoint server to query the Northwind database directly. However, for security and performance reasons we decided that's not a good idea. (If you're still wondering about this, ask your finance department how they'd feel about systems outside the firm's firewall querying their databases!)

■ **Tip** You can create SQL and XML web parts with identical formats: a SQL web part for internal users and an XML web part for external users. That way, internal users accessing a SharePoint server on the WAN will see the most current data, whereas extranet users accessing a SharePoint server in the extranet domain will see a "snapshot" of that same data, both in the same format.

XML Cache Loader

Now that the building blocks are in place, I'll put it all together to build the XML cache loader. For the purpose of this discussion, let's assume that the Northwind.Customers table contains the authoritative list of customer IDs. Because most firms have one system that provides the "master" customer list, with references to these customers used throughout other internal systems, this is a reasonable assumption.

The output of the cache loader will generate a collection of XML document files: one for each customer in the Customers table as well as some processing status data written to the Windows console. Figure 6-9 depicts the logic of the XML cache loader process.

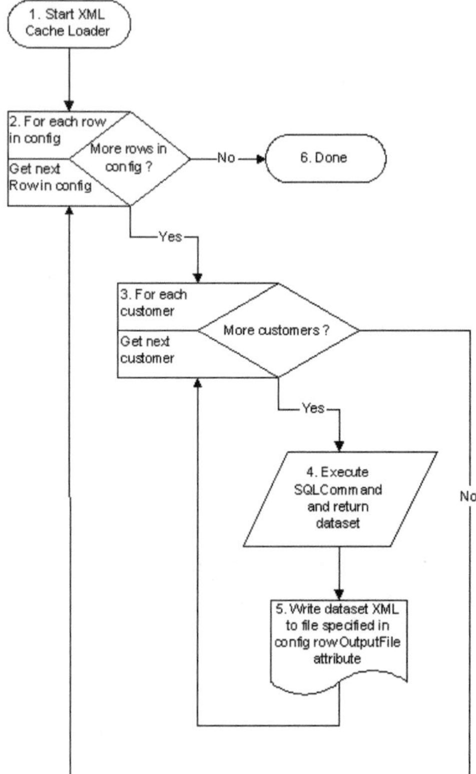

Figure 6-9. *XML cache loader process flow*

1. Start the cache loader .NET console application (see the next section).
2. Load the `CacheLoaderConfig.xml` file into a .NET DataSet, and loop through each row until you process the last row.
3. Load the customer list from the Northwinds.Customers table and loop through each customer for the current CacheLoaderConfig row.

4. Execute the SQL query to return the results into a .NET DataSet.
5. Write the DataSet as an XML file using the filename specified in the `CacheLoaderConfig.xml` file.

XML Cache Loader Metadata

The cache loading process is driven by an XML configuration file that describes which data sources to load and where to write the resulting XML files (are you getting the sense that we live in an XML world?). The configuration file to generate the Northwind orders XML documents looks like Listing 6-4.

Listing 6-4. *Cache Loader Metadata*

```
<?xml version="1.0"?>
<CacheLoader>
  <Request>
    <SQLConnection>user id=Pubs_Test;data source=spsdev;initial catalog
=Northwind</SQLConnection>
    <SQLCommand>
    SELECT Customers.CompanyName,Orders.OrderID,Products.ProductName,
      [Order Details].UnitPrice,[Order Details].Quantity,Orders.ShippedDate,
      [Order Details].Quantity*[Order Details].UnitPrice AS ExtPrice
      FROM Customers INNER JOIN Orders ON Customers.CustomerID=Orders.CustomerID
      INNER JOIN [Order Details] ON Orders.OrderID = [Order Details].OrderID
      INNER JOIN Products ON [Order Details].ProductID = Products.ProductID
      WHERE (Customers.CustomerID = '[CustomerID]')
    </SQLCommand>
    <OutputName>NorthwindOrders</OutputName>
  </Request>
  <Request>
    <SQLConnection>user id=Pubs_Test;data source=spsdev;initial catalog
=Northwind</SQLConnection>
    <SQLCommand>
    SELECT    CompanyName,ContactName,ContactTitle,Address,Phone,Fax
      FROM Customers
      WHERE (Customers.CustomerID = '[CustomerID]')
    </SQLCommand>
    <OutputName>NorthwindCustomers</OutputName>
  </Request>
</CacheLoader>
```

Cache Loader Source Code

As shown in Listing 6-5, the program processes the configuration file, writing out one XML document file for each request/customer combination.

Listing 6-5. *Cache Loader Program*

```
Sub Main()

  'Load the cache loader requests
  Dim dsRequests As New DataSet
  Dim drRequest As DataRow
  dsRequests.ReadXml("c:\NonSPSApps\XML\CacheLoaderConfig.xml")

  'Get a list of all customers
  Dim strConCustomers As String = "user id=Pubs_Test;data source=spsdev;" & _
"initial catalog=Northwind"
  Dim strQryCustomers As String = "select CustomerID from Customers " & _
"order by CustomerID"
  Dim saCustomers As New SqlClient.SqlDataAdapter(strQryCustomers, strConCustomers)
  Dim dsCustomers As New DataSet
  Dim drCustomer As DataRow
  saCustomers.Fill(dsCustomers)

  'Loop through each Request, and write one XML document for each customer
  Dim dsResultSet As New DataSet
  Dim saResultSet As New SqlClient.SqlDataAdapter
  Dim strConResultSet As String
  Dim strQryResultSet As String
  Dim strOutputName As String

  'Process each cache loader request
  For Each drRequest In dsRequests.Tables(0).Rows

      'Process for each customer
      For Each drCustomer In dsCustomers.Tables(0).Rows

           strQryResultSet = Replace(LCase(drRequest("SQLCommand")), _
               "[customerid]", _
               drCustomer("CustomerID"))
          strConResultSet = drRequest("SQLConnection")
          dsResultSet = New DataSet
          saResultSet = New SqlClient.SqlDataAdapter(strQryResultSet, _
               strConResultSet)
          saResultSet.Fill(dsResultSet)
          strOutputName = "c:\NonSPSApps\XML\" & drRequest("OutputName") & "_" & _
 drCustomer("CustomerID") & ".XML"
          dsResultSet.WriteXml(strOutputName)
          Console.WriteLine(strOutputName & " written.")

      Next
```

```
    Next

    Console.WriteLine("")
    Console.WriteLine("Processing complete.")
    Console.ReadLine()

End Sub
```

A partial listing of the output from running the cache loader is displayed in Figure 6-10.

```
C:\Documents and Settings\mgerow\My Documents\Visual Studio Projects\CacheLoader\...

Beginning cache loader process.
c:\NonSPSApps\XML\NorthwindOrders_ALFKI.XML written.
c:\NonSPSApps\XML\NorthwindOrders_ANATR.XML written.
c:\NonSPSApps\XML\NorthwindOrders_ANTON.XML written.
c:\NonSPSApps\XML\NorthwindOrders_AROUT.XML written.
c:\NonSPSApps\XML\NorthwindCustomers_ALFKI.XML written.
c:\NonSPSApps\XML\NorthwindCustomers_ANATR.XML written.
c:\NonSPSApps\XML\NorthwindCustomers_ANTON.XML written.
c:\NonSPSApps\XML\NorthwindCustomers_AROUT.XML written.

Processing complete.
```

Figure 6-10. *Output from XML cache loader*

Scheduling the XML Cache Loader

The Windows Scheduler, a standard part of the Windows operating system, provides a convenient way to automatically run the cache loader at regular intervals. To create a new scheduled job, choose the Scheduled Tasks option from the Systems Tools menu. To get there, click Program Files and then click Accessories from the Start menu, as shown in Figure 6-11.

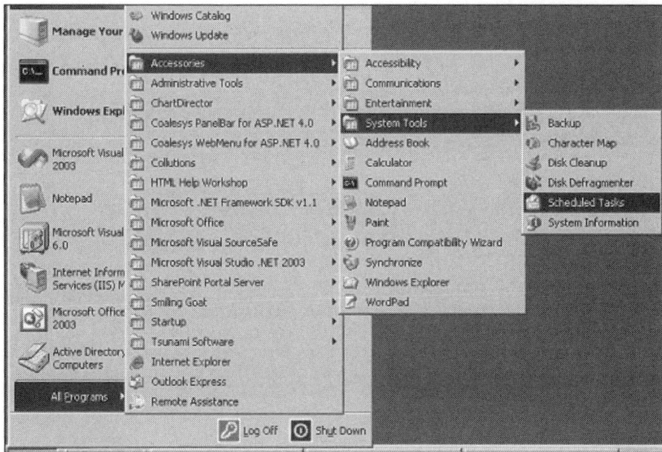

Figure 6-11. *Creating a scheduled task to run the cache loader*

To create a scheduled task to run the cache loader, follow these steps:

1. Double-click the Add Scheduled Task item at the top of the list of scheduled tasks.
2. Click the Browse button and then navigate to the `\bin` folder of the CacheLoader console application.
3. Double-click on `CacheLoader.exe`.
4. Choose Daily for the frequency to perform this task.
5. Click Next twice.
6. Enter a user name and password under which the task will run.
7. Click Next.
8. Click Finish.

Your Scheduled Tasks window should now include a CacheLoader task as shown in Figure 6-12.

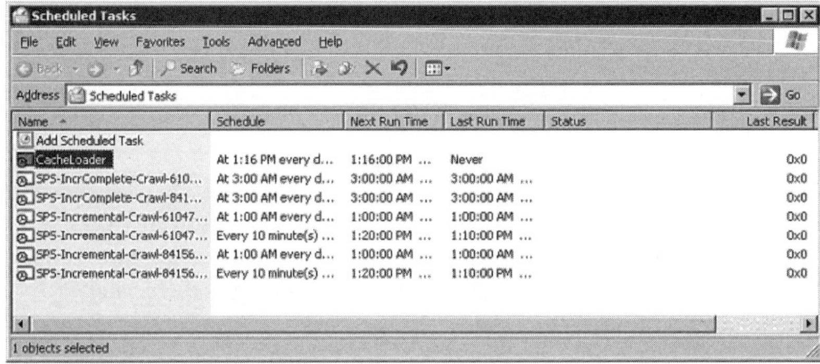

Figure 6-12. *The scheduled tasks window showing the XML cache loader process*

You can test the task by right-clicking CacheLoader and choosing the Run command. The display changes to indicate the run time and return code (see Figure 6-13).

Name	Schedule	Next Run Time	Last Run Time	Status	Last Result	Creator
Add Scheduled Task						
CacheLoader	At 1:16 PM every d...	1:16:00 PM ...	1:22:24 PM ...		0x0	mgerow

Figure 6-13. *Scheduled tasks display, showing a successful run of the XML cache loader*

A Last Result value of 0x0 indicates that no errors occurred. You should also verify that the XML files were written correctly to the target folder.

Summary

In this chapter you learned how to write data from internal system databases to XML documents in an XML cache that can be securely and reliably accessed by extranet users without the need to give those users access to the source systems. This approach has several benefits:

- Internal system security is not compromised.
- Extranet users do not need user accounts in source systems.
- Data is available to extranet users even if internal systems are offline for maintenance or other reasons.
- Performance is fast and predictable.

You can now integrate your SharePoint extranet with a wide range of systems while minimizing concerns about security, user account management, availability, and performance. Taking this approach enables you to create a robust SharePoint extranet, one that your clients will appreciate for its varied and valuable content.

Additional XSLT Resources

There are a vast number of resources available to help you master XSLT syntax. A few excellent places to start are these:

- `http://www.w3schools.com/xsl/`
- `http://www.w3.org/TR/xslt`

In addition, there are many XSLT editors available, both commercial and shareware. Here are some you might want to investigate:

- Stylus Studio Professional, Progress Software
- XML Spy, Altova
- Or simply search the web for "XSLT editors"

Books that you might find helpful include these:

- *Beginning XSLT*, by Jeni Tennison; Apress, 2004
- *XSLT Cookbook*, by Sal Mangano; O'Reilly, 2002
- *Learning XSLT*, by Michael Fitzgerald; O'Reilly, 2003

CHAPTER 7

Customizing Site Navigation

Windows SharePoint Services (WSS) comes with several built-in site templates that provide rudimentary navigation between and within sites. However, a common complaint of SharePoint users is that the built-in navigation is confusing and frustrating. Especially in an extranet environment, in which your client's perception of your firm will be affected by the quality of their experience on the site, it's important to provide the best possible user experience.

In this chapter, I'll discuss several ways in which you can customize or replace the SharePoint navigation features to improve the end user's experience. We'll explore the following three techniques:

- Customizing the standard Quick Launch menu
- Creating a replacement Quick Launch menu
- Creating a My Extranets page

At the conclusion of this chapter, you'll be able to make informed design choices regarding whether and how much customization is right for your extranet site.

Customizing the Quick Launch

Customizing the out-of-the-box Quick Launch is accomplished via two techniques:

- Modifying the CSS classes in `OWS.css` to alter the way the menu text displays
- Modifying the `default.aspx` page to exclude unwanted menu sections

Modifying OWS.css to Alter the Quick Launch Menu

Some of the simplest customizations you can make are to the color, size, or appearance of the Quick Launch category headings. Listing 7-1 shows some minor changes to the `.ms-navheader` CSS class of the `OWS.css` file.

Note The `OWS.css` file, as well as all SharePoint style sheets, can be found in `c:\Program Files\Common Files\Microsoft Shared\web server extensions\60\TEMPLATE\LAYOUTS\1033\STYLES` (assuming you installed SharePoint on the `c:` drive).

Listing 7-1. *Modifications to* `OWS.css` *to Change the Quick Launch Headings*

```
.ms-navheader A,.ms-navheader A:link, .ms-navheader A:visited {
    font-weight: bold;
    /* MG: Make the header italic */
    font-style: italic;
    /* MG: Make the header larger */
    font-size: larger;
    /* MG: Add a color to change the foreground */
    color: Green;
    /* MG: Add a background-color */
    background-color: Yellow;
}
```

■ **Caution** Prior to making changes to `OWS.css`, or to any SharePoint file, you should make a backup copy of the original, or preferably add the original to a source control system such as Microsoft Visual SourceSafe, so that you can easily restore the original if your modifications introduce an error.

Modifying Default.aspx

Another easy way to modify the Quick Launch menu is to edit the `default.aspx` page that is referenced in a site template. You might recall from earlier chapters that modifications to this file should be made with care (of course, you're using a source control so you can easily roll back to an earlier known-good version if you make a mistake). The changes here are simple. We will do the following:

1. Remove the Quick Launch watermark.
2. Remove the section displaying picture lists.
3. Remove the section displaying discussion lists.
4. Remove the section displaying survey lists.

In your extranet, you might choose to make any or all of these modifications. I chose these because a) the "Quick Links" watermark provides no useful information and takes up valuable browser space; b) the sites I create generally do not use picture, discussion, or survey lists.

■ **Note** One perfectly valid option not discussed here is to remove the Quick Launch menu section altogether. This can easily be accomplished by removing, rather than editing, the sections of `default.aspx` discussed following.

Removing the Quick Launch Watermark

Although the WSS Team Site watermark demonstrates some interesting HTML techniques, the watermark itself provides no real value to end users, and yet it takes up a significant amount of browser real estate. For these reasons, removing the default watermark is one of the first changes I always make to the standard site `default.aspx` file. Removing the watermark is simply a matter of finding and removing the HTML that produces it. Listing 7-2 shows the section of code that needs to be removed.

Listing 7-2. *HTML to Render the Quick Launch Watermark*

```
<!-- MG: To remove the watermark, delete the following <TD></TD> range. -->
<td valign=top id="onetidWatermark" class="ms-navwatermark" style="padding-top:
4px;padding-right: 0px;" dir="ltr">
  <!--[if gte vml 1]>
  <v:shapetype id="_x0000_t136" coordsize="21600,21600" o:spt="136" adj="10800"
path="m@7,l@8,m@5,21600l@6,21600e">
    <v:formulas>
      <v:f eqn="sum #0 0 10800"/>
      <v:f eqn="prod #0 2 1"/>
      <v:f eqn="sum 21600 0 @1"/>
      <v:f eqn="sum 0 0 @2"/>
      <v:f eqn="sum 21600 0 @3"/>
      <v:f eqn="if @0 @3 0"/>
      <v:f eqn="if @0 21600 @1"/>
      <v:f eqn="if @0 0 @2"/>
      <v:f eqn="if @0 @4 21600"/>
      <v:f eqn="mid @5 @6"/>
      <v:f eqn="mid @8 @5"/>
      <v:f eqn="mid @7 @8"/>
      <v:f eqn="mid @6 @7"/>
      <v:f eqn="sum @6 0 @5"/>
    </v:formulas>
    <v:path textpathok="t" o:connecttype="custom"
o:connectlocs="@9,0;@10,10800;@11,21600;@12,10800"
       o:connectangles="270,180,90,0"/>
    <v:textpath on="t" fitshape="t"/>
    <v:handles>
      <v:h position="#0,bottomRight" xrange="6629,14971"/>
    </v:handles>
    <o:lock v:ext="edit" text="t" shapetype="t"/>
  </v:shapetype>
```

```
  <v:shape id="navWatermark" type="#_x0000_t136" style='width:139pt;
height:17.25pt;rotation:-90' fillcolor="#cbdbf8;" stroked="f">
    <v:textpath style='font-family:"Arial";font-size:18pt;font-weight:bold; v-text-
spacing:2;v-text-spacing-mode:tightening' string="Quick Launch"/>
  </v:shape>
<![endif]-->
<script>
  if (browseris.ie5up && document.all("navWatermark") &&
document.all("onetidWatermark")) {
document.all("navWatermark").fillcolor=document.all("onetidWatermark"). _
currentStyle.color;
        }
</script>
</td>
```

Removing the Pictures Section

Another standard component of the Quick Launch menu is the Pictures category. In my experience, very few sites require libraries of pictures (if pictures are required, they can easily be added to document libraries), so I usually remove this section. Listing 7-3 shows the code to remove from `default.aspx` to accomplish this.

Listing 7-3. *HTML That Renders the Pictures Category on the Quick Launch Menu*

```
<!-- MG: Remove the "Picture" links. -->
<TR>
   <TD class="ms-navheader"><A
HREF="_layouts/<%=System.Threading.Thread.CurrentThread. _
CurrentUICulture.LCID%>
/viewlsts.aspx?BaseType=1&ListTemplate=109">Pictures</A>
  </TD>
</TR>
<TR>
  <TD style="height: 6px">
<!--webbot bot="Navigation" S-Btn-Nobr="FALSE" S-Type="sequence" S-Rendering="html"
 S-Orientation="Vertical" B-Include-Home="FALSE" B-Include-Up="FALSE" U-
Page="sid:1005" S-Bar-Pfx="<table border=0 cellpadding=4 cellspacing=0>" S-Bar-
Sfx="</table>" S-Btn-Nml="<tr><td><table border=0 cellpadding=0
cellspacing=0><tr><td><img src='_layouts/images/blank.gif' ID='100' alt='Icon'
border=0>&amp;nbsp;</td><td valign=top><a ID=onetleftnavbar#LABEL_ID#
href='#URL#'>#LABEL#</td></tr></table></td></tr>" S-Target TAG="BODY" startspan -
><SharePoint:Navigation LinkBarId="1005" runat="server"/><!--webbot bot="Navigation"
endspan -->
  </TD>
</TR>
```

Removing the Discussions Section

In a similar fashion, the Discussions section can be removed by eliminating the HTML shown in Listing 7-4.

Listing 7-4. *HTML That Renders the Discussions Category on the Quick Launch Menu*

```
<!-- MG: Remove the "Discussion" links. -->
<TR>
  <TD class="ms-navheader">
    <A HREF="_layouts/ ➥
<%=System.Threading.Thread.CurrentThread.CurrentUICulture.LCID%>
/viewlsts.aspx?BaseType=3">Discussions</A>
  </TD>
</TR>
<TR>
  <TD style="height: 6px">
<!--webbot bot="Navigation" S-Btn-Nobr="FALSE" S-Type="sequence" S-Rendering="html"
S-Orientation="Vertical" B-Include-Home="FALSE" B-Include-Up="FALSE" U-
Page="sid:1006" S-Bar-Pfx="<table border=0 cellpadding=4 cellspacing=0>" S-Bar-
Sfx="</table>" S-Btn-Nml="<tr><td><table border=0 cellpadding=0
cellspacing=0><tr><td><img src='_layouts/images/blank.gif' ID='100' alt='Icon'
border=0>&amp;nbsp;</td><td valign=top><a ID=onetleftnavbar#LABEL_ID#
href='#URL#'>#LABEL#</td></tr></table></td></tr>" S-Target TAG="BODY" startspan -
><SharePoint:Navigation LinkBarId="1006" runat="server"/><!--webbot bot="Navigation"
endspan -->
  </TD>
</TR>
```

Removing the Surveys Section

Finally, removing the following HTML from `default.aspx`, as shown in Listing 7-5, will remove the Surveys category (you get the idea . . .).

Listing 7-5. *HTML to Render the Surveys Category on the Quick Launch Menu*

```
<!-- MG: Remove the "Surveys" links. -->
<TR>
  <TD class="ms-navheader">
    <A HREF="_layouts/ ➥
<%=System.Threading.Thread.CurrentThread.CurrentUICulture.LCID%>
/viewlsts.aspx?BaseType=4">Surveys</A></TD></TR>
```

```
<TR>
  <TD style="height: 6px">
<!--webbot bot="Navigation" S-Btn-Nobr="FALSE" S-Type="sequence" S-Rendering="html"
S-Orientation="Vertical" B-Include-Home="FALSE" B-Include-Up="FALSE" U-
Page="sid:1007" S-Bar-Pfx="<table border=0 cellpadding=4 cellspacing=0>" S-Bar-
Sfx="</table>" S-Btn-Nml="<tr><td><table border=0 cellpadding=0
cellspacing=0><tr><td><img src='_layouts/images/blank.gif' ID='100' alt='Icon'
border=0>&amp;nbsp;</td><td valign=top><a ID=onetleftnavbar#LABEL_ID#
href='#URL#'>#LABEL#</td></tr></table></td></tr>" S-Target TAG="BODY" startspan -
><SharePoint:Navigation LinkBarId="1007" runat="server"/><!--webbot bot="Navigation"
endspan -->
    </TD>
</TR>
```

Removing the sections shown previously affects all sites based on the template containing the copy of `default.aspx` that you edit, so it's probably a good idea to test your changes on a sample site template prior to altering one in production. By making the preceding changes you can quickly give all sites based on this template a cleaner and more professional appearance.

Replacing the Quick Launch with a Custom Server Control

There are times when making minor alterations to the out-of-the-box Quick Launch menu just isn't enough to meet your needs. You might want more control over how the Quick Launch menu is formatted, or you might want to include only those links that the user has permissions to view—both of which require replacing the stock Quick Launch menu.

In this section, I'll show you how to create a replacement for the Quick Launch menu that provides complete control over its appearance.

Obtaining a List of All Document Libraries and Lists for the Current User

The first step is to obtain a list of all document libraries and lists the current user is authorized to view. I'll accomplish this by creating a custom web server control that will query the SharePoint object model to return a list of contacts, document libraries, events, tasks, and other lists for the current user. I'll then format this list using an XSLT.

The following code listings show how the `MyQuickLaunch` server control is written. Listing 7-6 shows the `Imports` statements required. Note that in addition to the standard imports I included references to the `Microsoft.SharePoint` and `Microsoft.SharePoint.WebControls` libraries. These provide access `SharePoint SPWeb` and `SPListCollections` classes and their associated members.

Listing 7-6. `MyQuickLaunch` *Imports*

```
Imports System.ComponentModel
Imports System.Web.UI
Imports Microsoft.SharePoint
Imports Microsoft.SharePoint.WebControls
```

The MyQuickLaunch control will have one public property: XSLTSource. This property allows me to pass the name of an XSLT file that will be used to format the output produced by the control (this is shown in Listing 7-7).

Listing 7-7. XSLTSource *Property*

```
<DefaultProperty("Text"), ToolboxData("<{0}:QL runat=server></{0}:QL>")>
Public Class QL
Inherits System.Web.UI.WebControls.WebControl
  Dim _xsltSource As String
  <Bindable(True), Category("Appearance"), DefaultValue("")>
  Property XSLTSource() As String  Get
        Return _xsltSource
    End Get
    Set(ByVal Value As String)
        _xsltSource = Value
    End Set
  End Property
```

The Render method is where all the work of processing the list and displaying the output is done. Listings 7-8 through 7-10 show sections of the method code.

Listing 7-8. MyQuickLaunch *Render Method*

```
Protected Overrides Sub Render(ByVal output As System.Web.UI.HtmlTextWriter)
  'Obtain a handle to the currently displayed website
```

As a first step, I instantiate an SPWeb object to obtain a collection of lists the current user is authorized to access. I also create a DataTable object to hold the results. Note the assignment web.Lists.ListForCurrentUser = True, which ensures that the only lists displayed are those the user is authorized to view. After a collection of lists is available in web.Lists, it's a simple matter to iterate through the collection, adding a row for each list to my DataTable.

Listing 7-9. *Getting the List of Lists*

```
      Dim web As SPWeb = SPControl.GetContextWeb(context)
      Dim list As SPList

       'Create a DataTable object to hold the results
      Dim dt As New DataTable("MyLists")
      Dim dr As DataRow
      dt.Columns.Add("Template")
      dt.Columns.Add("Title")
      dt.Columns.Add("Url")
      dt.Columns.Add("ImageUrl")
      dt.Columns.Add("Description")
      dt.Columns.Add("Type")
```

```
    'Only include lists that the current user is authorized to view
    web.Lists.ListsForCurrentUser = True

    'Iterate through the list items, adding to the DataTable those
    'that are flagged as visible and to be displayed on the Quick Launch
    For Each list In web.Lists
        If list.Hidden = False And list.OnQuickLaunch = True Then
            dr = dt.NewRow
            dr("Type") = list.BaseType
            dr("Title") = list.Title
            dr("Url") = list.DefaultViewUrl
            dr("ImageUrl") = list.ImageUrl
            dr("Description") = list.Description
            dr("Template") = list.BaseTemplate
            dt.Rows.Add(dr)
        End If
    Next
```

The last section of code (see Listing 7-10) creates a new XML web control, assigns the XML from `DataTable` to it, transforms the XML using the supplied XSLT, and renders the resulting HTML to the output stream.

Listing 7-10. *Rendering the Output to the Page*

```
    'Display the list on the page.
    Dim xml As New Web.UI.WebControls.Xml
    Dim ds As New DataSet("MyLists")
    ds.Tables.Add(dt)
    xml.DocumentContent = ds.GetXml
    xml.TransformSource = XSLTSource
    xml.RenderControl(output)

End Sub
```

■ **Note** The preceding code provides an important improvement over the stock Quick Launch routine; it only displays those lists that the user is authorized to view. The stock Quick Launch, on the other hand, displays any lists that are flagged for inclusion on the Quick Launch menu, even if the end user is not authorized to view them. It is only when the user clicks a link that SharePoint verifies the user's permissions and, for unauthorized users, displays a login dialog box requesting that they provide a new user name and password.

Figure 7-1 shows the unformatted data retrieved from the `SPWeb` object displayed in a DataGrid. Note that the Url column is relative to the current site (in this example `http://localhost`). This data provides the raw material to create a nicely formatted list of lists from which your users can navigate to the list of their choice.

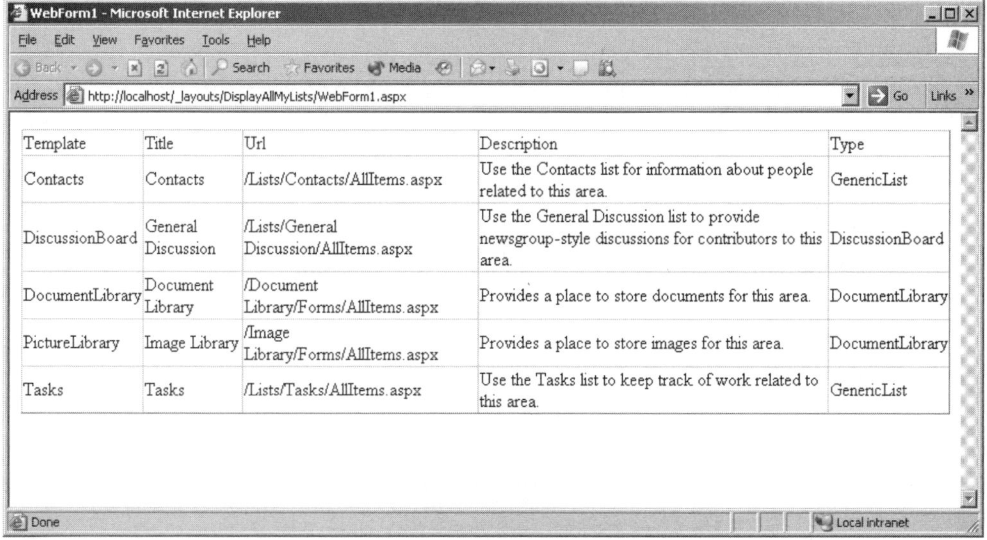

Template	Title	Url	Description	Type
Contacts	Contacts	/Lists/Contacts/AllItems.aspx	Use the Contacts list for information about people related to this area.	GenericList
DiscussionBoard	General Discussion	/Lists/General Discussion/AllItems.aspx	Use the General Discussion list to provide newsgroup-style discussions for contributors to this area.	DiscussionBoard
DocumentLibrary	Document Library	/Document Library/Forms/AllItems.aspx	Provides a place to store documents for this area.	DocumentLibrary
PictureLibrary	Image Library	/Image Library/Forms/AllItems.aspx	Provides a place to store images for this area.	DocumentLibrary
Tasks	Tasks	/Lists/Tasks/AllItems.aspx	Use the Tasks list to keep track of work related to this area.	GenericList

Figure 7-1. *Data used by* `MyQuickLaunch`

Creating an XSLT to Format MyQuickLaunch

After we have our list of lists, it's easy to format it using XSLT. The variety of output formats that can be produced for this web control is limited only by your requirements and imagination. Listing 7-11 shows the XSLT document that produces the output, as shown in Figure 7-2. The version of the `MyQuickLaunch` shown provides collapsible sections for each list type, and, as noted earlier, shows only those lists the end user is authorized to view.

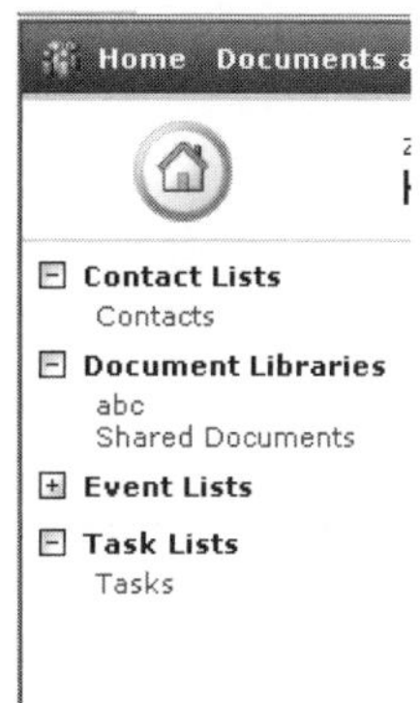

Figure 7-2. *Sample* `MyQuickLaunch` *format*

The XSLT to produce the preceding layout highlights some of the more interesting XSLT formatting capabilities. The first major block after the standard `<xsl>` elements is a bit of JavaScript that will be inserted verbatim into the rendered document. This function allows the user to click the +/– icon on the left of the heading to expand or collapse that section.

Listing 7-11. *Sample XSLT to Format* `MyQuickLaunch`

```
<?xml version='1.0'?>
<xsl:stylesheet version="1.0" xmlns:xsl="http://www.w3.org/1999/XSL/Transform">
<xsl:output method="html"/>

<xsl:template match="/">
...
```

Listing 7-12 shows the JavaScript helper function to show/hide the detail for a given menu section.

Listing 7-12. *XSLT JavaScript to Show/Hide Details*

```
...
<script language="javascript">
  function toggleRssItem(theParentDiv, resourcePath)
  {
    // get the div id
    var parentId = theParentDiv.id;

    // get the child div
    var childDiv = document.getElementById(parentId + "__child");

    // toggle the display
    if (theParentDiv.src.indexOf("collapsePlus.gif") &gt; -1) {
        theParentDiv.src = resourcePath + "/collapseMinus.gif";
        childDiv.style.display = "";
    }
    else {
        theParentDiv.src = resourcePath + "/collapsePlus.gif";
        childDiv.style.display = "none";
    }
  }
</script>
...
```

Using subtemplates simplified and reduced the size of the template. The `<xsl:with-param>` statement, as shown in Listing 7-13, allows the calling template to pass parameters to the subtemplate.

Listing 7-13. *XSLT to Call Subtemplate*

```
...
    <!-- Display all Contacts -->
    <xsl:call-template name="sectionBody">
        <xsl:with-param name="sectionTitle" select="'Contact Lists'"/>
        <xsl:with-param name="template" select="'Contacts'"/>
    </xsl:call-template>
```

```
    <!-- Display all Contacts -->
    <xsl:call-template name="sectionBody">
        <xsl:with-param name="sectionTitle"
                     select="'Document Libraries'"/>
        <xsl:with-param name="template" select="'DocumentLibrary'"/>
    </xsl:call-template>

    <!-- Display all Event Lists -->
    <xsl:call-template name="sectionBody">
        <xsl:with-param name="sectionTitle" select="'Event Lists'"/>
        <xsl:with-param name="template" select="'Events'"/>
    </xsl:call-template>

    <!-- Display all Task Lists -->
    <xsl:call-template name="sectionBody">
        <xsl:with-param name="sectionTitle" select="'Task Lists'"/>
        <xsl:with-param name="template" select="'Tasks'"/>
    </xsl:call-template>

</xsl:template>
...
```

The sectionBody template, shown in Listing 7-14, produces the section heading and all menu links for the section. Note the <div> tag, which is hidden by default using the style= "display: none;" clause. The onclick="toggleRssItem(this,'/_layouts/images');" clause of the heading enables users to toggle the visibility of the detail section by clicking the +/– icon.

Listing 7-14. *Subtemplate That Formats the Section Data*

```
...
<xsl:template name="sectionBody">
<xsl:param name="sectionTitle"/>
<xsl:param name="template"/>
<table width="90%" cellpadding="0" cellspacing="0">
  <tr>
    <td vAlign="top" align="center" width="3%" class="ms-WPBody" valign="middle">
    <img id="{$template}"
               onclick="toggleRssItem(this,'/_layouts/images');"
               alt="Click here to expand/collapse item detail"
               src="/_layouts/images/collapsePlus.gif" border="0"/>
    </td>
    <td class="ms-WPBody">
    <strong><xsl:value-of select="$sectionTitle"/></strong>
    <br/>
    </td>
  </tr>
</table>
```

```
<div id="{$template}__child" style="display: none;">
  <table width="90%" cellpadding="0" cellspacing="0">
    <tbody>
    <xsl:for-each select="/MyLists/MyLists">
      <xsl:if test="$template=Template">
        <tr>
             <td width="5%"/>
        <td class="ms-WPBody" valign="middle">
          <a href="{Url}" target="_top">
            <xsl:value-of select="Title"/>
          </a>
              </td>
            </tr>
          </xsl:if>
        </xsl:for-each>
      </tbody>
    </table>
</div>
</xsl:template>

</xsl:stylesheet>
...
```

Because the MyQuickLaunch server control derives its format from an XSLT template, you can quickly and easily alter the appearance of the menu without the need to recompile. Next, I'll cover the processes of placing the server control on the page and deploying the server control assembly so SharePoint can use it.

Deploying the Server Control

Deploying a server control for use by a SharePoint page is simply a matter of copying the .DLL to the inetpub\wwwroot\bin folder (or the bin folder under the root for the SharePoint virtual server you're deploying to). Once deployed, the control can be used on any SharePoint web page.

Placing the Server Control on the Page

To add the MyQuickLaunch control to the default.aspx page I must first tell .NET where to find its assembly file. I do this with a page directive, as follows:

```
<%@ Register TagPrefix="cc1" Namespace="MyQuickLaunch" Assembly="MyQuickLaunch" %>
```

This directive should be placed at the top of the page, just following the <%@ Page language="C#" ...> directive. Now that .NET knows about the new control, I can place it anywhere on the page by adding the following statement:

```
<!-- Navigation -->
<TD id="webpartpagenavbar" widthchange="175" height=100% class=ms-nav>
<cc1:QL id="QL1" runat="server" XSLTSource="/xslt/mylists.xslt"></cc1:QL>
</TD>
```

If you compare the previous code fragment with the corresponding section of the stock `default.asp` you will see that I've removed all the pre-existing `Navigation` code and replaced it with a single call to `MyQuickLaunch`. You can also see how the value for the XSLT is passed to the server control through the `XSLTSource` parameter. By editing the underlying `mylists.xslt` or changing the reference here to another XSLT file, you can quickly alter the appearance of the `MyQuickLaunch` control on the page.

■ **Caution** In the example I placed the `mylists.xslt` file in the path `http://localhost/xslt/mylists.xslt`, which is represented by the `XSLTSource` value of `/xslt/mylists.xslt` and stored in the location `c:\inetpub\wwwroot\xslt\mylists.xslt` on disk. By default, SharePoint intercepts all requests for pages under `c:\inetpub\wwwroot`—that is, `http://localhost` (assuming that you installed WSS to the default website in Internet Information Server [IIS])—and attempts to resolve them by reading the SharePoint content database. Any attempts to read pages under this directory will produce a "page not found" error. To allow pages and files in `c:\inetpub\wwwroot\xslt` to be read directly, I need to *exclude* that path from SharePoint's list of managed paths. I can do this through the Define Managed Paths page of the Windows SharePoint Services administrative application. This page can be found at `http://localhost:31272/scprefix.aspx?VirtualServer=[servername]` where `[servername]` is replaced with the actual server name of your site.

■ **Note** You might be more familiar with adding web controls and custom server controls through the Visual Studio design interface. However, SharePoint `.aspx` pages use inline code rather than code-behind pages, and do not support this approach. Therefore all changes must be made directly in the `.aspx` page.

Creating a My Extranets Page

In large extranet environments, it's quite likely that some of your users (either internal or external) have permissions to more than one extranet site. Providing them with a single page from which they can see and access all their extranets will be greatly appreciated and have a positive impact on their perceptions of your extranet.

In this section, I'll show you how to create a My Extranets page that provides the user with a consolidated view of available extranets.

Creating the MyExtranets.aspx ASP.NET Application

As with any ASP.NET project that needs to access the SharePoint site context, the MyExtranets project should be created under the `http://localhost/_layouts` web directory, as shown in Figure 7-3.

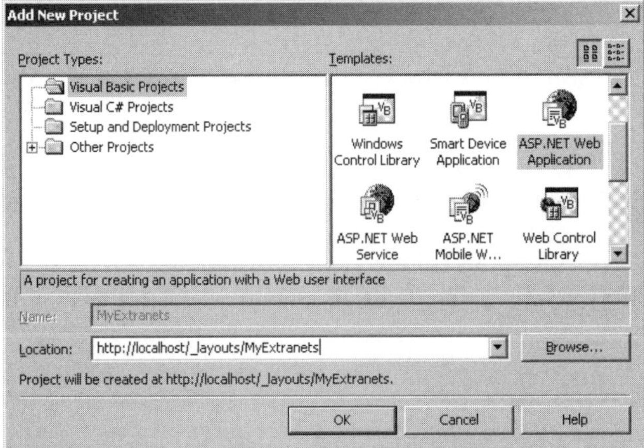

Figure 7-3. *Creating the MyExtranets ASP.NET project*

And, as with all .NET applications of any type that use the SharePoint object model, I need to add a reference to the `Microsoft.SharePoint` assembly as shown in Figure 7-4.

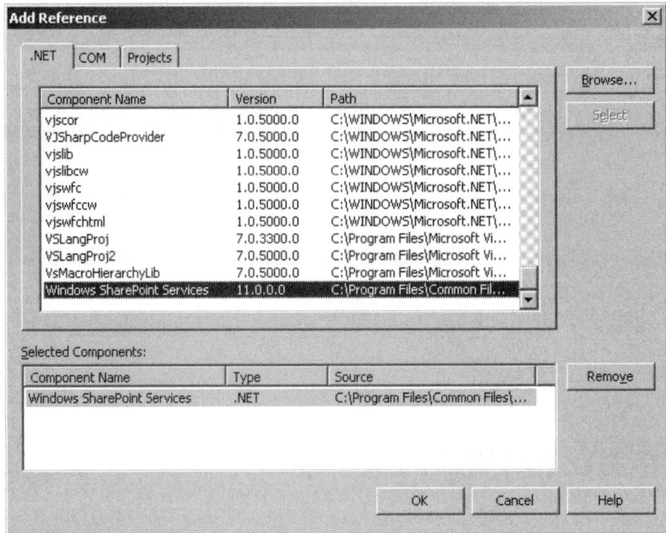

Figure 7-4. *Adding a reference to the* `Microsoft.SharePoint` *library*

Next, I'll open the `MyExtranets.aspx.vb` code-behind file and add two `Imports` statements referencing two libraries in the `Microsoft.SharePoint` assembly. As you might recall from earlier examples, the `Microsoft.SharePoint` library contains most general-purpose classes such as `SPWeb`, whereas the `Microsoft.SharePoint.WebControls` contains the `SPControl.GetContextWeb (context)` class, which I'll need to get access to the current website's context.

```
Imports Microsoft.SharePoint
Imports Microsoft.SharePoint.WebControls
```

The `Web.Config` file needs to be modified to tell ASP.NET to impersonate the current user. The SharePoint `SPWeb.GetSubwebsForCurrentUser` method then knows what user it should return extranets for. The `<identity impersonate="true" />` should be inserted immediately following the `<authentication...>` tag in `Web.Config`, as shown following:

```
<authentication mode="Windows" />
<identity impersonate="true" />
```

Writing the MyExtranets Program

The listings in this section, starting with Listing 7-15, show the complete source code necessary to display, sort, and filter a list of sites for the current user.

Listing 7-15. *MyExtranets* `Page_Load` *Routine*

```
Private Sub Page_Load(ByVal sender As System.Object, _
    ByVal e As System.EventArgs) Handles MyBase.Load

  If Not IsPostBack Then

      'Build a table to hold the results of search
      Dim dt As New DataTable("ClientSites")
      dt = GetMySites(dt)

      'Display results in the data grid.
      DataGrid1.DataSource = dt
      DataGrid1.DataBind()

      'Add list of site types to drop down list
      Dim strTemplateList As String = ""
      Dim dr As DataRow
      Dim li As ListItem
      DropDownList1.Items.Clear()
      DropDownList1.SelectedIndex = 0
      DropDownList1.AutoPostBack = True

      li = New ListItem("(All)", "%")
      DropDownList1.Items.Add(li)

      For Each dr In dt.Rows
          If InStr(strTemplateList, dr("Template")) = 0 Then
              strTemplateList = strTemplateList & "," & dr("Template")
              li = New ListItem(dr("Template"), dr("Template"))
              DropDownList1.Items.Add(li)
          End If
      Next

  End If

End Sub
```

The GetMySites() function, shown in Listing 7-16, returns a list of those sites to which the current user has access. Note the web.GetSubwebsForCurrentUser call, which is key to making sure that only those sites for the current user are displayed.

Listing 7-16. *MyExtranets* GetMySites() *Routine*

```
Private Function GetMySites(ByVal dt As DataTable) As DataTable

  Dim web As SPWeb = SPControl.GetContextWeb(context)
  Dim subwebs As SPWebCollection = web.GetSubwebsForCurrentUser
  Dim subweb As SPWeb
  Dim dr As DataRow

  dt.Columns.Add("Image")
  dt.Columns.Add("Name")
  dt.Columns.Add("Title")
  dt.Columns.Add("Description")
  dt.Columns.Add("Template")
  dt.Columns.Add("Type")
  dt.Columns.Add("Url")

  'Get a list of all webs (sites) the user has access to
  For Each subweb In subwebs
      dr = dt.NewRow
      dr("Image") = GetImage(subweb.WebTemplate)
      dr("Name") = subweb.Name
      dr("Title") = subweb.Title
      dr("Description") = subweb.Description
      dr("Template") = subweb.WebTemplate
      dr("Url") = subweb.Url
      dt.Rows.Add(dr)
  Next
  Return dt

End Function
```

The GetImage() function returns an <IMG> HTML tag for use in the data table. In this example, the image is the same regardless of site template, but you might want to display different image icons for different site templates.

```
Private Function GetImage(ByVal strTemplate As String) As String
  'Modify as needed to associate different icons with different templates.
  Return "<img src='/_layouts/images/folder.GIF' border='0' />"
End Function
```

When the user changes the selected item of the drop-down list, you need to filter the list of sites based on the selected template. The following routine creates a view, sets its filter based on the selected template, and assigns the view as the DataSource of DataGrid1.

```
Private Sub DropDownList1_SelectedIndexChanged(ByVal sender As System.Object, _
    ByVal e As System.EventArgs) Handles DropDownList1.SelectedIndexChanged
  Dim dt As New DataTable("ClientSites")
  dt = GetMySites(dt)
  Dim dv As New DataView
  dv.Table = dt
  dv.RowFilter = "Template LIKE '" & sender.selectedvalue & "'"
  DataGrid1.DataSource = dv
  DataGrid1.DataBind()
End Sub
```

Formatting the Output

A DataGrid web control is used to format the resulting list of sites. And the easiest way to configure the DataGrid is to use the Property Builder Wizard that can be accessed by right-clicking the DataGrid control in the Visual Studio design view. Then select the Property Builder menu option, as shown in Figure 7-5.

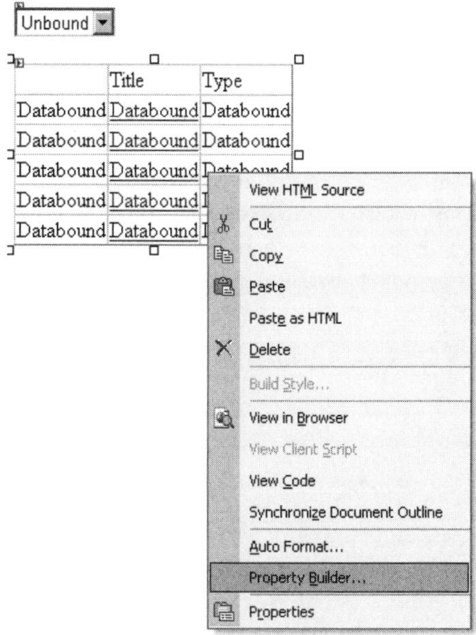

Figure 7-5. *Opening the DataGrid Property Builder*

In the `Columns` panel of the Property Builder, deselect the Create Columns Automatically At Run Time option so that only the columns you explicitly define will be shown in the DataGrid. Next add three columns: `Image`, `Title`, and `Type`, which will contain the data from the `Image`, `Title`, and `Template` columns of the DataTable. Figure 7-6 shows the `Columns` panel with the information for the `Title` column (which is a `HyperLink` column) that the user can click to navigate to the selected site.

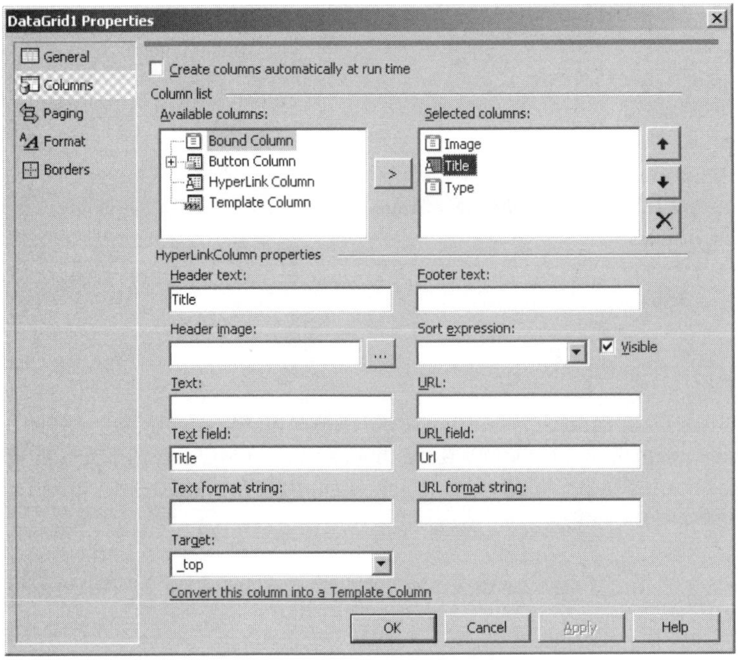

Figure 7-6. *Visual Studio DataGrid Property Builder*

Next I'll change the color scheme of my DataGrid to provide a more professional appearance. This is easily done by again right-clicking the DataGrid in design view, selecting Auto Format from the context menu, and selecting one of the predefined schemes shown in Figure 7-7.

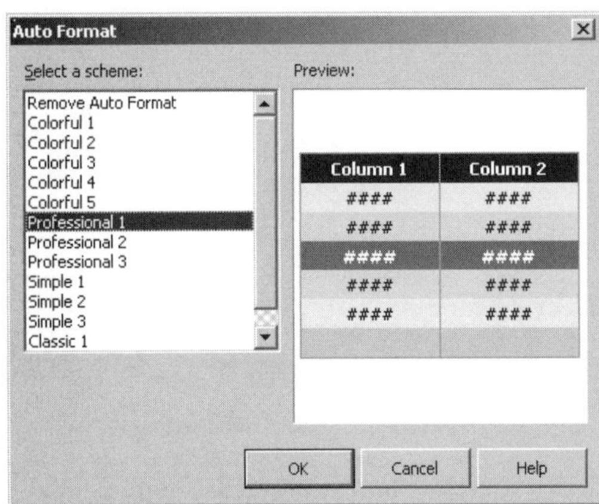

Figure 7-7. *Setting the DataGrid's color scheme*

We also need to include a reference to the standard WSS style sheet so that we can format the various components on this page using the same CSS classes as those used by standard SharePoint pages. To do so, add the following statement to the `MyExtranets.aspx` file:

```
<Link REL="stylesheet" Type="text/css" HREF="/_layouts/1033/styles/ows.css">
```

For best effect, I'll set the CssClass or Class property of the text, DropDownList, and DataGrid controls to `ms-WPBody`. The page should now look as shown in Figure 7-8.

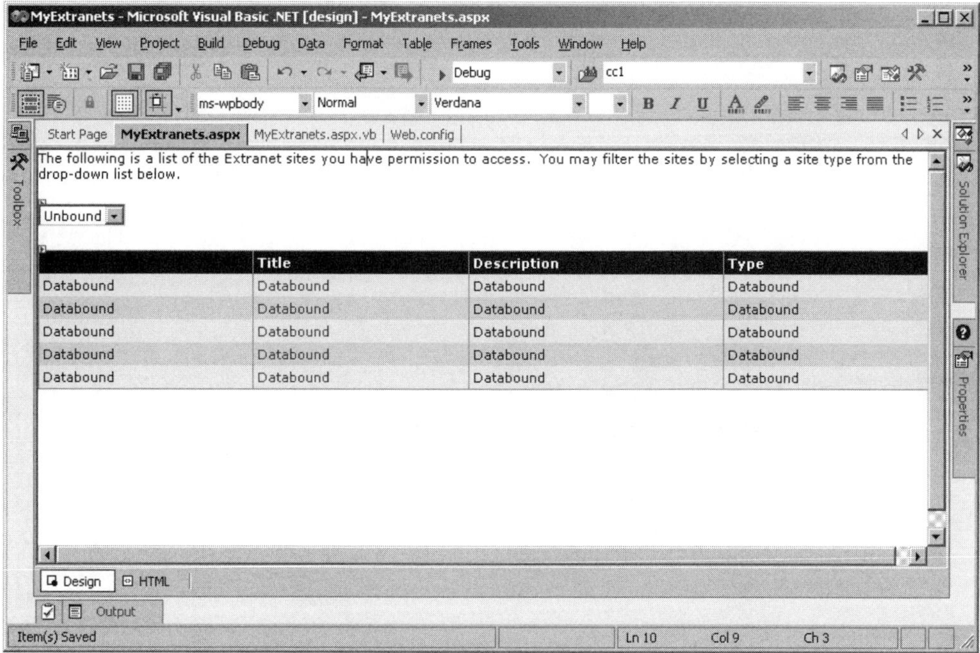

Figure 7-8. *The formatted MyExtranets page*

The MyExtranets application is now ready for use in a Page Viewer web part on any site in which we want to provide a nicely formatted list of subsites.

Displaying the List in a Page Viewer Web Part

In this case, all extranet users start on `http://localhost/allclients` and navigate to their extranet sites from there. All that's required is to drag a new Page Viewer web part onto the `http://localhost/sites/AllClients/default.aspx` page, setting the page location as shown in Figure 7-9.

Note The web page location entered into the PageViewer web part is relative, so it begins with `_layouts/...`. This is important because it determines the context in which the MyExtranets application will run and thus the list of subsites it will return.

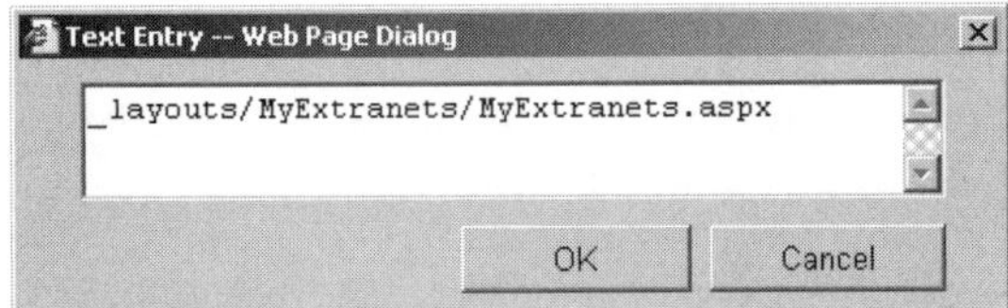

Figure 7-9. *The My Extranets landing page with the MyExtranets application displayed*

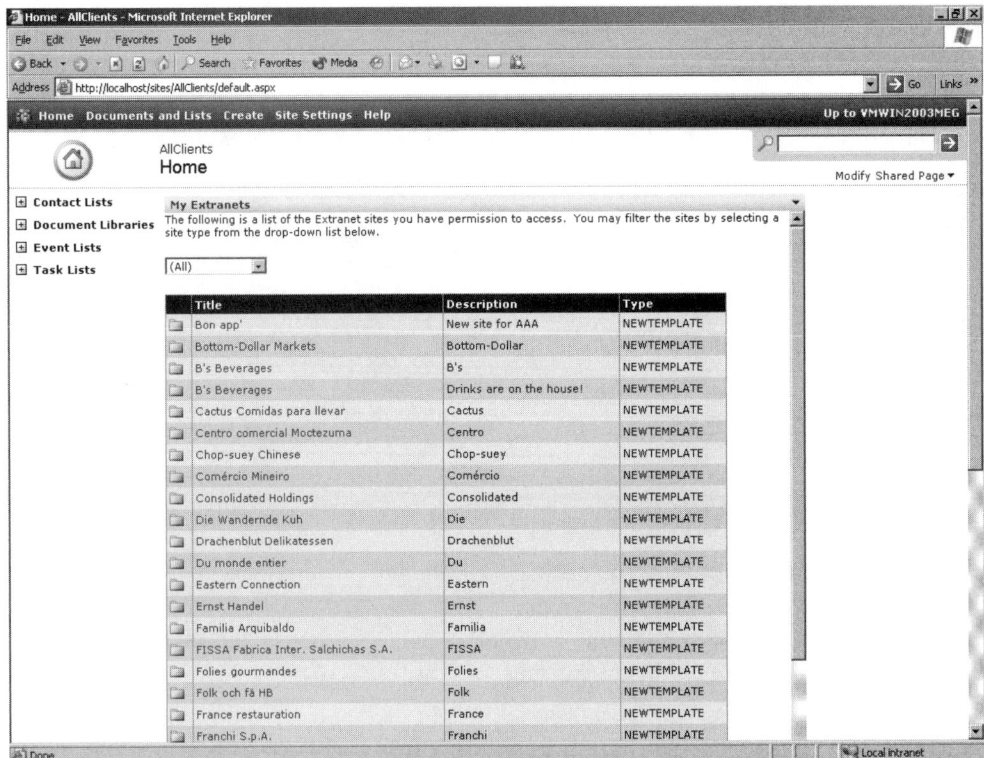

Figure 7-10. *Completed My Extranets page*

Summary

In this chapter, you learned how to customize the built-in Quick Launch menu using style sheet settings and modifications to the `default.aspx` page of a site template. In addition, you saw how to create a replacement Quick Launch menu using a .Net server control that provides you with complete control over the appearance of the menu. Finally, you learned how to create a My Extranets page that provides a convenient home page for your extranet users, giving them easy access to any extranets they have rights to access.

CHAPTER 8

Creating Custom Site Templates

One of SharePoint's most powerful features is its support for custom site templates; you can use it to generate multiple sites with a consistent look and functionality. This feature is particularly important in an extranet environment, in which you need the ability to create new client sites quickly and/or apply updates to a group of sites. You can use SharePoint site templates to control the following:

- Style sheets and headers for site administration pages
- `.aspx` program files you want to include in a site (for example, `default.aspx`)
- Web parts you want to include on each web part page in a site
- Lists and document libraries you want to create as part of the site

In addition to the templates, you can customize the base `.aspx` files such as `default.aspx` or `allitems.aspx`, which are executed when SharePoint displays a site. Although these files must be edited with care, learning how to modify them allows you to quickly alter the behavior of all sites that inherit from a given site template. This makes it possible to efficiently administer hundreds or even thousands of sites.

Five Methods of Site Definition

There are essentially five methods you can use to create a SharePoint site or modify its characteristics:

- Method 1: Use the browser-based interface to add, remove, or modify web parts and lists.
- Method 2: Use FrontPage 2003 to add, remove, modify web parts and lists, or alter the look and feel of the underlying web part pages.
- Method 3: Save an existing site as a template through the web interface, and optionally install that site template using the `STSADM` utility.

- Method 4: Create a new site template in Collaborative Application Markup Language (CAML) and select that site definition when creating a new site.
- Method 5: Write a .NET program that uses the SharePoint SDK to create and customize a site, and add or edit web parts and lists.

Each of these methods has its benefits and drawbacks. As shown in Figure 8-1, you can think of them forming a continuum, with the first method requiring little technical knowledge and providing limited impact and control; ending with the fifth method that requires the most technical knowledge, but provides the greatest impact and control. Table 8-1 describes the pros and cons of each method.

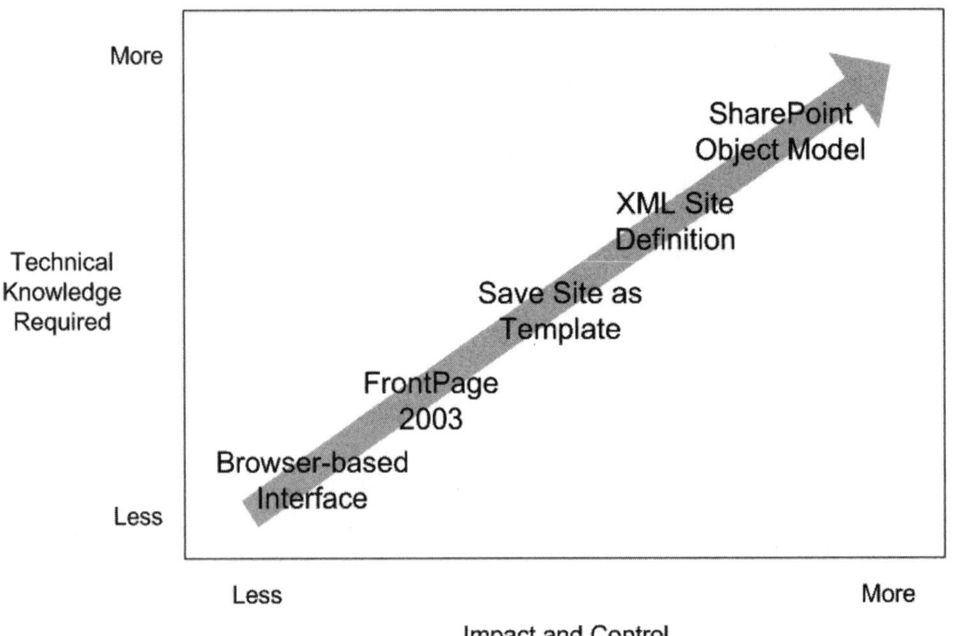

Figure 8-1. *The five methods of site definition*

It's important to realize that each of these methods has its place, and none should be considered the preferred method for all situations. There are times when you will want to modify a single web part on a single site, in which case you should choose the first method. Other times you will want to perform some custom page layout on a single site, which you can accomplish more easily with FrontPage 2003. The third approach allows you to package the edits to a site made using either of the first two methods so that you can create new sites in a single step.

The fourth method is the one SharePoint uses out of the box to create new sites, and is the one you'll find documented in the SharePoint SDK. Although it is more difficult to master, it minimizes database access and improves performance. This performance edge can be important if you are supporting an extranet with a large number of active sites.

You can use the fifth method to create utilities to automate the creation of sites that require moderate-to-complex customizations as part of the site-generation process. An example of this might involve the news feed XML web part that I showed you how to create in an earlier chapter. Imagine that you have hundreds of customers for whom you want to create extranets. Each customer is listed in a table in your Customer Relationship Management (CRM) system along with a stock sticker symbol. You want to automate the creation of sites, each of which will have a different news feed URL based on the ticker symbol of the customer. Using the SharePoint object model you can automate the process of creating these sites and configuring the news feed URL, which is far easier than creating the sites one at a time and editing the news feed web part's properties manually.

Table 8-1. *Pros and Cons of Different Site Definition Methods*

Method	How Achieved	Pros	Cons	Scope
Browser-based	Use the SharePoint Modify Shared Page option to add/edit web parts or the Site Settings option to modify more global settings	Easy to learn, appropriate for end users and quick "one-off" changes	Breaks link between the site being modified and the underlying site definition on disk, site might load more slowly due to increased database I/O	Current site
FrontPage 2003	Open SharePoint page using FrontPage 2003 to add, edit, remove web parts or other page elements	Provides full editing capabilities in a WYSIWYG environment	Breaks link between site being modified and underlying site definition on disk, some edits in FrontPage can "break" the page and make it unusable, site might load more slowly due to increased database I/O	Current site
Save site as template	Using the Site Administration ➤ Save Site As Template option, save the site definition to an `.stp` file; optionally install as global template using `STSADM` command	Can create a template from a site defined using either browser-based or FrontPage 2003 methods	Requires several steps to install site as global template, sites created from this type of template might load more slowly due to increased database I/O	Affects site definition at time of creation, after site creation has no impact
XML site definition	Copy an existing site definition under `...\60\TEMPLATE\1033` folder on SharePoint server	Site definition can be read more quickly from disk than database	Process is complex, requiring understanding of CAML syntax and file structures, incorrectly editing files can result in nonfunctional sites	All sites created from this template will continue to read some of their definition from the template
SharePoint object model	Create custom .NET applications that instantiate the `Microsoft.SharePoint` library, using its classes to add or edit sites and web part pages	Provides fine-grained control over site customization, allows large numbers of sites to be processed programmatically	Requires knowledge of SharePoint object model and .NET programming	Current site or multiple sites, depending on program logic

I will focus on these last two methods in this chapter and the next. I will show you how to create an XML-based site template as the basis for extranet sites that include the custom web parts created earlier in this book. In the next chapter I will discuss how to use the SharePoint object model to automate the creation of multiple sites from a single template, and how to further customize a site programmatically.

The Big Picture—Creating a Site Template

You can think of SharePoint site templates as containing the data SharePoint uses to create the site, as well as references to the pages that are loaded each time a site based on that template is displayed. The file containing the data is `ONET.XML`. The files read each time a site is displayed are those contained in the folder `..\60\TEMPLATE\1033\`*`<sitename>`* and its subfolders.

Note There are two other configuration files, `STDVIEW.XML` and `VWSTYLES.XML`, which are used to define a site, but should not be edited.

To create a site template, follow these steps:

1. Make a copy of the `..\60\TEMPLATE\1033\STS` folder (or a previous copy if you want), using all capital letters for the name of the copy.
2. Make a copy of the `..\60\TEMPLATE\1033\XML\WEBTEMP.XML` file using `WEBTEMP`*`<some additional characters of your choice>`*`.XML` for the name of the copy.
3. Edit the copy of `WEBTEMP.XML` to refer to the copy of the `STS` folder, giving it a unique template name and number.
4. Edit the `ONET.XML` file found in the XML subfolder of the new copy of the `STS` folder as needed to customize the pages, lists, document libraries, web parts, and other features of the site.
5. Add or edit `.aspx` files (such as `default.aspx` in the root of the new copy of the `STS` folder) to change their appearance, add or remove zones, or add server controls.

You need only the first three steps to create a new template, but if you stop after completing step 3 your new template will generate sites that are identical to those created using the original template. It's the edits you make in steps 4 and 5 that give the new template its unique characteristics. In the following sections, we'll walk through each step of the process in detail.

Copying the STS Folder

When Windows SharePoint Services (WSS) is installed, all the configuration data and files it needs to configure new Team sites are placed in the folder `C:\PROGRAM FILES\COMMON FILES\MICROSOFT SHARED\WEB SERVER EXTENSIONS\60\TEMPLATE\1033\STS`.

■ **Note** The folder `1033` refers to the "culture" of the WSS installation. `1033` refers specifically to an installation using United States English. If your version of SharePoint was installed using a different language/culture, you should substitute the appropriate number for that part of any path that refers to `1033` in this book.

To create a new copy of the `STS` folder, simply select it in Windows Explorer, choose the Edit ➤ Copy command, or press Ctrl-C; then select the parent `1033` folder and choose the Edit ➤ Paste command, or press Ctrl-V. At this point, you will see in Figure 8-2 that you will have a copy of the directory named `Copy of STS`.

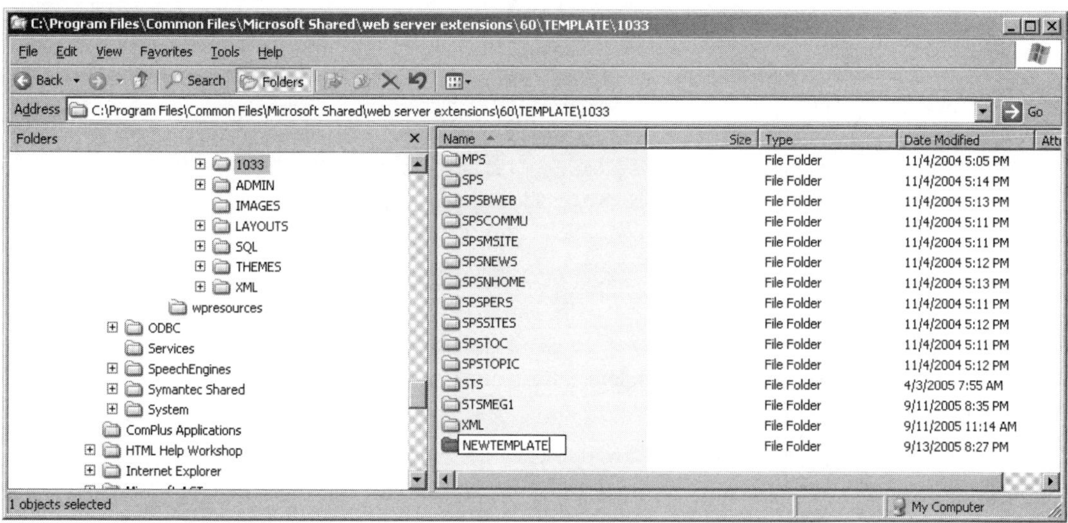

Figure 8-2. *Copying STS folder*

Simply rename this folder, being sure to use all capital letters (remember earlier we learned that XML is case-sensitive). I'll name this folder `NEWTEMPLATE`.

Modifying WEBTEMP.XML

We now have a new template definition, but SharePoint doesn't know that it exists. To correct the situation I need to copy the WEBTEMP.XML file found in the C:\PROGRAM FILES\COMMON FILES\MICROSOFT SHARED\WEB SERVER EXTENSIONS\60\TEMPLATE\1033\STS folder creating a new file whose name begins with WEBTEMP and having an .XML extension.

■ **Caution** Although it is possible to add a reference to your new site template to the existing WEBTEMP.XML file, this is not recommended, because a mistake editing the original file could render SharePoint inoperative. SharePoint will concatenate all files whose name begins with WEBTEMP and have .XML extensions, so it is best to leave the original file unchanged.

In this instance, I'll name my copy WEBTEMPNEW.XML. The following shows the content of this new file:

```
<?xml version="1.0" encoding="utf-8" ?>
<!-- _lcid="1033" _version="11.0.5510" _dal="1" -->
<!-- _LocalBinding -->
<Templates xmlns:ows="Microsoft SharePoint">
  <Template Name="NEWTEMPLATE" ID="10001">
    <Configuration ID="0" Title="New Team Site" Hidden="FALSE"
      ImageUrl="/_LAYOUTS/IMAGES/STONEHENGE.jpg"
      Description="New customized Team Site template.">
    </Configuration>
  </Template>
</Templates>
```

Most of what I did here is to delete extraneous content, but one line in particular must be edited:

```
  <Template Name="NEWTEMPLATE" ID="10001">
```

Note that the Template Name must be the same as the name you gave the copy of the STS folder and must be all capital letters. Also, note that the ID number must be unique for all templates on this SharePoint server and should be 10001 or greater because Microsoft reserves the right to use ID numbers 10000 and below. The values you enter for Title and Description will be displayed in the list of possible templates when a user creates a new site through the browser interface. You can also change the ImageUrl attribute to provide a thumbnail of the site available in the site gallery to help the user select the correct template.

Finally, because SharePoint reads all template definitions at startup, you need to issue the IISRESET command at the Windows command prompt to force SharePoint to load the new site template definition. Figure 8-3 shows the Template Selection page with the new template highlighted.

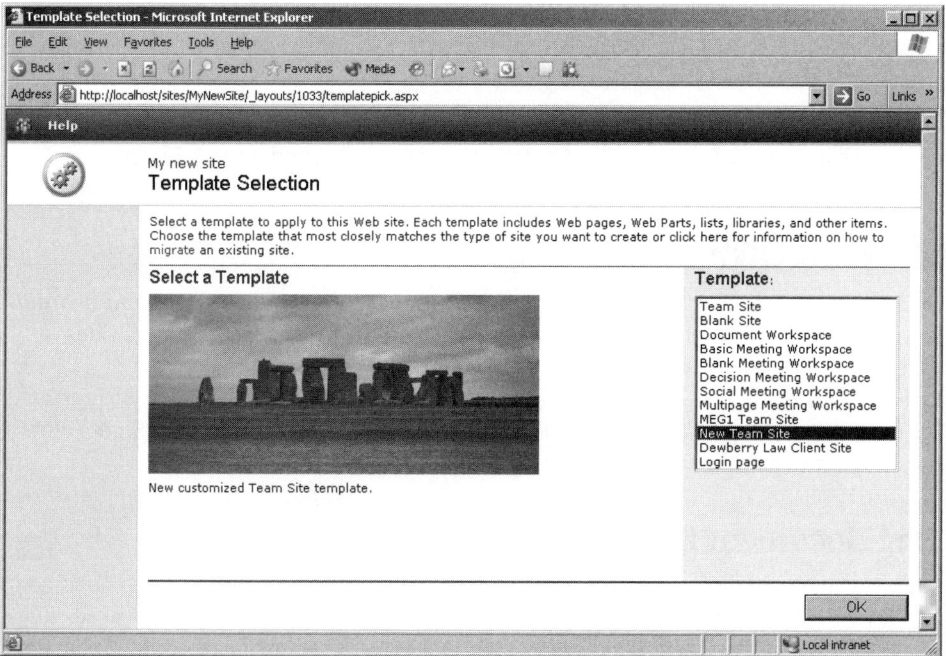

Figure 8-3. *New template displayed on the Template Selection page*

When you click OK, a new site will be created using the `New Team Site` template, but because the only part of the definition we changed so far is the name, description, and image, the resulting site will be identical to one created with the standard `Team Site` template. There is one important difference, however. The new site is permanently linked to the template that was used to create it. You can see this by querying the SharePoint site database, as shown in Figure 8-4.

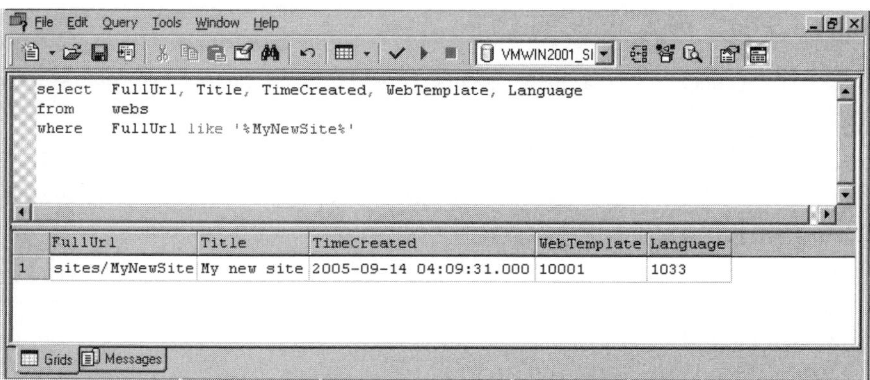

Figure 8-4. *Site definition data in SharePoint site database*

The significance of this is that any site created using the `New Team Site` template is permanently linked to that template. Should the template be deleted or become otherwise inaccessible, all sites based on it will become unusable.

■ **Caution** If a template is deleted or inaccessible, any sites created using that template will become unusable.

Next, we'll look at customizing the site definition further by modifying `ONET.XML`.

Modifying ONET.XML

This section covers how to modify the `ONET.XML` file to add a couple of document libraries and a web part. In the process, you'll learn how to make two of the most useful modifications to `ONET.XML`.

You can think of `ONET.XML` as a "punch list" of things for SharePoint to add to a newly created site when using that template. The data in `ONET.XML` is transformed into data in the SharePoint SITES database and permanently associated with that site.

Adding Document Libraries

The following fragment of the `ONET.XML` file shows the section that determines which document libraries will be created for the new site (see Listing 8-1). Note that I added an element starting with the text `<List Title="Secure Documents"`. This tells SharePoint to create a new document library when adding the site. The Secure Documents library will be used to store documents that will be visible only to a limited subset of users.

Listing 8-1. *Configurations Element of* `ONET.XML`

```
<Configurations>
    ...
    <Configuration ID="0" Name="Default">
        <Lists>
            <List Title="Shared Documents"
                Url="Shared Documents"
                QuickLaunchUrl="Shared Documents/Forms/AllItems.aspx"
                Type="101" />
            <List Title="Secure Documents"
                Url="Secure Documents"
                QuickLaunchUrl="Secure Documents/Forms/AllItems.aspx"
                Type="101" />
        </Lists>
        <Modules>
            <Module Name="Default"/>
            <Module Name="WebPartPopulation"/>
        </Modules>
    </Configuration>
    ...
```

Adding Web Parts

I also edited the Modules section to insert a TreeView web part during site creation (see Listing 8-2).

Listing 8-2. *Modules Element of* `ONET.XML`

```
<Modules>
    <Module Name="Default" Url="" Path="">
        <File Url="default.aspx" NavBarHome="True">
            <View List="104" BaseViewID="0" WebPartZoneID="Left"/>
            <View List="106" BaseViewID="0" WebPartZoneID="Left" WebPartOrder="2"/>
        ...
           <AllUsersWebPart WebPartZoneID="Left" WebPartOrder="2">
               <![CDATA[
               <WebPart xmlns="http://schemas.microsoft.com/WebPart/v2"
 xmlns:iwp="http://schemas.microsoft.com/WebPart/v2/Image">
                   <Assembly>MG.WebParts.DLTV, Version=1.0.0.0, Culture=neutral,
 PublicKeyToken=dc85e9c54eade9c5</Assembly>
                   <TypeName>MG.WebParts.DLTV.WebPart1</TypeName>
                   <FrameType>Default</FrameType>
                   <Title>Site Documents</Title>
                   <DetailLink></DetailLink>
                   <DoclibName xmlns="MG.WebParts.DLTV">Shared Documents,
 Secure Documents</DoclibName>
               </WebPart>
               ]]>
           </AllUsersWebPart>
        ...
           <View List="103" BaseViewID="0" WebPartZoneID="Right" WebPartOrder="3"/>
           <NavBarPage Name="Home" ID="1002" Position="Start"> </NavBarPage>
           <NavBarPage Name="Home" ID="0" Position="Start">  </NavBarPage>
       </File>
   </Module>
```

The `<Module>` element specifies one or more files you want to include as part of a site. Typically, this will include the `default.aspx` web part page, but might include other pages as desired. The module name is referenced in the `<Configuration>` element that we used in the preceding section to add a document library. The `<View List="104" BaseViewID="0" WebPartZoneID="Left"/>` refers to an announcement list (list type = 104) that is to be added to the page in the left zone. Likewise, `<View List="106" BaseViewID="0" WebPartZoneID="Left" WebPartOrder="2"/>` indicates that an events list will be added to the left zone in the second position.

Things get interesting when you come to the `<AllUsersWebPart>` tag. First, you might be wondering about the `<![CDATA [ ... ]]>` tag. This is an XML tag that allows any text between the start and end brackets to be treated a simple text. The most common use of these tags is to allow < and > characters to appear within XML content without the XML parser treating them as tag delimiters.

■ **Tip** Sometimes a web part definition requires a `<![CDATA[...]]>` construct as input to one or more of its properties. Most commonly this construct appears within the `<Content></Content>` element of a Content Editor web part definition to allow the inclusion of < and > characters. You cannot nest `<![CDATA[...]]>` elements, but you can replace < with `<` and > with `>` to accomplish the same result.

The next likely question is where the data for the `<WebPart>...</WebPart>` element came from. Fortunately, you don't have to come up with this from scratch because SharePoint provides all the XML you need for the `<WebPart>` section when you export a web part definition. To see how this works, I'll export an instance of the TreeView web part (see Figure 8-5).

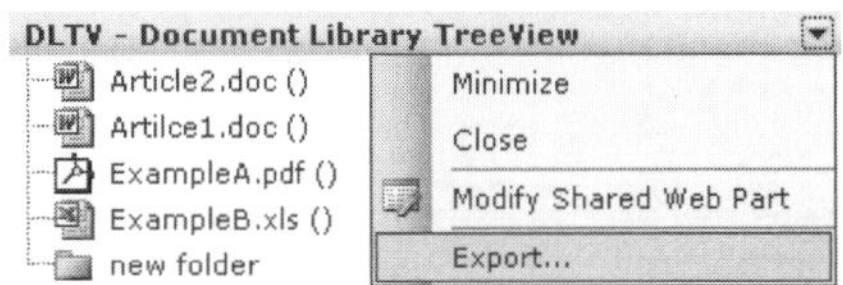

Figure 8-5. *Exporting the web part definition*

Next, I open the resulting `.DWP` file to examine its contents (see Listing 8-3).

Listing 8-3. *Web Part Definition XML from a* `.DWP` *File*

```
<?xml version="1.0" encoding="utf-8"?>
<WebPart xmlns:xsd="http://www.w3.org/2001/XMLSchema"
      xmlns:xsi="http://www.w3.org/2001/XMLSchema-instance"
      xmlns="http://schemas.microsoft.com/WebPart/v2">
  <Title>DLTV - Document Library TreeView</Title>
  <FrameType>Default</FrameType>
  <Description>Display a document library in a tree view.</Description>
  <IsIncluded>true</IsIncluded>
  <ZoneID>Left</ZoneID>
  <PartOrder>5</PartOrder>
  <FrameState>Normal</FrameState>
  <Height />
  <Width />
  <AllowRemove>true</AllowRemove>
  <AllowZoneChange>true</AllowZoneChange>
  <AllowMinimize>true</AllowMinimize>
  <IsVisible>true</IsVisible>
  <DetailLink />
  <HelpLink />
  <Dir>Default</Dir>
  <PartImageSmall />
  <MissingAssembly />
  <PartImageLarge />
  <IsIncludedFilter />
```

```
  <Assembly>MG.WebParts.DLTV, Version=1.0.0.0, Culture=neutral,
      PublicKeyToken=dc85e9c54eade9c5</Assembly>
  <TypeName>MG.WebParts.DLTV.WebPart1</TypeName>
  <DoclibName xmlns="MG.WebParts.DLTV">Shared Documents</DoclibName>
  <DaysBack2Include xmlns="MG.WebParts.DLTV">3650</DaysBack2Include>
</WebPart>
```

With the exception of the `<?xml ...>` header, the contents of the `<AllUsersWebPart>` element is identical to that of a `.DWP` file. In fact, you can think of that section of the `ONET.XML` file as simply automating the process of importing web part definitions onto a page during site configuration. Therefore, the approach I recommend for adding module definitions to `ONET.XML` is to do the following:

1. Manually place a web part you want to include in your site definition on a web part page.
2. Configure the web part properties as desired.
3. Export the web part to a `.DWP` file.
4. Open the `.DWP` file and select all text except the `<?xml ...>` header.
5. Paste the text selected into `ONET.XML` between the `<![CDATA[ ... ]]>` tags of an `<AllUsersWebPart></AllUsersWebPart>` element.

Repeat this process for all web parts you want on a page; if you have multiple `<File>` elements, do the same for each web part page you are including in your site template.

Modifying Default.aspx

The `<Modules>` section of `ONET.XML` allows you to place web parts on the page. What if you want the `default.aspx` page to have a different layout or you want to include server controls in addition to web parts? To accomplish it I need to edit the `.aspx` page directly.

■ Caution Editing `default.aspx` or any `.aspx` page that is referenced in `ONET.XML` will affect all existing sites that were created using the site definition of which the `.aspx` file is a part . Therefore, you should thoroughly test your changes prior to making them in a production environment.

In this section, I will edit the `default.aspx` page to accomplish three things:

- Change the heading displayed.
- Remove the Quick Launch menu.
- Add two new zones.

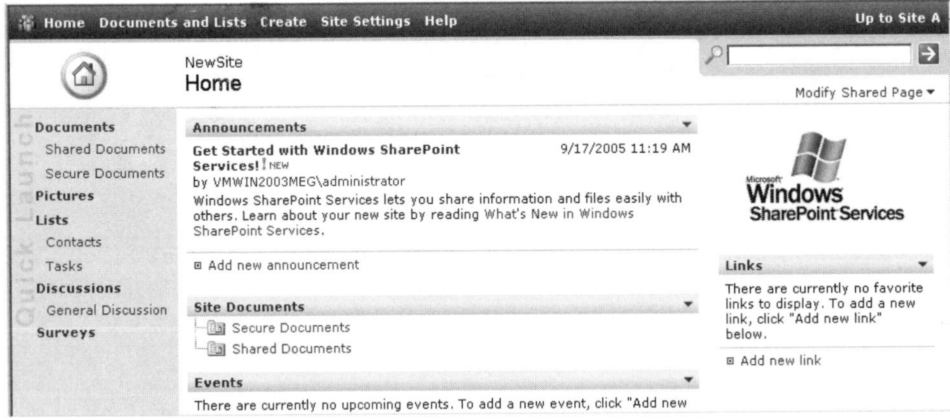

Figure 8-6. *Changes to* `default.aspx`

Changing the Page Heading

Although SharePoint provides some support for customizing WSS headings, I typically want more control at the site template level than SharePoint provides. To achieve this level of control I will edit the section of the `default.aspx` file that displays the heading, replacing the default text and SharePoint content.

■ **Tip** The HTML in the `default.aspx` file that ships with WSS is poorly indented, which makes it difficult to identify where various page elements start and end. Although I recommend using Visual Studio for all program editing, you can use FrontPage 2003 to apply standard indenting, which will dramatically improve the readability of the HTML. To do this, open the `default.aspx` file in FrontPage 2003, switch to code view, right-click anywhere in the code window, and choose the Reformat HTML menu option. Save the file back to disk.

The heading can be found immediately following the `<!--Top bar-->` comment. I want to change this, removing the image and the link to the parent site, and adding some text. The edited HTML looks like Listing 8-4.

Listing 8-4. *Modifications to* `default.aspx` *Top Bar*

```
<!--Top bar-->
<table class="ms-bannerframe" border="0" cellspacing="0" cellpadding="0"
    width="100%">
<tr>
    <td nowrap valign="middle"></td>
    <td class="ms-banner" width="99%" nowrap id="HBN100" valign="middle">
        <H2>Hello World!</H2>
    </td>
```

```
    <td class="ms-banner">  </td>
    <td nowrap class="ms-banner" style="padding-right: 7px"></td>
</tr>
</table>
```

I also want to remove the home icon and the word "home" from the heading, leaving just the site title. To do so, I change the <!--Title--> section, as shown in Listing 8-5.

Listing 8-5. *Modifications to* default.aspx *Title*

```
<!-- Title -->
<tr>
  <td colspan="3" class="ms-titleareaframe">
    <div class="ms-titleareaframe">
      <table width="100%" border="0" class="ms-titleareaframe" cellpadding="0"
         cellspacing="0">
        <tr>
          <td style="padding-bottom: 0px">
            <table style="padding-top: 0px;padding-left: 2px" cellpadding="0"
               cellspacing="0" border="0">
              <tr>
                <td align="center" nowrap style="padding-top: 4px" width="132"
                   height="46">
                  <!-- Home.gif image tag removed -->
                </td>
                <td></td>
                <td nowrap width="100%" style="padding-top: 0px">
                  <table cellpadding="0" cellspacing="0">
                    <tr>
                      <td nowrap class="ms-titlearea">
                        <!-- Site title displayed in H2 style -->
                        <H2><SharePoint:ProjectProperty Property="Title"
                          runat="server" /></H2>
                      </td>
                    </tr>
                    <tr>
                      <td id="onetidPageTitle" class="ms-pagetitle"/>
                        <!-- Text "Home" removed -->
...
```

Removing the Quick Launch Menu

Although the Quick Launch menu can be useful for intranet sites, it provides access to features that extranet users do not need or want, so it needs to be removed. To eliminate the Quick Launch, remove all the HTML beginning with the <!-- Navigation --> tag up to but not including the <!-- Contents --> tag.

Adding Top and Bottom Zones

Finally, I want to add a Top and Bottom zone to the page, which is easily accomplished by editing the `<!-- Contents -->`, as shown in Listing 8-6.

Listing 8-6. *Modifications to* `default.aspx` *Zones and Contents*

```
<!-- Contents -->
<td><img src="/_layouts/images/blank.gif" width="5" height="1" alt=""></td>
<td class="ms-bodyareaframe" valign="top" style="width:100%">
  <form runat="server">
    <table style="margin-top: 4px" cellpadding="3" cellspacing="0" border="0"
          width="100%">
      <tr>
        <td class="ms-descriptiontext" valign="top" colspan="4">
          <SharePoint:ProjectProperty Property="Description" runat="server" />
        </td>
      <tr>
        <!-- Top zone -->
        <td valign="top" width="100%" colspan="3">
          <WebPartPages:WebPartZone runat="server" FrameType="TitleBarOnly" ID="Top"
             Title="loc:Top" /></td>
        </td>
      </tr>
      <tr>
        <!-- Middle column -->
        <td valign="top" width="70%">
          <WebPartPages:WebPartZone runat="server" FrameType="TitleBarOnly"
             ID="Left"
              Title="loc:Left" />
            </td>
        <td> </td>
        <!-- Right column -->
        <td valign="top" width="30%">
          <WebPartPages:WebPartZone runat="server" FrameType="TitleBarOnly"
              ID="Right"
              Title="loc:Right" />
          </td>
        <td> </td>
      </tr>
      <tr>
        <!-- Bottom zone -->
        <td valign="top" width="100%" colspan="3">
          <WebPartPages:WebPartZone runat="server" FrameType="TitleBarOnly"
              ID="Bottom" Title="loc:Bottom" /></td>
        </td>
      </tr>
    </table>
...
```

The new sections begin with `<!-- Top zone -->` and end with `<!-- Bottom zone -->`. The `<WebPartPages:WebPartZone ... />` tag tells SharePoint to define a zone at this location. You need to change the `ID` and `Title` attributes of these elements to be unique; otherwise, SharePoint will throw an error when the page is displayed. In this case I set the `ID` and `Title` to be `Top` and `loc:Top`, respectively, for the top zone, and `Bottom` and `loc:Bottom`, respectively, for the bottom zone. Figure 8-7, shows the resulting zone configuration in design view.

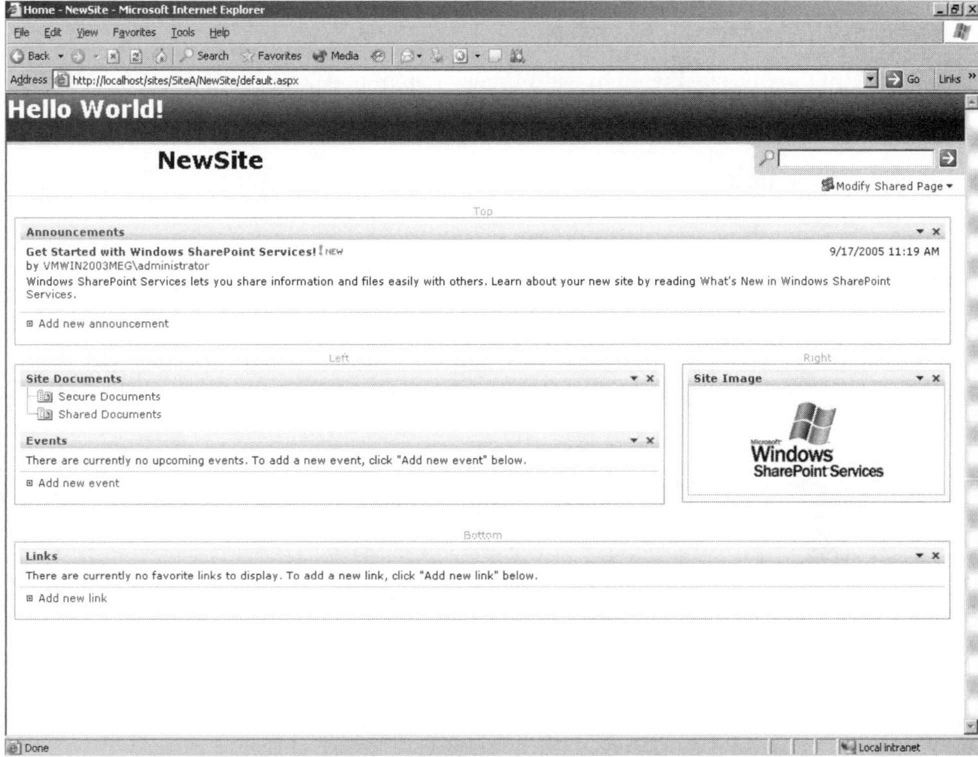

Figure 8-7. `Default.aspx` *with modifications shown in design view*

Adding a Breadcrumb Server Control to Default.aspx

You can also customize a template by adding .NET server controls to the `.aspx` template pages to provide functionality that is not provided by SharePoint. I assume that you are familiar with server controls; if not, you can think of them as equivalent to the web controls, such as the `TextBox` control, that ship with .NET. When used in a SharePoint `.aspx` page you can use server controls to access the SharePoint object model.

This section shows you how to create a breadcrumb server control that can be placed in the heading of the `default.aspx` page, which allows users to easily see where they are in relation to the site hierarchy.

Note Web parts are simply a special kind of server control that must be placed within a zone.

The breadcrumb server control needs to do several things:

- Get the current web page's URL.
- Obtain the title of the current web page.
- "Walk" up the web site hierarchy, getting each parent page's URL and title.
- Build a series of links that the user can click to navigate up the hierarchy.
- Display these links on the current page.

Creating a Server Control Project

Creating a new server control project is no more difficult than creating any other type of project in Visual Studio 2003. Simply open Visual Studio and select the File ➤ New ➤ Project option and then select the Web Control Library template. We will name the new project Breadcrumb. The completed New Project dialog box is shown in Figure 8-8.

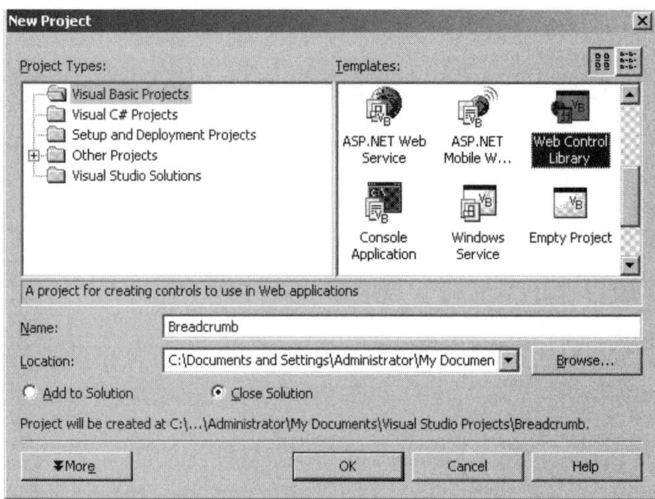

Figure 8-8. *Creating a new server control project*

Writing the Breadcrumb Code

Let's look at how the breadcrumb server control accomplishes all these goals. First I need the standard `Imports`:

```
Imports System.ComponentModel
Imports System.Web.UI
Imports Microsoft.SharePoint
Imports System.Web
```

Notice the similarity between the server control's "decoration" and that of the custom web parts we built in earlier chapters. This similarity exists because web parts are simply a special type of server control:

```
<DefaultProperty("Text"), _
    ToolboxData("<{0}:BreadCrumb1 runat=server></{0}:BreadCrumb1>")>
Public Class BreadCrumb1
  Inherits System.Web.UI.WebControls.WebControl
  Dim m_SpWeb As SPWeb
```

The `Render()` method is the server control equivalent of the `RenderWebPart()` method we used in web part definitions:

```
Protected Overrides Sub Render(ByVal output As System.Web.UI.HtmlTextWriter)
```

Here's where I get the current page's context, which tells the server control what page we're building a breadcrumb for:

```
    'Get the context of the current web site being displayed
    Dim objWeb As SPWeb =
           Microsoft.SharePoint.WebControls.SPControl.GetContextWeb(Context)
```

The rest of the `Render()` method simply calls my routine to create the breadcrumb (see Listing 8-7).

Listing 8-7. *Creating the Breadcrumb Trail*

```
Dim breadcrumbTrail As String = ""
Try
  'Recursively "walk" up the site hierarchy to display a breadcrumb.
  BuildBreadcrumb(objWeb, output, breadcrumbTrail)
  output.Write("<div width='100%' class='ms-WPBody' style='' ><b>Breadcrumb server
       control: " + breadcrumbTrail + "</b></div><br/>")
    Catch ex As Exception
      output.Write("Error:  " + ex.Message)
    End Try
  End Sub
```

This is the routine that does the work of reading the current web site's title and URL, building an `<A>` tag and appending it to the breadcrumb trail (see Listing 8-8).

Listing 8-8. *The* `BuildBreadcrumb()` *Routine*

```
Private Sub BuildBreadcrumb(ByVal objWeb As SPWeb, ByVal output As HtmlTextWriter,
          ByRef breadcrumbTrail As String)
```

```
    ' Set current web as we recurse
    m_SpWeb = objWeb
    If Trim(breadcrumbTrail) = "" Then
       ' If current page is default.aspx, just show text, don't make a link.
       If objWeb.Url.ToString + "/default.aspx" = context.Request.Url.ToString Then
          breadcrumbTrail = objWeb.Title.ToString()   ' Do not link to itself
       Else
          breadcrumbTrail = "<b><a href=" + objWeb.Url.ToString() + ">" +
             objWeb.Title.ToString() + "</a></b>"
      End If
    Else
       ' Provide link
       breadcrumbTrail = "<a href=" + objWeb.Url.ToString() + ">" +
          objWeb.Title.ToString() + "</a> > " + breadcrumbTrail
    End If

    ' Here's where recursion is used to "walk" up the site hierarchy.
    ' If there is a parent, go to it and continue to build breadcrumb
If (Not (objWeb.ParentWeb) Is Nothing) Then
    BuildBreadcrumb(objWeb.ParentWeb, output, breadcrumbTrail)
End If

  End Sub

End Class
```

Deploying the Breadcrumb Server Control

Deploying a server control for use by a SharePoint page is simply a matter of copying the .DLL to the inetpub\wwwroot\bin folder (or the bin folder under the root for the SharePoint virtual server you're deploying to).

Adding the Server Control to the Default.aspx Page

The last step is to update default.aspx to include the server control. There are two things that I need to do: First, I register the server control. Second, I place an instance of the server control on the page.

To register the server control, I place the following page directive at the top of the page:

```
<%@ Register TagPrefix="cc1" Namespace="BreadCrumb" Assembly="BreadCrumb" %>
```

This process creates a reference ="cc1" to the "BreadCrumb" class library so that it can be used later in the page. Then I add the control to the Title section of the page, as shown in the following code.

```
...
<table cellpadding="0" cellspacing="0">
  <tr>
    <td nowrap class="ms-titlearea">
      <!-- Site title displayed in H2 style -->
      <H2><SharePoint:ProjectProperty Property="Title" runat="server" /></H2>
      <!-- Text "Home" removed -->
      <!-- Breadcrumb added -->
      <cc1:BreadCrumb1 id="BreadCrumb11" runat="server"></cc1:BreadCrumb1>
    </td>
  </tr>
</table>
...
```

Figure 8-9 shows the results.

A sub-site

Breadcrumb server control: Site A > NewSite > **A sub-site**

Figure 8-9. *Example breadcrumb*

The parent and grandparent site titles are links, but the current site is simply text because the code in the BuildBreadcrumb() routine checks to see whether the SPWeb.Url is the same as the context's URL. We now have a general-purpose server control that can be used on any page on our extranet to improve the user's ability to navigate between pages.

Summary

This chapter covered various ways to customize a SharePoint site definition. By modifying WEBTEMP.XML and ONET.XML you can alter the way a template is presented to new users when they are creating a new site. You can alter the files and web parts that will be included as part of that site. Making changes to default.aspx (or any .aspx page you choose to include through the ONET.XML <Modules> section) allows you to remove or add headings, the Quick Launch, or web part zones. Creating server controls allows you to add any .NET functionality you want, including the ability to use the SharePoint object model.

The next chapter looks at automating the site-creation process to ease the burden of fulfilling requests for new client extranets in a corporate environment.

Additional Resource

Advanced SharePoint Services Solutions by Scot P. Hiller, Apress, 2004; Chapter 1: "Collaborative Application Markup Language"

CHAPTER 9

■ ■ ■

Automating Site Creation

The previous chapter covered SharePoint's support for custom site templates, which enable the developer to define complex and varied templates that can generate correspondingly sophisticated sites. However, all sites generated with a given template will start out being identical. Any customization beyond that point must be done manually.

This chapter introduces you to two techniques to move beyond the inherent limitations of this template-based approach to automate the production of new sites. Two scenarios will be explored. First, I'll cover creating a standalone utility that builds sites by combining a custom template with .NET programming. Second, I'll discuss how you can create a web application that SharePoint executes after the end user has selected the template, providing you with the ability to gather additional information from the site requestor, external databases, or SharePoint, and then make modifications to the site based on these inputs.

At the conclusion of this chapter, armed with the techniques you'll learn, you'll be able to automate complex site creation and provide your end users with much more control over the characteristics of the sites they create.

Object Model Classes Related to Site Creation

Before we start, let's look at the classes that you'll be working with to create and edit a website. The classes are shown in Table 9-1.

Table 9-1. *SharePoint Classes Used When Automating Site Creation*

Class	Purpose
`SPSite`	Provides handle to a site collection
`SPWeb`	Provides handle to a single site
`SPWebPartCollection`	Provides handle to collection of all web parts on a single site
`WebPartPages.WebPart`	Represents a single web part
`WebPartPages.ContentEditorWebPart`	Provides access to content editor web part properties
`MG.WebParts.DLTV.WebPart1`	Provides access to TreeView custom web part properties
`MG.WebParts.SQL.WebPart1`	Provides access to SQL custom web part properties

The last two classes, which were created earlier in this book, are needed to add either of these web parts or to modify any of the custom properties that exist only as part of their definitions.

Creating a Console Application

The demands on administrators and developers responsible for a SharePoint extranet increase in direct proportion to the number of sites hosted by that extranet. To support a large installation and provide a robust and customized environment, you will need to automate as many processes as possible. As you saw in the preceding chapter, one important form of automation is through the creation of custom site templates. This section covers the creation of a .NET application that makes possible data-driven customization beyond what we could achieve with our custom template alone. At the completion of this section, you will have the skills necessary to program a wide range of utilities for creating and manipulating SharePoint sites.

Let's start by creating a single site programmatically through a console application that can be run from the command prompt. Console applications are a good choice for administrative utilities or for applications that must be scheduled to be run on a regular basis. Conceptually, our program needs to do the following:

- Gather data that will define the new site.
- Add the new site.
- Delete any unwanted web parts.
- Add new web parts.
- Edit existing web parts.

Creating the Project

To get started, I will create a new console application project in Visual Studio .NET called CreateSites. After you create the project, as with our earlier projects, you need to add a reference to the `Microsoft.SharePoint` library and two of our custom web part assemblies. The following references need to be added to the project references section so that the source code can access the associated classes:

- `Microsoft.SharePoint`
- `MG.WebParts.TreeView`
- `MG.WebParts.SQL`

`MG.WebParts.SQL` and `MG.WebParts.TreeView` should be project references rather than .NET references. To add project references, first add the existing projects for these web parts to the solution (see Chapters 4 and 5, respectively, for a discussion of these projects) and then choose the Add Reference option from the Project menu and click the Projects tab. Figure 9-1 shows the two projects selected for inclusion as references.

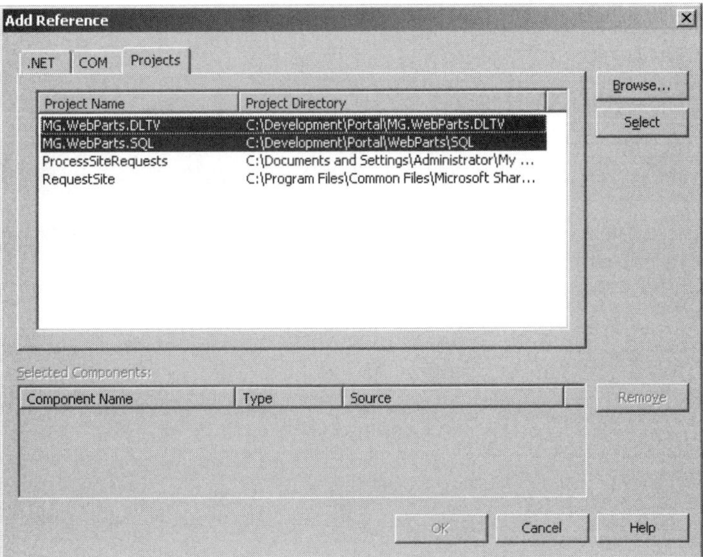

Figure 9-1. *Adding references to custom web parts*

Writing the Program

Now that the references are in order, let's turn to the program itself, break it down into its component parts, and walk through the code:

Imports

```
Imports System.Configuration
Imports Microsoft.SharePoint
Imports System.Web.UI
Imports System.Xml
```

The first `Imports` statement provides access to .NET configuration settings; the second provides access to the base SharePoint classes. The `System.Web.UI` class is required because even though this is a console application, it will be manipulating objects based on web classes, so it needs access to the functions of those class libraries. Finally, the `System.Xml` class is required because you must specify the content property of a ContentEditor web part as an XML element.

Global Variables

Next, I need to define some variables that will provide control data. I grouped them by what part of the process they support, as shown in Listing 9-1.

Listing 9-1. *CreateSites Control Variables*

```
'Site definition variables
Private strParentSite As String = "http://localhost/sites/AllClients/"
Private strSiteName As String
Private strSiteTitle As String
Private strSiteDescrip As String
Private strTemplateName As String = "NEWTEMPLATE"
Private uInt32LocId As UInt32 = System.Convert.ToUInt32(1033)
Private strNorthwindConnectionString As String _
    = "user id=Northwind_test_user;" &_
"data source=(local);persist security info=False;" &_
"initial catalog=Northwind"

'Content editor web part variables(s)
Private strWelcomeMsg As String

'SQL web part variables(s)
Private strCustomerID As String
```

Two of the preceding variables might be puzzling to you: `strParentSite` contains the path to the site collection that will hold the new site, and `uInt32LocId` stores the location ID for the language/culture of our installation—remember that 1033 is for U.S. English. (The Microsoft authors of the `SPWeb.Add()` method decided to use a `Uint32` type for this parameter, so I need to create a value that conforms to that type.) A third variable, `strTemplateName`, provides the name of the SharePoint template created in the previous chapter. In general, the `strTemplateName` variable needs to provide the name of a valid template from which to create the new site.

Reading User-Supplied Parameters

For this application to be useful, it needs to accept a couple of data items that will be used to define new sites: the ID of the customer for whom the new site will be created and the site description. Given the customer ID, I want to look up the contact information and address of the customer so it can be added to the new site (see Listing 9-2).

Listing 9-2. *Retrieving User Input and Obtaining Customer Information*

```
Try
  'Site name is same as customer id
  strSiteName = args(0)
  strCustomerID = args(0)

  'Provide a friendly description
  strSiteDescrip = args(1)
```

```
  'Set the site title to the customer name in the customers table, and provide a
  'custom message that includes the contact information for this customer.
  Dim da As New SqlDataAdapter(String.Format("select * from customers where " &_
"CustomerId='{0}'", strCustomerID), strNorthwindConnectionString)
  Dim ds As New DataSet
  Dim dr As DataRow
  da.Fill(ds)
  dr = ds.Tables(0).Rows(0)
  strSiteTitle = dr("CompanyName")
  strWelcomeMsg = String.Format( _
      "<br/>Welcome <strong>{0}</strong>.  The contact " & _
      "information we have on record for you " & _
      "is:<br/><br/><strong>{1}</strong><br/>{2}<br/>{3}, {4}  {5}"  &_
      "<br/>{6}<br/>{7}", _
      dr("ContactName"), dr("ContactTitle"), dr("Address"), _
      dr("City"), dr("Region"), dr("PostalCode"), _
      dr("Country"), dr("Phone"))

'Don't let a SQL failure spoil our day.
Catch ex As Exception
  Console.WriteLine("Error: one or more parameters were incorrect.")
  Console.WriteLine()
  Console.WriteLine("Syntax:")
  Console.WriteLine()
  Console.WriteLine("CREATESITES <customerid> <site description>")
  Console.WriteLine()
  Exit Sub
End Try
```

Creating the Site

With all the input data in hand, I'm now ready to create the site, as shown in Listing 9-3.

Listing 9-3. *Creating the New Site*

```
'Get handle to parent site of new site
Dim site As New SPSite(strParentSite & "/default.aspx")

'Create the site
site.AllWebs.Add(strSiteName, _
    strSiteTitle, _
    strSiteDescrip, _
    uInt32LocId, _
    strTemplateName, _
    False, _
    False)
```

The second-to-last parameter of the Add() method determines whether the site should use unique permissions or inherit its permissions from the parent site (False indicates that they should be inherited). The last parameter determines whether an existing site of the same name should be converted to a SharePoint site if it exists (False indicates that SharePoint should throw an error if the site already exists).

Deleting Unwanted Web Parts

I want to keep only the TreeView web part on the page. So I need to iterate through the web part collection for the default.aspx page and remove any web parts not of the TreeView class (see Listing 9-4).

Listing 9-4. *Deleting Unwanted Web Parts Programmatically*

```
'Get handle to web parts default.aspx page, and iterate through web parts
Dim strThePage As String = strParentSite & strSiteName & "/default.aspx"
Dim web As SPWeb = site.OpenWeb(strSiteName)
Dim webParts As SPWebPartCollection = web.GetWebPartCollection(strThePage,
Microsoft.SharePoint.WebPartPages.Storage.Shared)
Dim wp As WebPartPages.WebPart
Dim i As Integer
Console.WriteLine("")
For i = webParts.Count - 1 To 0 Step -1
    wp = webParts(i)
    Console.Write(wp.Title & ": " & wp.GetType.ToString)
    If wp.GetType.ToString <> "MG.WebParts.DLTV.WebPart1" Then
        webParts.Delete(wp.StorageKey)
        Console.WriteLine(".... Deleted.")
    Else
        Console.WriteLine(".... Kept.")
    End If
Next
```

Adding New Web Parts

Now that the web part page contains only the TreeView web part that was included in the NEWTEMPLATE site template, I need to add two additional web parts: a “Welcome” content editor web part and a SQL web part to display client orders. Listing 9-5 shows you how to do it.

Listing 9-5. *Adding New Content Editor Web Part Programmatically*

```
'Add a "Welcome" content editor web part
Console.WriteLine("")
Console.Write("Adding content editor web part.")
Dim ce As New WebPartPages.ContentEditorWebPart
```

```
' Create an XmlElement to hold the value of the Content property.
Dim xmlDoc = New XmlDocument
Dim xmlElement As XmlElement = xmlDoc.CreateElement("MyElement")
xmlElement.InnerText = strWelcomeMsg
ce.ZoneID = "Right"
ce.PartOrder = 1
ce.Title = String.Format("Welcome message for {0}...", strSiteTitle)
ce.Content = xmlElement
webParts.Add(ce)
Console.WriteLine("... Added.")
```

■ **Note** Because of the way the `ContentEditorWebPart` class is constructed, you cannot simply add text to the content element (as nice as that would be). You must construct a fully formed `XmlElement` object and assign it to the `Content` property of the web part.

Listing 9-6. *Adding New SQL Web Part Programmatically*

```
'Add a SQL web part to display client orders
Console.WriteLine("")
Console.Write("Adding SQL web part.")
Dim sql As New MG.WebParts.SQL.WebPart1
sql.ConnectionString = strNorthwindConnectionString
sql.Query = "SELECT TOP 10 dbo.Customers.CompanyName, dbo.Orders.OrderID, " &_
"dbo.Products.ProductName, " & _
"dbo.[Order Details].UnitPrice, dbo.[Order Details].Quantity, " &_
"dbo.Orders.ShippedDate," & _
"dbo.[Order Details].Quantity * dbo.[Order Details].UnitPrice AS ExtPrice " & _
"FROM dbo.Customers INNER JOIN dbo.Orders " & _
"ON dbo.Customers.CustomerID = dbo.Orders.CustomerID " & _
"INNER JOIN dbo.[Order Details] ON dbo.Orders.OrderID = " &_
"dbo.[Order Details].OrderID " & _
"INNER JOIN dbo.Products ON " & _
"dbo.[Order Details].ProductID = " & _
"dbo.Products.ProductID " & _
"WHERE (dbo.Customers.CustomerID = N'" & strCustomerID & "') " & _
"ORDER BY ExtPrice DESC"
sql.XSLTPath = "XSLT/NorthwindSQL.xsl"
sql.FormatUsing = MG.WebParts.SQL.WebPart1.enumFormatUsing.XSLT
sql.ZoneID = "Left"
sql.PartOrder = 2
sql.Title = "TOP 10 Orders for: " & strSiteTitle
webParts.Add(sql)
Console.WriteLine("... Added.")
```

Note We need to create an instance of the `MG.WebParts.SQL.WebPart1` custom web part class to access its custom properties. That's why we created a reference to the source.

Editing Existing Web Parts

Let's return to the TreeView web part to edit several of its properties. Specifically, we need to customize the web part title for the site customer and we want to make sure that the web part is placed in the correct zone and order on the page. Finally, we want to display the TreeView without lines connecting its nodes (see Listing 9-7).

Listing 9-7. *Modifying a TreeView Web Part Programmatically*

```
'Editing the existing TreeView web part
Console.WriteLine("")
Console.Write("Editing TreeView web part.")
Dim tv As New MG.WebParts.DLTV.WebPart1
tv = webParts(0)
tv.Title = "Extranet documents for: " & strSiteTitle
tv.ZoneID = "Left"
tv.PartOrder = 1
tv.UseLines = False
webParts.SaveChanges(tv.StorageKey)
Console.WriteLine("... Edited.")
```

Caution One of the easy traps to fall into is failing to call the `SaveChanges()` method after the properties have changed. Failing to do so can lead to many hours of fruitless debugging trying to figure out why your changes didn't stick!

Testing from a Command Window

Now we're ready to test out the work. To do so, open a command, move to the directory where the `CreateSites.exe` file is, and type the following command: **`CreateSites CONSH "This is a new site for Consolidated Holdings"`**.

```
>CreateSites
Error: one or more parameters were incorrect.

Syntax:

CREATESITES <customerid> <site description>

>CreateSites CONSH "This is a new site for Consolidated Holdings"

Site: http://localhost/sites/AllClients/CONSH successfuly created.

Links: Microsoft.SharePoint.WebPartPages.ListViewWebPart.... Deleted.
Site Documents: MG.WebParts.DLTV.WebPart1.... Kept.
Site Image: Microsoft.SharePoint.WebPartPages.ImageWebPart.... Deleted.
Events: Microsoft.SharePoint.WebPartPages.ListViewWebPart.... Deleted.
Announcements: Microsoft.SharePoint.WebPartPages.ListViewWebPart.... Deleted.

Adding content editor web part.... Added.

Adding SQL web part.... Added.

Editing TreeView web part.... Edited.

>
```

Figure 9-2. *Output of Console application*

Note that all but the TreeView web part were deleted in the first pass, a content editor and SQL web part were added, and finally the TreeView web part was edited. Figure 9-3 shows the resulting site with various modifications noted.

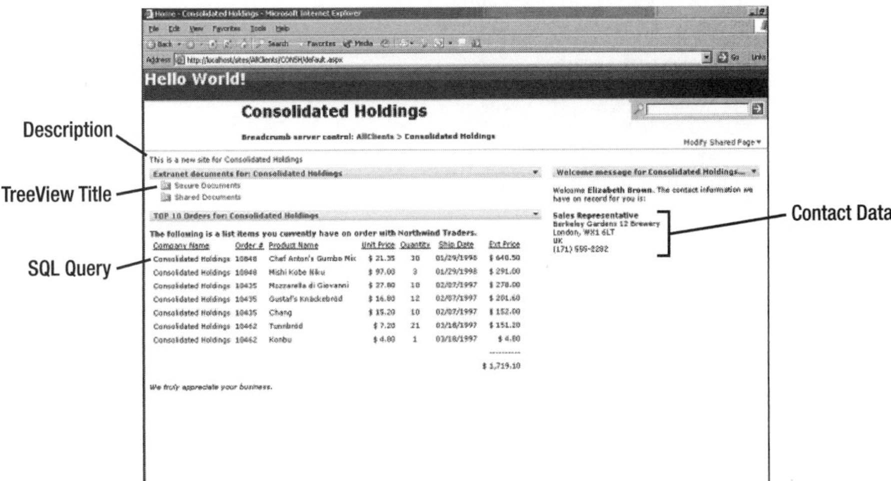

Figure 9-3. *Resulting site*

Creating a "Driver" Application to Process Multiple Sites

Now let's say you have a database of 500 customers, all of whom need extranet sites. Given the preceding work on the CreateSites application, we can now automate the process of creating these sites. To do so, I will write a simple "driver" application that reads the customer table, passing the necessary parameters to the CreateSites routine.

■ **Tip** I could have combined the following functionality with the CreateSites routine, but by keeping them separate, I have both a single and multisite generation utility.

Driver Application

The driver application is quite simple: it runs the CreateSites application iteratively, once for each customer in the `Northwind.Customers` table. Let's take a look at how Listing 9-8, when executed, gets a list of customers, creates a site for each customer in the list, and updates each customer's record indicating that a site was created.

Listing 9-8. *Driver Application to Process Multiple Sites*

```
Private strSiteRequestConnectionString As String = "user id=Northwind_test_user;" &
"data source=(local);persist security info=False; " & _
"initial catalog=Northwind"
Private con As New SqlClient.SqlConnection(strSiteRequestConnectionString)
Private sql As New SqlClient.SqlCommand

' Get a list of all customers without extranet sites
Private da As New SqlClient.SqlDataAdapter( _
"select * from Customers where Status='' " & _
"or Status IS NULL order by CustomerID", _
strSiteRequestConnectionString)
Private ds As New DataSet
Private dr As DataRow

Sub Main()

    da.Fill(ds)
    'Loop through SiteRequest queue, processing all requests with a 'Pending'
    'status.
    For Each dr In ds.Tables(0).Rows
        Try

    'Call our CreateSites command with the CustomerID of the customer that needs a
    'site.
    Shell("C:\Documents and Settings\Administrator\My Documents\" & _
        "Visual Studio Projects\CreateSites\bin\CreateSites.exe " & _
        "dr(0) & " " & dr(1) & "", AppWinStyle.Hide, True)
        UpdateRequestStatus(dr("CustomerID"), "Complete", "")
        Catch ex As Exception
            UpdateRequestStatus(dr("CustomerID"), "Failed", ex.Message)
        End Try
    Next
```

```
End Sub
'Lastly, update the status for this customer indicating that the
'site has been created.
Private Sub UpdateRequestStatus(ByVal strCustomerID As String, _
    ByVal strStatus As String, ByVal strNotes As String)

    'Update status to reflect fact that request(s) has/have been processed.
    con.Open()
    sql.CommandText = String.Format("Update Customers set Status='{2}', _
        "ProcessDateTime='{0}', ProcessNotes='{3}' where CustomerId='{1}'", Now, _
        strCustomerID, strStatus, strNotes)
    sql.Connection = con
    sql.ExecuteNonQuery()
    con.Close()

 End Sub

End Module
```

Preparing the Northwind.Customers Table

I also added three columns to the `Northwind.Customers` table, which will be used to record whether a site has been created for a given customer, along with the date and time of creation; or if an error occurred, what the error was.

- `Status varchar (10)`
- `ProcessDateTime datetime`
- `ProcessNotes text`

Testing the Driver Application

To test the application, open a command window and navigate to the folder on your hard drive where the `Driver.exe` file is. For example:

```
Cd \Documents and Settings\Administrator\My Documents\Visual Studio
Projects\Driver\bin
```

Type the command **`Driver.exe`** and you should see output similar to the following:

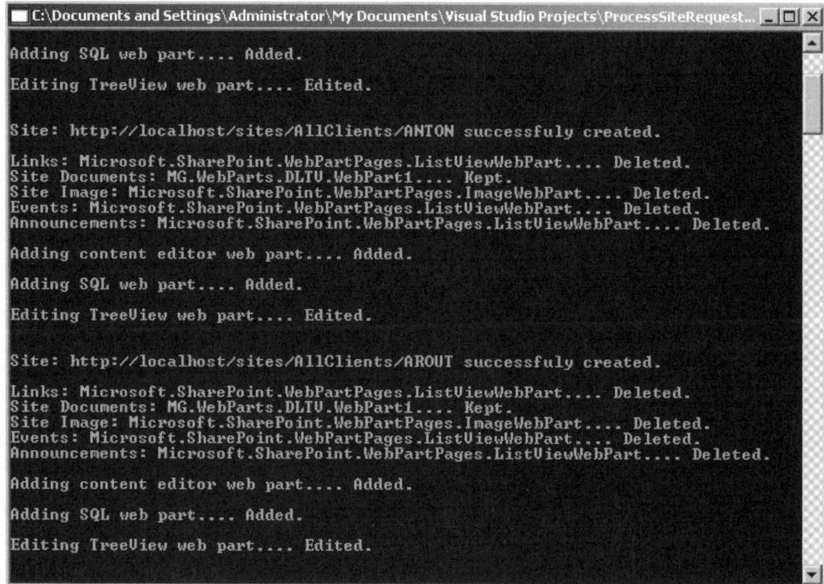

Figure 9-4. *Partial console output from driver application execution*

You can check that the driver application is also updating the status in the `Northwind.Customers` table by querying the table using SQL Server Query Analyzer, as shown in Figure 9-5.

SQL Query Analyzer - [Query - VMWIN2003MEG.Northwind.VMWIN2003MEG\Administrator - Untitled4*]

File Edit Query Tools Window Help

Northwind

```
select CustomerID,CompanyName,Status,ProcessDateTime,ProcessNotes from customers
```

	CustomerID	CompanyName	Status	ProcessDateTime	ProcessNotes
1	ALFKI	Alfreds Futterkiste	Complete	2005-10-01 07:55:48.000	
2	ANATR	Ana Trujillo Emparedados y ...	Complete	2005-10-01 07:57:01.000	
3	ANTON	Antonio Moreno Taquería	Complete	2005-10-01 07:57:54.000	
4	AROUT	Around the Horn	NULL	NULL	NULL
5	BERGS	Berglunds snabbköp	NULL	NULL	NULL
6	BLAUS	Blauer See Delikatessen	NULL	NULL	NULL
7	BLONP	Blondesddsl père et fils	NULL	NULL	NULL
8	BOLID	Bólido Comidas preparadas	NULL	NULL	NULL
9	BONAP	Bon app'	NULL	NULL	NULL
10	BOTTM	Bottom-Dollar Markets	NULL	NULL	NULL
11	BSBEV	B's Beverages	NULL	NULL	NULL

Figure 9-5. *Results after partial run of driver application*

The possibilities for automating site-related processes are limited only by your needs and programming abilities. By following a few basic "design patterns" for accessing and updating SharePoint site objects you can add, remove, and modify the web parts on a page, or change the properties (such as Title) of the page itself. You also can leverage those techniques to create a driver application that can make modifications to an arbitrary number of sites—giving you the ability to manage installations of hundreds or even thousands of sites efficiently.

Extending the SharePoint Site Creation Process

The previous section focused on developing tools for SharePoint installation administration that empower you to do more with less. In this section I'll show you how to extend the SharePoint user interface (UI) to provide your end users with more subtle control over the definition of the sites they create. The ultimate objective here is to place more control in the hands of end users, offloading as much of the trivial customization work as possible, so that you can focus on higher-level tasks. By the end of this section, you'll know how to port the programming logic developed in the preceding sections to an ASP.NET application that SharePoint can call as part of its own site creation process. This application will prompt the end user for some additional data beyond what is normally requested by SharePoint, modify the site, and display the completed site to the end user.

ExecuteUrl Site Template Option

The `ExecuteUrl` attribute of the `ONET.XML Project` element can be used to tell SharePoint to execute an ASP.NET page immediately after the user has selected a site template. This page can prompt the user for additional information to customize the site. In the following example, the `ExecuteUrl` page will prompt the user for the same two pieces of information: CustomerID and site description, which were provided to the CreateSites console application. The web application will perform the same set of customization steps and then redirect the user to the completed site. To apply the `ExecuteUrl` directive, do the following:

1. Open the file `C:\Program Files\Common Files\Microsoft Shared\web server extensions\60\TEMPLATE\1033\NEWTEMPLATE\XML\ONET.XML` (or whichever `ONET.XML` file applies to the custom template you wish to update).
2. Find the line `<Configuration ID="0" Name="Default">`.
3. Find the corresponding `</Configuration>` tag.
4. Immediately before the `</Configuration>` tag, place the text `<ExecuteUrl Url="_layouts/CreateSitesWeb/CreateSitesWeb.aspx"/>`.
5. Save `ONET.XML`.
6. Open a command window and type **`IISRESET`** to restart Internet Information Server (IIS) and force SharePoint to reload all site definitions.

The next time someone asks SharePoint to create a new site based on the `NEWTEMPLATE` template, SharePoint will call the `CreateSitesWeb.aspx` application immediately after adding the new site.

Creating CreateSitesWeb Under LAYOUTS

SharePoint reserves a special location on disk for custom applications that end users will interact with through the SharePoint web interface:

```
[drive:]\Program Files\Common Files\Microsoft Shared\Web ServerÂ
Extensions\60\TEMPLATES\LAYOUTS
```

Applications in this location appear to exist at the relative path `_layouts/[application path]` for any SharePoint site. For example, if we create a new ASP.NET project called `CreateSitesWeb` under the `LAYOUTS` folder that has a web page named `CreateSitesWeb.aspx`, we can access that page from any site on SharePoint by the relative path `_layouts/CreateSitesWeb/CreateSitesWeb.aspx`. Further, the SharePoint object model has a simple way of providing the current site context to any application running under the `LAYOUTS` folder. SharePoint takes advantage of this feature when calling a web application specified in the `ExecuteUrl` parameter of `ONET.XML`.

Creating the New ASP.NET Project

Figure 9-6 shows the Visual Studio New Project dialog box filled in with the information necessary to create the CreateSitesWeb project.

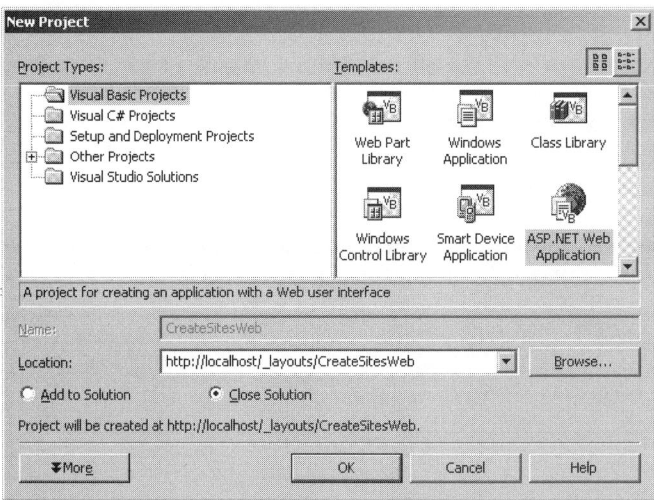

Figure 9-6. *Creating the CreateSitesWeb project*

Notice the location for the application is under `_layouts`. This is the virtual IIS directory that is created by Windows SharePoint Services when it is installed that maps to the `LAYOUTS` folder described previously. It's important that you tell Visual Studio to create the new project under that virtual directory.

After Visual Studio has created the CreateSitesWeb project, you will need to rename the default web page WebForm1.aspx to `CreateSitesWeb.aspx`. Next, add references to the `Windows.SharePoint.Services`, `MG.WebParts.DLTV`, and `MG.WebParts.SQL` .dlls (see previous section on creating a console application for a discussion of how to add web part references to the CreateSitesWeb project).

Creating the Web Form

As shown in Figure 9-7, the web form that we want SharePoint to display immediately after the site has been created contains two fields: Customer ID and Site Description. It also contains a button that, when clicked, passes the values in the two fields to the code-behind routine that will customize the new website. After the customization is complete, the CreateSiteWeb routine will redirect the user to the completed site.

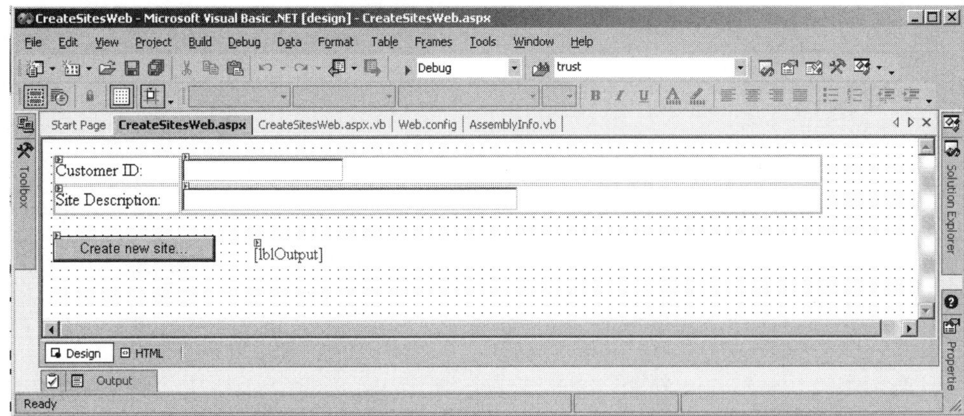

Figure 9-7. *CreateSiteWeb form in design mode*

The form will contain four web controls, shown in Table 9-2.

Table 9-2. *Web Controls on the CreateSitesWeb.aspx Page*

Control Id	Type	Purpose
`TxtCustomerId`	TextBox	User input field for Customer ID of new site
`TxtSiteDescrip`	TextBox	User input field for site description (optional)
`LblOutput`	Label	Displays any errors that occurred during site customization
`CmdCreateSite`	Button	When clicked, passes the Customer ID and site description to back-end program, initiating final site customization

Copying the Code from CreateSites Console Application

Most of the code in the CreateSitesWeb application will be identical to that of its console application cousin. A few differences are important to note, however.

Because the site has been created for us by SharePoint, we use the `SPControl.GetContextWeb(Context)` method to get a handle to the new site, instead of explicitly referencing it by its URL.

```
...
'Get handle to new site
Dim web As SPWeb = SPControl.GetContextWeb(Context)
...
```

In the Page_Load event, I initialize my form fields using the website name that the user entered through the standard SharePoint create web dialog box.

```
...
Private Sub Page_Load(ByVal sender As System.Object, _
    ByVal e As System.EventArgs) Handles MyBase.Load

    'Default customer ID, site description to site name.
    If Not IsPostBack Then
        txtCustomerID.Text = web.Name
        txtSiteDescrip.Text = "New site for " & web.Name
    End If

End Sub
...
```

The Console.WriteLine() commands are replaced with assignments to a form label, which will be displayed if an error occurs.

```
...
lblOutput.Text = lblOutput.Text & ("Error: one or more parameters were incorrect.")
lblOutput.Text = lblOutput.Text & "<BR/>"
...
```

In the console application, I assigned the title and description as part of the site.AllWebs.Add()method call. Because SharePoint has already added the new site at the time the CreateSitesWeb page is displayed, I don't need to add it. However, I do need to assign and directly update the values of the title and description properties.

```
...
'Set the title of site = to customer id.
web.AllowUnsafeUpdates = True
web.Title = strSiteTitle
web.Description = strSiteDescrip
web.Update()
...
```

■Caution The SPWeb.AllowUnsafeUpdates = True statement tells SharePoint that this program will be making updates to the website or web parts collection. Without this command, SharePoint will throw the cryptic error "The Security Validation For This Page Is Invalid. Click Back in your web browser, refresh the page, and try your operation again" if you attempt to assign a value to a website property or add or modify a web part. Because console applications execute at a higher trust level, the earlier application did not require this command.

```
...
'Enable updates to web part collection.
webParts.Web.AllowUnsafeUpdates = True
...
```

■ **Caution** When updating the web parts collection of a page, you must set the `SPWebPartCollection.Web.AllowUnsafeUpdates` property to `True`, even if you already set the parent web's property of the same name. Failure to set this property prior to edits will result in the same security validation error noted previously.

When all processing is complete, the user is redirected to the completed site.

```
...
'Customizations complete, take user to site's main page.
Response.Redirect(web.Url)
...
```

Testing the Application

Now let's test the application by creating a new site. Follow these steps:

1. Go to the parent site.
2. Click the Create link at the top of the page.
3. Click Sites And Workspaces at the bottom of the Create page.
4. Enter a title and URL for the new site (note: the title will be replaced by that entered into the custom CreateSitesWeb page) and click Create.
5. Select the New Team Site template from the Template Selection page and click OK.
6. Enter a valid Customer ID from the `Northwind.Customers` table into the Customer ID field.
7. Enter any text description into the Site Description field, as shown in Figure 9-8.

Customer ID: FURIB
Site Description: This is my new site...
Create new site...

Figure 9-8. *Completed CreateSitesWeb form*

8. Click the Create New Site button and voila! Figure 9-9 shows the results.

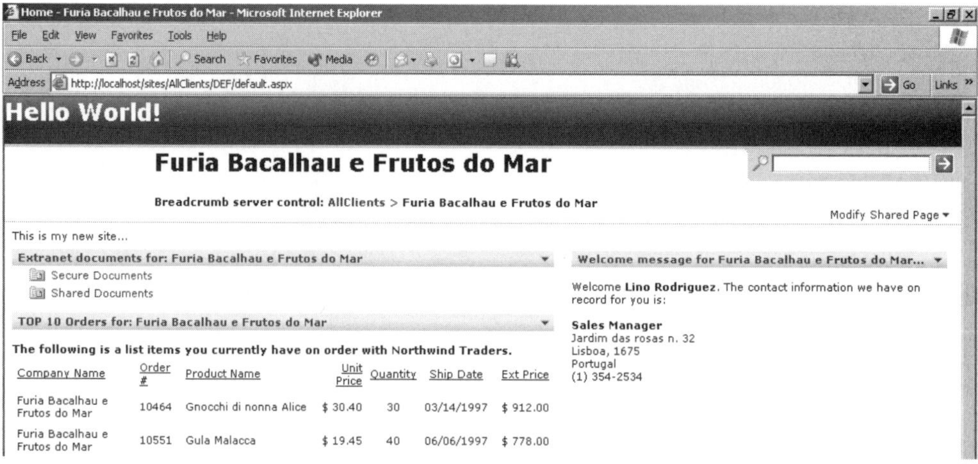

Figure 9-9. *Completed site*

Summary

This chapter showed you how to create a command-line application that creates a new SharePoint site, and that modifies the content of that site programmatically. You also saw how to create an application that can generate an arbitrary number of sites based on data from an external source—such as a customer database.

You also learned how to extend the site creation process by using the `ExecuteSQL` `ONET.XML` attribute. If you choose to do so, you can gather any additional information from your end user that you need to complete the site. Your application can read or write to external databases and systems, and update the site definition using the SharePoint object model. Although the previous section was about how to make your life as a SharePoint administrator easier by creating specialized tools to meet your unique needs, this section has been about how to empower the end user so that you can focus on higher-level tasks.

With these techniques in hand, combined with .NET's capability to customize SharePoint sites through the SharePoint object model, you can now efficiently manage large SharePoint installations while providing your end users with sophisticated and robust site designs.

CHAPTER 10

Putting It All Together

SharePoint is one of those products, like SQL Server, that can be installed in 20 minutes or become a focus of your work for years. One aspect of SharePoint that fascinates me is the variety of technologies and techniques embodied in the product, and thus called into play when you attempt to truly customize it. The genius behind SharePoint is that as you learn more and more about customizing SharePoint, you also build skills that have general web development applicability.

The more you work with SharePoint, the more malleable you will find it becomes, more like a painter's canvas; a foundation upon which to create your extranet. Stepping back from this canvas is an opportunity for you to picture your client extranets as they will look when completed and to decide which techniques and technologies that are covered here—or new ones you will create—to use.

In this chapter, we'll bring together all the conceptual threads that have been woven throughout the preceding chapters. Given the breadth of topics covered so far, you might find that you need to go back to one or more of the earlier chapters to review the details of that topic. Regardless, it's useful to get a 30,000-foot view of what we've covered, putting all the moving parts of our extranet environment in their proper places.

In this book we've touched on several technologies and techniques, including:

- SSL and Proxy Servers
- SQL and SharePoint Backup and Restore
- .NET programming
- XML and XSLT
- SQL query language
- CAML
- Web Services
- CSS
- HTML

We'll start our review with a look at server and Windows SharePoint Services (WSS) configurations, followed by a review of how we have customized each. Then we'll walk through the process of creating an extranet site using our customized SharePoint installation, and adding users to that site. Figure 10-1 shows the high-level activities, all of which were discussed earlier in the book, which are required to launch the extranet environment. The order of the activities is somewhat artificial in that they will be revisited throughout the life of the extranet as needed. However, the sequencing does generally track with when the activity will first need to be addressed.

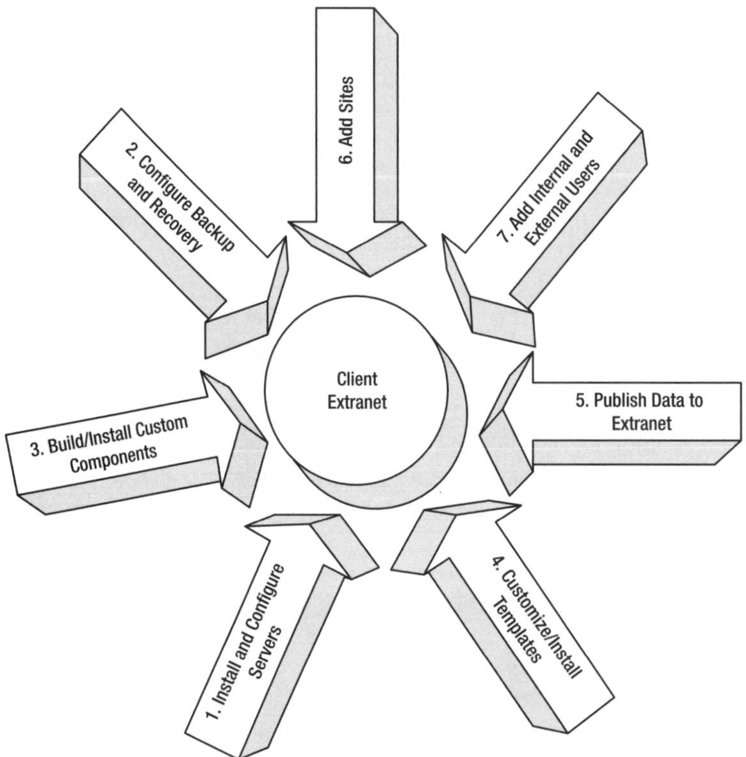

Figure 10-1. *The high-level activities required to launch an extranet environment*

Install and Configure Servers

In Chapters 1 and 2, you learned about the SharePoint server architecture required to support an extranet environment. The ideal architecture provided the following:

- User-level authentication and authorization
- Data encryption
- Isolation of the SharePoint server from the Internet
- Employee access to the extranet without reauthenticating

To accomplish these results, we installed several components (shown in Figure 10-2):

- Active Directory one-way trust to enable internal users to seamlessly access the extranet
- IIS and WSS

- SSL to encrypt all transmissions between SharePoint and the external user
- ISA to act as a reverse proxy, preventing external users from connecting directly to the SharePoint server

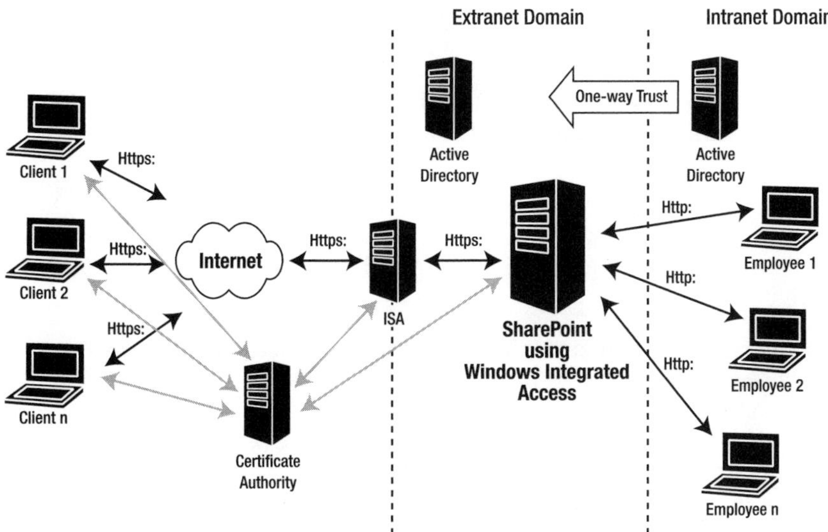

Figure 10-2. *Extranet server configuration*

Active Directory One-Way Trust

An Active Directory trust tells Windows to accept the network credentials of users who have already authenticated in the trusted domain. For example, if the EXTRANET domain trusts the INTRANET domain, a user who has previously logged in as INTRANET\Jdoe will be accepted as Jdoe on the EXTRANET domain. This does not mean that the any server on the EXTRANET domain need provide authorization to access any of its resources, only that it will accept that Jdoe is who the INTRANET domain says she is.

A one-way trust operates in one direction only. For example, a one-way trust between the EXTRANET and INTRANET domains can be configured so that the EXTRANET domain accepts authentication by the INTRANET domain, but not vice versa. By making the trust between EXTRANET and INTRANET one way, an external user attempting to access resources in the INTRANET domain will be forced to provide a valid INTRANET user name and password. On the other hand, an internal user who has already been authenticated on the INTRANET domain need not log in again to gain access to resources on the EXTRANET domain.

IIS and SSL

Internet Information Server (IIS) is the only web server that supports SharePoint. We configured IIS to encrypt transmissions between SharePoint and the external user by installing a Secure Sockets Layer (SSL) certificate. Certificates for public use are generally obtained from a commercial certificate authority such as VeriSign. Once obtained, these certificates are installed on the IIS server, and the websites are configured to require SSL-encrypted transmissions.

You also learned that it is possible to use Microsoft's Certificate Services to create and install a certificate, acting as your own certificate authority, which is useful for testing or for production use within your firm. However, most clients will feel more comfortable accessing secure sites using certificates from a third-party provider.

ISA

We covered the installation and configuration of Internet Security and Acceleration (ISA) Server, Microsoft's proxy server solution, which provides several features that improve the security of a SharePoint extranet solution, including the following:

- Reverse proxy to prevent external users from connecting directly with the SharePoint server
- Firewall to limit which servers are published through the proxy and which protocols can be used
- Caching of content as appropriate for improved performance and reduced load on the SharePoint servers

Configure Backup and Recovery

Backup and restore are planning activities that are too easily ignored until a problem arises. However, given a little bit of upfront planning you can be prepared to quickly recover part or all of your extranet environment in the case of human or machine failure. Because WSS stores its content in a SQL Server database, it's not surprising that SQL backup is one of your backup/recovery options. SharePoint also supports two other backup options: STS backup for site collections and `SMIGRATE` for individual sites. In practice, you will probably use all these methods at various times to ensure the recoverability of your sites or to move sites from one location to another.

SQL Server

We saw how SQL Server backup can be used to schedule a full backup of the SharePoint content and configuration databases. You should periodically run a full backup to ensure that the site can be recovered in total should the database server on which the SharePoint databases reside suffers a catastrophic failure.

STS Backup and Restore

The STS administrative utility includes backup and restore commands that allow you to back up a top-level site and all its subsites. This capability can be used to create backups between full SQL Server database backups, or to move or copy a site collection. We also saw how a simple command script can be created to automate the backup of multiple sites using the STS backup command.

SMIGRATE

The SMIGRATE command was originally conceived as a way to migrate sites from one location to another, either on the same SharePoint server or between servers and possibly between different versions of SharePoint. Nonetheless, this command can also be used as a backup option if you have a particularly important lower-level site and do not want to back up the entire site collection of which the site is a member.

Build/Install Custom Components

A phenomenon of the SharePoint ecosystem is the explosion of third-party web parts. This is very similar to the situation after Visual Basic 5 was introduced, when Microsoft made available a well-documented API for creating add-on components. It was the vast array of add-on components that made Visual Basic the platform of choice for corporate developers. I believe the large and growing number of off-the-shelf components for SharePoint will have the same impact on this platform. However, it's early in this process, and many of the add-on web parts are still rudimentary. In addition, the choice of whether to build or buy a new web part (ideally) should not be based on whether you have the knowledge or skills to build it, but what will be the best use of your scarcest resource: time. With that in mind, we spent a large part of the book looking at how to work with the SharePoint object model to build our own web parts and other components. Depending on the size of your firm, number of application development resources, and availability of off-the-shelf components to meet your needs, you might choose to buy rather than build most if not all your components. Having the ability to build your own, however, will allow you to make more informed build/buy decisions.

Let's now review the components we created earlier in this book.

Web Parts

Web parts are a basic building block of the SharePoint user interface (UI). They are also a bit tricky to create, requiring more steps to deploy than a typical server control, user control, or ASP.NET application. Having said that, custom web parts, which provide the tightest integration with the SharePoint user interface, can be connected to the stock web parts in many useful ways. Given the relative difficulty of creating and deploying web parts, I try to make them as general-purpose as possible, so the effort required can be put to use in the broadest range of applications. The web parts we created are described in the following sections.

Base

As the name implies, this is the Base web part class. One of the nice things about web parts is that they adhere to the .NET object-oriented development model. I can subclass my Base web part to produce any number of new parts while inheriting the methods and properties of the Base class. The Base web part provides one primary feature: it queries Active Directory (through the Authorization web service) to discover which security groups the current user belongs to and then checks them against the security groups that should be able to view that particular web part. If the user is in one of those groups, the web part displays itself; if not, the web part is rendered invisible. This provides the much-needed targeting that is missing from SharePoint 2003.

SQL

Another common task is to integrate structured data from external sources such as accounting, Customer Relationship Management (CRM), data warehouses, or document management systems. We created the SQL web part to provide a general-purpose tool for querying and formatting data from these types of sources.

■ **Note** SharePoint does come with a DataView web part, which can also query SQL data sources and provide formatted output. However, to create and edit the DataView web part you must use FrontPage 2003, which introduces the "ghosting" problem—breaking the direct link between a page and the underlying `CAML` template. For that reason, many SharePoint developers, including the author, avoid the use of FrontPage and thus DataView web parts. Further, the DataView does not support the show/hide capability provided by the custom SQL web part, which is based on the `Base` web part class.

You learned how to use XSLT to format the result set produced by the SQL query. Although not specifically discussed here, XSLTs can be constructed to format SQL queries (or stored procedures) that produce multiple result sets. So you can return and format queries of arbitrary complexity using this web part.

TreeView

One of the glaring omissions in SharePoint 2003 is the inclusion of a visual representation of the hierarchical folder structure of a document library. End users have come to expect this, based on their experience with Windows Explorer and other applications. This web part uses a freely available JavaScript library to display the folder structure on the page, and allows the user to click a folder to open its default view or to click a document within a folder to display that document. Creating this web part also allows us to delve into the object model classes for lists, folders and files—a set of classes that will come in handy any time you need to manipulate the content of document libraries programmatically.

■ **Note** There are a number of third-party document library web parts that provide features beyond what we've created here. However, to my knowledge none provides source code, so these web parts are therefore not extensible by you. Further, the skills you acquired by creating the TreeView web part will be useful in any scenario where you need to traverse and manipulate the contents of a document library or list programmatically.

XML

To be an IT professional today is to live in an XML world! From document storage to commercial applications to Really Simple Syndication (RSS) feeds, we're finding that XML is the common denominator. We saw that XML is nothing more than taking the raw data of whatever we want to represent and wrapping it in tags denoting fields, records, and result sets. When you consider that .NET stores all DataSet data as XML, you can see the truly universal quality of this technology for managing structured data.

Like the SQL web part, the XML part is a general-purpose component for taking any well-formed chunk of XML and formatting it using XSLT. The XML web part, when combined with the XML cache loader process, has the advantage of not requiring a live connection to back-end SQL databases. This capability to create an "arms-length" relationship between source internal systems and data displayed on the extranet is important because we don't want to expose internal systems to the threat of malicious access.

Installing the Server Controls

In a SharePoint environment, server controls are close cousins of web parts. They share many of the same characteristics, including the ability to access the SharePoint object model and display content on the page. Where they differ is in the level of integration with the SharePoint user interface and the difficulty of deployment. Specifically, server controls provide no inherent integration with web parts, but are easier to deploy. Server controls are a good choice when you want to place a component on a page (or as part of a template) that the user will not need to move or remove, particularly if that content will not exist within a web part page zone (the `Breadcrumb` and `Quick Launch` navigational components are examples).

Breadcrumb

A *breadcrumb* is a common navigational element that shows end users where they are now and where they've been. We saw how the SharePoint object model could be used to discover the current location and the path back to the top-level My Extranets page through use of the `SPWeb` class. Once created, the `Breadcrumb` server control can be placed on any page to improve its usability. This simple customization will be greatly appreciated by your end users.

Quick Launch

You saw that the built-in Quick Launch element had significant drawbacks, both in terms of personalization and in terms of formatting. For example, if a document library is defined for a site and designated to appear on the built-in `Quick Launch`, a link will appear for it, whether or not the end user has permission to view documents in that library. In general, the built-in `Quick Launch` will display links to lists (document libraries, contact lists, and so on) that the end user does not have permission to access. When users click one of them, they are prompted to log in using a different user name and password. Not only does it frustrate the end user but it also violates one of the basic tenets of UI design: don't show users options they can't use! Our customized `Quick Launch` server control solved this problem by using the SharePoint object model to show the user only those choices that they can access, and has the added benefit of allowing us to format the choices any way we want by using XSLT. Using this formatting technique, you can present the `Quick Launch` as a simple list, a series of nested menus, or any other visual representation that meets your users' needs.

Installing the ASP.NET Web Services

Along with XML, web services are a foundational element of the emerging computing paradigm. In fact, SharePoint has numerous web services that it exposes to the developer, and entire books could be written just on the topic of using the native SharePoint web services and creating new ones. You saw that web services are a good candidate for reusable classes that might be called from a variety of web parts or applications.

In our work, we created a single Authorization web service that queries Active Directory to discover which security groups the current user is a member of. This capability to retrieve the current user's Active Directory group membership enabled our Base web part to determine whether it should show or hide itself (and, by implication, web parts subclassed from it) on the page.

Installing the ASP.NET Applications

Extranet installations can potentially spawn huge amounts of administrative work. As we all know, there are only 32 hours in an IT professional's day, so we need to find ways to work smarter, not harder. In several earlier chapters, we explored how to create administrative utilities to ease the burden of creating new sites. We also created a utility to extract data (in the form of XML documents) from the internal systems to the extranet server, in which they can be presented to the end user without compromising internal systems security. Finally, we created an application to allow the user to easily navigate to all sites they have permission to view.

CreateSites

The CreateSites application allows you to automatically generate 1, 10, or 1,000 sites quickly based on data from an external accounting or CRM system. When your management comes to you and says they need extranet sites for the firm's top 250 clients, you can look them in the eye and tell them you can get it done in a day or two (even though you know it will take about 30 minutes!) This utility also demonstrated the use of .NET console applications with the SharePoint object model, which is often a better choice for administrative tasks that need to be run and scheduled on the SharePoint server.

CreateSitesWeb

Microsoft exercised real forethought when it included the `ExecuteUrl` parameter in `ONET.XML`. This one parameter opens the door to limitless automation and user configurability during the site-creation process by allowing you to point to a custom ASP.NET application that can gather data from the end user, external systems, or SharePoint. You can then have the application use this information to add or remove web parts, lists, pages, or other site elements or customize the new site in numerous other ways. The CreateSitesWeb application you built prompts for customer ID and site title, finds the associated record in the accounting system, adds key data and configures web parts, and then displays the page. I have used this method to allow end users to select web parts and other site elements from a menu of checkboxes, which allows the end user a significant degree of control over the completed site within parameters that you determine.

■Note If the ASP.NET application specified in the `ExecuteUrl` parameter is designed correctly, it can be used during site creation and later to add or remove site elements. Such a custom page configuration application provides an alternative to the web part gallery, which requires a higher authority level than you may want to give your users, and requires a higher level of knowledge about the workings of the individual web parts, while providing very little control over placement or use.

MyExtranets

In a typical extranet environment, the end user might have rights to access multiple sites (perhaps your firm is working on multiple engagements for a given client, or a partner or vendor is working with you across multiple client engagements). Regardless, you need to provide your extranet users with an easy way to access all of their sites, without having to remember or bookmark URLs.

The MyExtranets application you developed shows how to create a list of sites underneath the current top-level site that the user has permissions to view. This list can then easily be formatted with a .NET DataGrid to support filtering and sorting. On your MyExtranets page, you will probably want to add other elements, such as client-specific news or announcements, or a disclaimer informing unauthorized users that they should exit the site.

XML Cache Loader

The key to presenting data from core internal systems available on your extranet is finding a way to make that data available without letting external users (or the extranet sites) query those core systems directly. To allow such direct access would sidestep our requirements regarding security of internal systems, as well as create potential performance and system availability risks. A simple workaround, discussed in Chapter 6, is to build an XML cache loader, which periodically extracts the needed datasets from the core systems, writing them to one or more XML documents on a shared drive in the EXTRANET domain. By combining the XML cache loader with a simple configuration file, the Windows Scheduler, and the XML web part, we created a powerful tool for making any type of structured data available in a controlled way to our extranet users.

Customize/Install Template(s)

One step up from individual web parts, server controls, or ASP.NET applications are the templates that contain them. SharePoint provides a rich, if arcane, language for defining these templates called Collaborative Application Markup Language (`CAML`), which is simply a set of XML schemas for defining the base set of data that will be used to create new sites. We saw how to create our own custom template by making a copy of the stock `STS` template and then editing the associated `ONET.XML` file. You also saw how to edit the `default.aspx` file to alter the end user's navigation experience and how to customize the look and feel to present your firm's brand. You now understand the relationship between the `CAML` templates, which SharePoint uses at site creation, and the files that exist under the root site folder (for example, `STS`).

■ **Caution** It's my opinion that to create truly robust extranet sites with an appealing and professional appearance tailored to your firm and its clients, you need to modify many of the files under the site directory (for example, `NEWTEMPLATE`). Microsoft, however, does not support those changes, so you should always customize by creating new templates rather than editing the stock templates in place, and you should use source control (such as Visual SourceSafe) to allow a rollback to an earlier version if needed.

Publish Data to Extranet

In addition to providing an online space in which you and your clients can collaborate on documents, you will want your client extranets to provide the capability to display structured data such as invoices, contact information, product lists, or other information drawn from your core internal systems. However, for security and administrative efficiency reasons, you do not want your clients (or the EXTRANET SharePoint server for that matter) making connections to your back-end systems. The solution in this case is to extract the data from your core systems in a controlled way and push those extracts from the INTRANET to the EXTRANET for presentation to the client.

One way to accomplish this, as noted in Chapter 6 and earlier in this chapter, is to create a cache of internal data in the EXTRANET domain using an XML cache loader, shown in Figure 10-3.

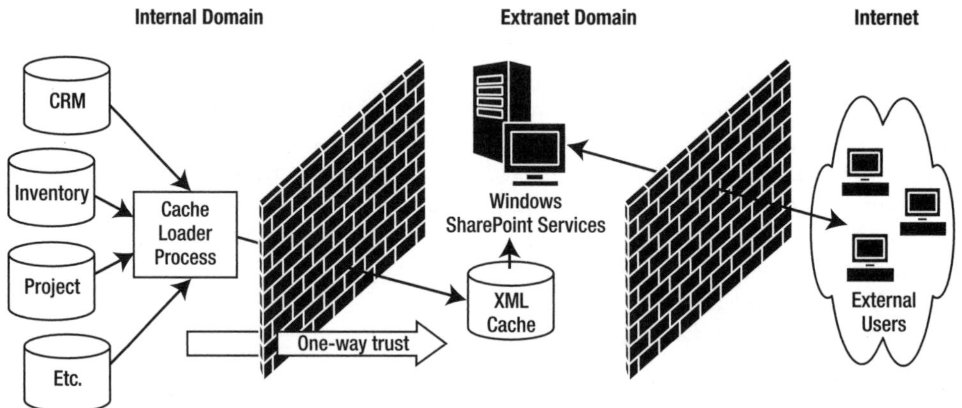

Figure 10-3. *XML cache loader data flow*

The XML cache loader runs as a scheduled task in the INTRANET domain, periodically extracting data from specific core systems, converting the data to XML documents, and writing those documents to the EXTRANET domain. The custom XML web part can then read the documents, format them with XSLT, and present them to the end user. Note that the one-way trust, discussed earlier in this chapter, is key to enabling the XML cache loader process to authenticate to the EXTRANET domain.

In this example, we used an XML configuration file to drive the cache-loading process, similar to the snippet shown in Listing 10-1.

Listing 10-1. *XML Cache Loader Configuration Data*

```
<CacheLoader>
  <Request>
    <SQLConnection>user id=Pubs_Test;data source=spsdev;initial catalog
=Northwind</SQLConnection>
    <SQLCommand>
    SELECT Customers.CompanyName,Orders.OrderID,Products.ProductName,
      [Order Details].UnitPrice,[Order Details].Quantity,Orders.ShippedDate,
      [Order Details].Quantity*[Order Details].UnitPrice AS ExtPrice
      FROM Customers INNER JOIN Orders ON Customers.CustomerID=Orders.CustomerID
      INNER JOIN [Order Details] ON Orders.OrderID = [Order Details].OrderID
      INNER JOIN Products ON [Order Details].ProductID = Products.ProductID
      WHERE (Customers.CustomerID = '[CustomerID]')
    </SQLCommand>
    <OutputName>NorthwindOrders</OutputName>
  </Request>
```

The two primary elements are `SQLConnection` and `SQLCommand`. These two bits of data, combined with the assumption that each SQL command will be executed for each customer in our customer database, will generate one XML document containing the result set for one SQL command for each customer. The generated documents will have unique names such as `NorthwindOrders_0001`, `NorthwindOrders_0002`, where `0001` and `0002` are customer IDs in the database.

Although the XML cache loader we built in Chapter 6 was designed to create documents for each customer ID, this program, with minor modifications, could create unique documents for each part, invoice, region, or any other key column.

Add Sites

After a custom site template is defined as noted previously, and the appropriate `WEBTEMPxxx.XML` file added, you simply restart IIS and add a new site as you would by using one of the out-of-the-box templates. When you select the custom template for the new site (`NEWTEMPLATE`, in this case), SharePoint displays the CreateSitesWeb page to allow entry of custom parameters. Remember that this ASP.NET application can be of arbitrary complexity and can add any elements to the site that the SharePoint object model allows, including web parts, lists, document libraries, web part pages, and so on. You have a great deal of control over the completed site, especially when combined with the capabilities of `CAML` to define site layout and content.

Add Internal and External Users

There are really two steps to adding new users. First, you must add the user to Active Directory, which can be accomplished through the Active Directory Users And Computers application. Figure 10-4 shows the New Object - User dialog box in Active Directory.

■ **Note** You need to add a user to Active Directory only once, regardless of the number of sites or lists to which the user is given access.

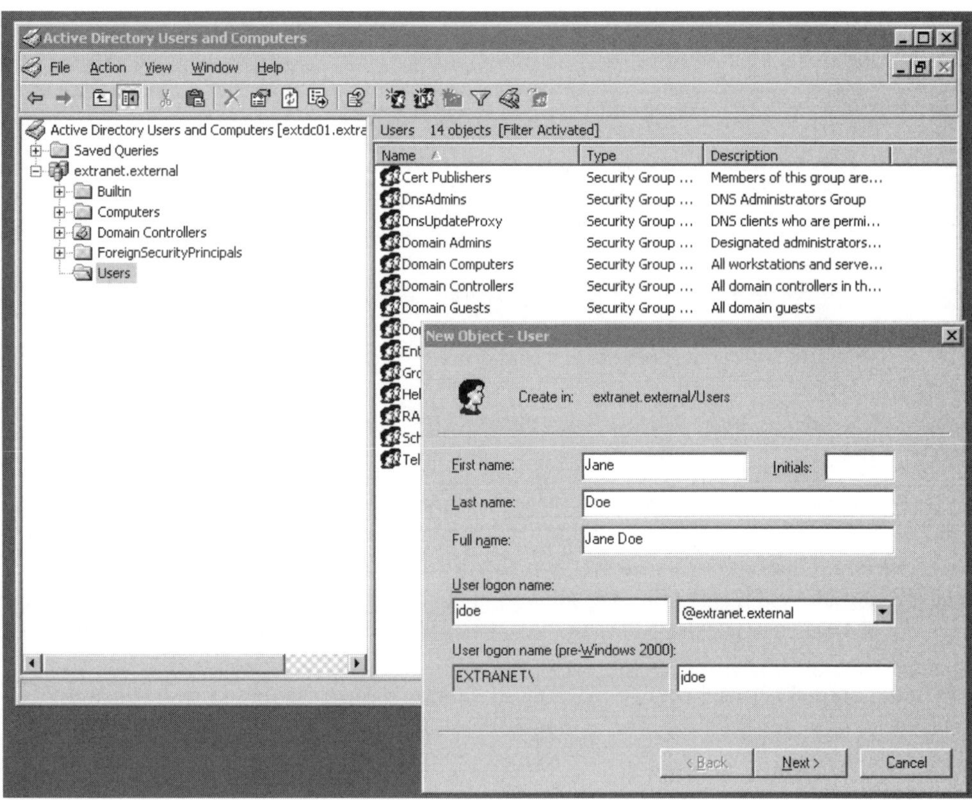

Figure 10-4. *Example Active Directory add user dialog box*

After adding a new external user, you are prompted to assign an initial password. You should check the Password Never Expires checkbox and uncheck the User Must Change Password At Next Logon checkbox. Leave the other two checkboxes unchecked. If you require users to change their password at first logon, they cannot access any secure sites because browsers don't provide the ability for users to change their password, and SharePoint will not allow them to log on until they do. This results in a "Catch 22," in which the user is continually prompted to log in but never is authenticated by SharePoint. Figure 10-5 shows the Active Directory dialog box for setting the new user's password.

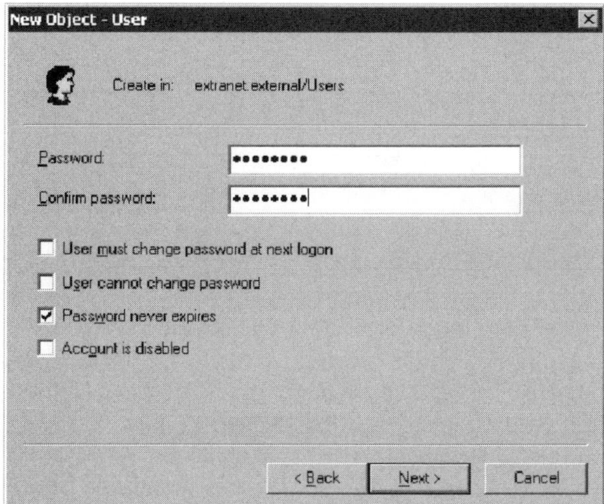

Figure 10-5. *Active Directory set password dialog box*

■ **Caution** Because there is no facility within the browser authentication scheme to allow users to change their password at first login, you should check the Password Never Expires checkbox when adding a new user. If you want to periodically force a change of password through Active Directory security policies, you need to provide end users a web page in which they can change their password.

By default, any user created in the EXTRANET domain will be a member of EXTRANET\Domain Users security group. You might want to assign users to other Active Directory security groups to allow you to target web parts based on the Base web part and to control access to site content. Figure 10-6 shows a user being assigned to the External Users - High Security Clearance group.

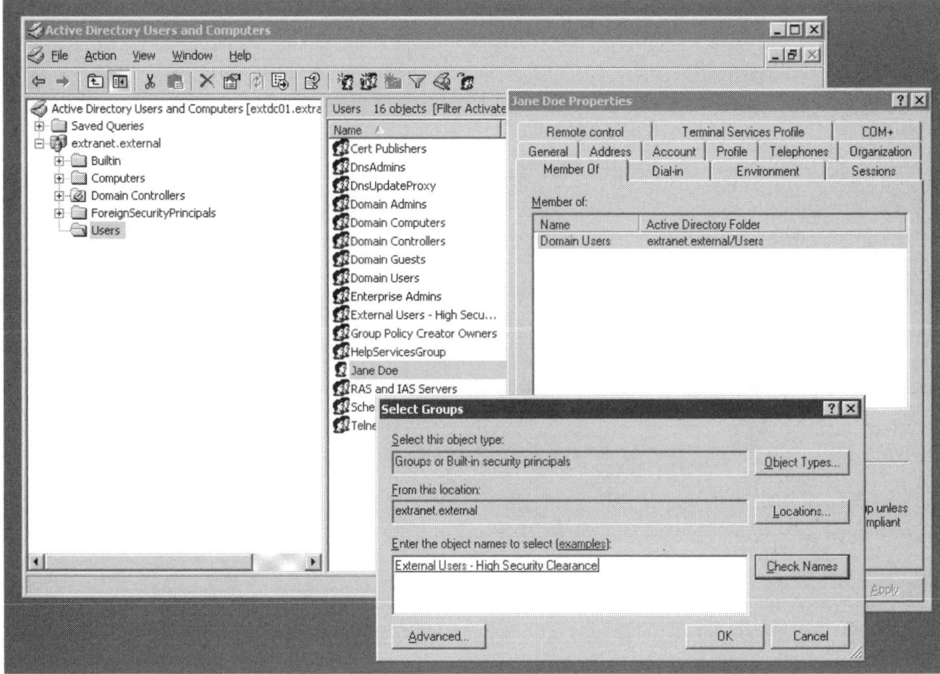

Figure 10-6. *Assigning a user to an Active Directory security group*

At this point, the new user has a valid user name and password in Active Directory, and can be added to one or more SharePoint sites. Recall that one of the properties of the Base web part we created is a list of Active Directory security groups that might view the output of this web part. To limit visibility of any SQL or XML web part based on the External User - High Security Clearance security group, you simply have to enter the name of that group in the AD Groups property field. Figure 10-7 shows the property sheet for the Base web part.

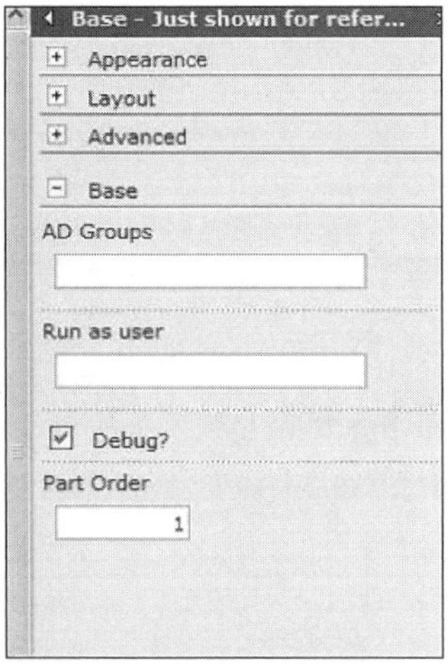

Figure 10-7. *Base web part property sheet*

Before users can access a site, they must be added as a user, either explicitly by using their DOMAIN\Username or implicitly by adding a domain security group to which they belong, to the list of authorized groups. To add a user or a security group, go to the Site Settings page of the site to which you want to grant access and then click Manage Users. A list of authorized users (along with site group affiliations) displays, as shown in Figure 10-8.

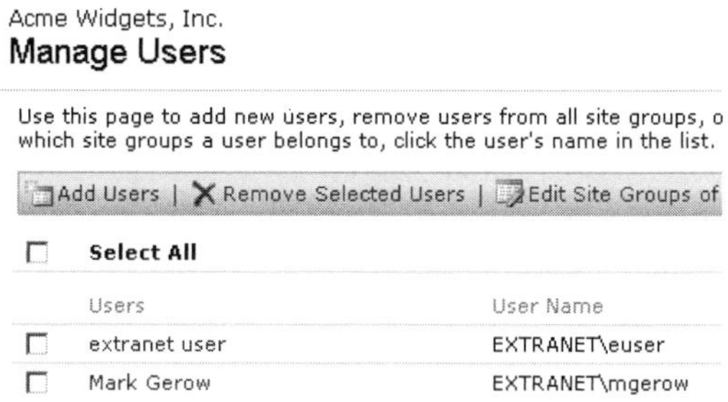

Figure 10-8. *SharePoint Manage Users administrative page*

The Add Users dialog box allows you to enter one or more domain users in the form DOMAIN\Username, as shown in Figure 10-9. You can select from any of the groups defined for the current site. The default groups are Reader, Contributor, Web Designer, or Administrator, but you can define other groups as needed.

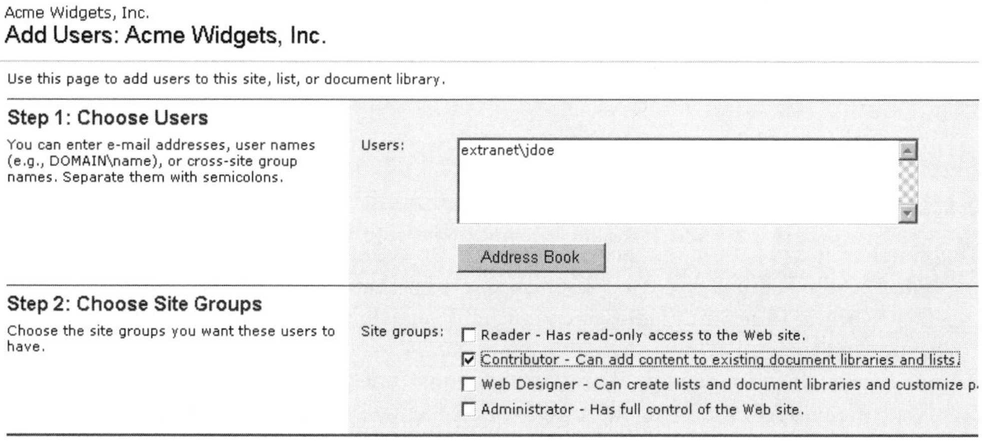

Figure 10-9. *SharePoint Add Users administrative page*

Finally, you have the option of sending an email to users, notifying them that they are being added as users of this site. Figure 10-10 shows the final Add Users page (I filled in the blocks for email address, subject, and body of the message).

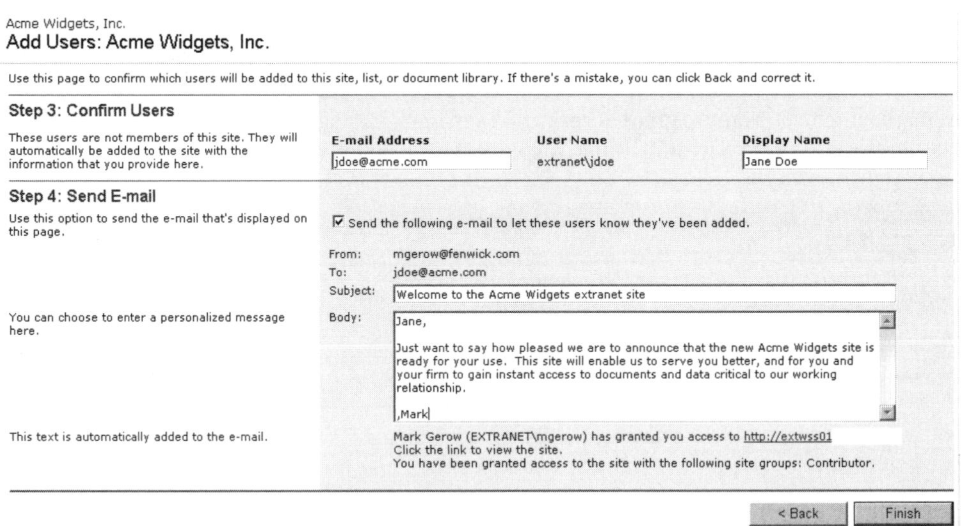

Acme Widgets, Inc.
Add Users: Acme Widgets, Inc.
Use this page to confirm which users will be added to this site, list, or document library. If there's a mistake, you can click Back and correct it.
Step 3: Confirm Users
These users are not members of this site. They will automatically be added to the site with the information that you provide here.
E-mail Address
User Name
Display Name
jdoe@acme.com
extranet\jdoe
Jane Doe
Step 4: Send E-mail
Use this option to send the e-mail that's displayed on this page.
Send the following e-mail to let these users know they've been added.
From: mgerow@fenwick.com
To: jdoe@acme.com
Subject: Welcome to the Acme Widgets extranet site
You can choose to enter a personalized message here.
Body: Jane,
Just want to say how pleased we are to announce that the new Acme Widgets site is ready for your use. This site will enable us to serve you better, and for you and your firm to gain instant access to documents and data critical to our working relationship.
,Mark
This text is automatically added to the e-mail.
Mark Gerow (EXTRANET\mgerow) has granted you access to http://extwss01
Click the link to view the site.
You have been granted access to the site with the following site groups: Contributor.
< Back
Finish

Figure 10-10. *Add Users email notification page*

■ **Caution** You should transmit the password to the new user in a way that does not compromise security. One approach is to instruct the new user to call the system administrator so the password can be communicated verbally. Another approach is to transmit the password in a separate email. The least-secure approach is to include the password in the body of the email message; doing so allows an eavesdropper to discover both the user name and password and thus impersonate the new user on your extranet site.

Summary

This chapter reviewed the steps necessary to install and configure the various server components and customizations discussed throughout earlier chapters. These components fit together to provide a secure, highly functional, and appealing environment within which your colleagues and clients can share documents and data. The technologies and techniques you learned here enable you to create SharePoint extranets that take full advantage of the platform's security model, document-management capabilities, template-driven site creation, and web part framework. In Chapter 11, I will discuss WSS 3.0 (scheduled to be released in late 2006), as well as .NET 2.0, Visual Studio 2005, and Windows Workflow Foundation. I will also discuss an expanded use of web services to make the underlying data displayed on an extranet available to clients for inclusion in their internal systems and websites.

CHAPTER 11

Conclusion

In this book, we have explored a set of technologies, techniques, and customizations to Windows SharePoint Services (WSS) that will allow you to deploy robust, manageable, and visually appealing extranets. In the process, we touched on many of the inherent capabilities of SharePoint, getting a glimpse of the full spectrum of possible ways in which this platform can be molded to meet your firm's unique requirements.

You can now see that SharePoint is actually made up of a collection of technologies working in concert, with foundations in .NET, SQL Server, and XML. Your efforts in learning these technologies have been rewarded with the ability to shape SharePoint to meet your specific extranet needs. As Microsoft continues to enhance SharePoint and integrate it more closely with technologies such as Visual Studio 2005, .NET 2.0, and Windows Workflow Foundation, the skills you've gained throughout this book will position you to take full advantage of each of these integrated platforms, as well as any extensions you choose to create with non-Microsoft systems.

In this concluding chapter, we'll look at the impact of a few of the developments relevant to those of us creating SharePoint extranets. The first three are entirely technical, involving the evolution of SharePoint itself. The fourth development is the trend (of which extranets are one manifestation) toward tearing down the barriers between your firm's information systems and those of your clients.

Windows SharePoint Services (WSS) 3.0

As of this writing, information about the next version of WSS has begun to emerge. As with any software product from Microsoft, the target feature set and ship date are closely guarded secrets and are subject to change at any time; however, it's unlikely that a fully baked version of the product will be available before late 2006 or early 2007. And until the new features can be put to the test, it's premature to say whether or how any given enhancement will affect the customizations we developed in earlier chapters.

The following is a list of the features slated for inclusion in the next version of WSS that I find most intriguing:

- Better navigation, including breadcrumbs and improved QuickLaunch.
- Item-level security on lists and libraries—a key improvement over the current version, which provides only list-level security.
- Recycle bin with user and administrator restore features for document libraries and list items. Although it's possible to create a recycle bin today, it's more difficult than it should be and requires custom programming.

- Customizable and extensible search.
- Built-in support for the show/hide capability we developed in the Base web part. However, the ability to target web parts based on arbitrarily complex business rules will not be provided, so the techniques covered in this book will still prove useful.
- All lists and libraries have Really Simple Syndication (RSS) feeds with site-level rollups, which allow authorized clients to subscribe to lists and libraries just as they would online news services.
- All lists (not just document libraries) will have version history capability, which will provide an important audit trail when documents and other list items are edited by multiple parties.
- WSS 2.0 web parts will continue to work, which will protect any investment in web parts developed or purchased today.
- Lists can have lookup fields that connect to a SQL Server table or a web service, which will make lists more useful as data-entry vehicles for complex data.

There are many more features planned; many of them (such as better integration with Microsoft Outlook) will be of more interest to users within your firm. One question that always comes to mind when faced with an impending upgrade—even one many months away—is this: Does it make more sense to continue to develop solutions with the current version or wait until the upgrade is released? My answer is generally to continue to develop solutions. One thing that's certain in life (along with death and taxes, of course) is a never-ending stream of business information management problems that need to be addressed; problems that need solutions in days or weeks, not months and years. By continuing to develop collaborative solutions with WSS 2.0, you are delivering real value today. Because all web parts, and presumably most customizations, that you create will work in WSS 3.0 when it ships, the need to rework significant portions of your customizations should be minimal.

Windows Workflow Foundation

Windows Workflow Foundation (WWF) will be part of the next version of the .NET Framework (WinFX). The design goal for WWF is to provide a common framework for workflow applications of all types.

For example, imagine the process a software development consultancy might go through when developing a software application for a client:

1. A business analyst works with the client to define requirements.
2. A systems architect reviews the requirements and produces a design specification. The development team then produces a schedule based on the design.
3. The client approves the schedule, and work begins.
4. Throughout the development, work-in-progress is reviewed with the client, who approves work or requests changes.
5. When the application is complete, it is installed, and the client provides final sign off.

A simplified flowchart of this process is shown in Figure 11-1.

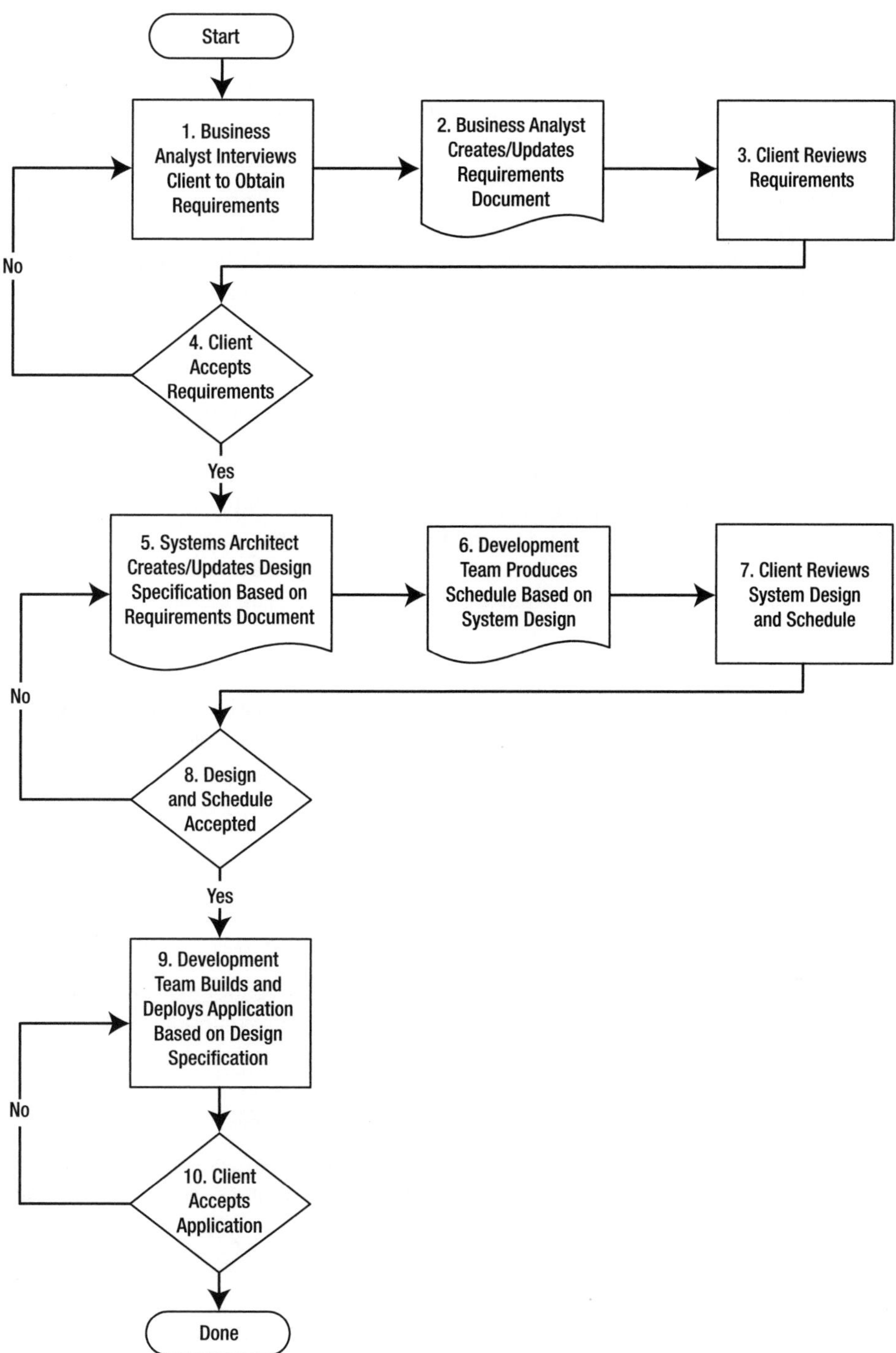

Figure 11-1. *Flowchart depicting the application development process*

Steps 1–8 of the application development process center around three documents: requirements, design specification, and project schedule. Because WWF will integrate with the next version of WSS, it will be possible to create a SharePoint document library that supports this process by changing the state of the document and notifying various parties when the process moves from one step to the next. Further, the workflow can include state- or time-based triggers that notify the client when a document is ready for review; notify the business analyst or systems architect if the client has not reviewed a draft of the requirements, design, or schedule documents within a specified period; or notify the development team of a change request. Management could be notified if a requirements document is not approved within three iterations (which might indicate that the business analyst is not communicating clearly with the client) or if the application is not approved within five iterations (an indication of quality problems on the part of the development team).

This example is artificially simplified, and real-world workflows typically include tens or hundreds of steps, but it is illustrative of how workflow can be used within a SharePoint extranet. The fundamental benefit of automated workflow management is that it promotes the consistent application of business process rules across all processes of a given class (for example, developing and deploying a software application) and offloads much of the work of tracking the status of each individual workflow to the workflow application.

Using WWF and future versions of WSS, it will be possible to create extranets that provide both an online space for collaboration as well as processes to ensure that collaboration is effective.

■ **Note** You can create the workflow application described above by using just WSS document library events and a custom .NET application. The advantage of WFF is that the workflow engine is more loosely coupled to the host platform (for example, WSS), making it easier to maintain, expand, or integrate with non–SharePoint technologies.

Visual Studio 2005 and .NET 2.0

As of this writing, Visual Studio 2005 and .NET 2.0 have been released, but they are not compatible with version 2.0 of WSS. In fact, some parts of .NET 2.0, such as support for ASP.NET web parts, conflict directly with SharePoint.

■ **Caution** .NET 2.0 should not be installed on a computer running WSS 1.0, 1.1, or 2.0; and it should not be used to develop web parts, server controls, or other applications for use by these versions of SharePoint.

The preceding caution notwithstanding, one of the more interesting features of .NET 2.0 is support for ASP.NET web parts. Microsoft has taken the web part framework developed for SharePoint and made it generic so that it can be used by web applications that are not connected to SharePoint. This provides all the benefits that SharePoint developers and users have realized through the use of web parts to non-SharePoint web applications. In addition, because the design of ASP.NET web parts has been carried over from SharePoint, the skills you've already acquired in developing the various SharePoint web parts earlier in this book will carry over as well.

My advice to you is to begin using Visual Studio 2005 and ASP.NET 2.0 for non-SharePoint development, both to take advantage of the many new features that will allow you to create better applications in less time and because it will be your development platform for the next version of WSS.

Turning the Organization Inside Out

More than a decade ago, William Davidow and Michael Malone wrote this in their book, *The Virtual Corporation*:

> *Business success in the global marketplace of the future is going to depend upon corporations providing "virtual" products high in added value, rich in variety and available instantly in response to customer needs. At the heart of this revolution will be fast new information technologies; increased emphasis on quality; accelerated product development; changing management practices, including new alignments . . . between company, supplier, and consumer.*

In some ways, the change Davidow and Malone foresaw has come more slowly than one might expect. The pace of change was partly driven by social and organizational factors; human beings don't change their attitudes and behaviors quickly, particularly when that change affects who has control of business information. Human factors notwithstanding, the technology needed to realize this vision just wasn't available in 1992 when Davidow and Malone wrote their book. Only through a seemingly haphazard stream of technical advances have we reached the point where turning the organization inside out is truly a possibility. The World Wide Web provides a ubiquitous virtual network that firms and their clients can tap into. Data encryption standards allow secure transmission of data over an unsecured Internet. XML provides a common framework for exchanging structured data. SOAP, RSS, and other XML standards allow the rapid dissemination of information without the need for sender and receiver to create an agreed-upon format themselves.

Beyond Extranets: Just Give Me the Data

I believe that client extranets will remain an important component of a layered approach to collaboration within and between firms for many years to come. Figure 11-2 provides a visual representation of the emerging structure for sharing data and documents in a "virtual" firm.

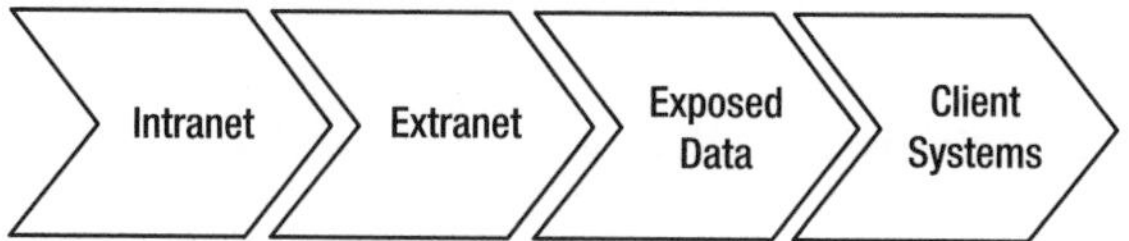

Figure 11-2. *Interlocking information layers in a virtual firm*

Throughout this book, we've discussed the first two layers; intranet and extranet. What about the last two layers? These two come about because your clients, particularly the larger or more technically sophisticated ones, have a need to integrate the data you expose via an extranet into their own back-end systems, such as intranets, financial systems, document management systems, client relationship management systems, or any other applications that can make use of the data exposed via your extranet.

Suppose, for example, that an extranet you've created displays a list of individuals at your firm who are responsible for working with the client on a particular engagement. In a law practice, these individuals might include the responsible attorney, all associate attorneys working on the matter, one or more paralegals, and administrative support staff. Your clients might want to display this information on an internal website for use by their employees who are also involved in this engagement. Of course, they could just place a link to your extranet on their internal site, but that would require that their users click the link and log in to your site to view the list. What your clients really want is a way to get just the data in some form that they can present on their internal site.

The solution to this and similar cases is to expose the data through web services that return the underlying data as XML. We touched on web services when developing our Base web part as a way to access Active Directory, but what we're talking about here is much broader: creating a library of web services that authorized clients can call to obtain the base data and documents exposed on an extranet so they can integrate those data and documents with *their* internal systems.

Of course, the whole notion that data transfer occurs in only one direction, as shown in Figure 11-2, is artificial. Your clients also need to provide you with information. After all, that's what collaboration is all about. They can upload and edit documents and data using our SharePoint extranet, but what if there's data in their core systems that we want to provide on the extranet site or incorporate into our internal systems? Figure 11-3 shows a revised picture of what information sharing looks like in a bidirectional world.

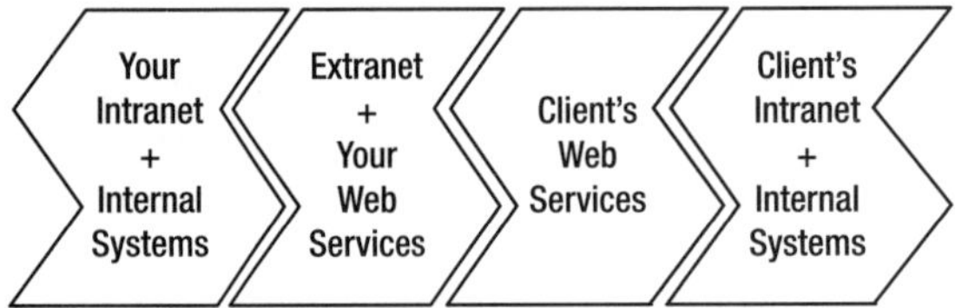

Figure 11-3. *Bidirectional data and document sharing in a virtual firm*

Considering that your firm probably has hundreds or thousands of clients, vendors, and partners, and that each of these clients, vendors, or partners in turn has their own clients, vendors, and partners, the number of interlocking data connections becomes mind-boggling. (As does the potential to unlock value by collaborating on the data and documents related to the even greater number of engagements, projects, and transactions that those connections represent.) If creating client extranets is a clear first step in realizing this interdependent world, building the web services that enable your clients to integrate your systems with theirs, and theirs with yours, is its logical complement.

The trend toward layered interfaces between firms and their clients, vendors, and partners will continue as standards mature and as all parties become more knowledgeable about the available technologies. Client extranets will be a key layer in the collaboration "stack" connecting your firm to your clients, and WSS provides a rich foundation upon which to build that layer today and into the future.

APPENDIX

Additional Resources

Although every effort has been made to include all the information you will need to successfully deploy client extranets with Windows SharePoint Services (WSS), as you peel back the layers of the technical onion, there are always more details, and thus more information needed.

In the past 18 months, there has literally been an explosion of resources to help you learn and use SharePoint. In an effort to save you the time of ferreting out the most useful books, websites, and products, I've listed my favorites here. Of course, you will likely find others that you want to add to your toolkit. I have also included a brief description of the areas of SharePoint and related technologies covered in each resource.

SharePoint—Advanced SharePoint Services Solutions

- Topic All
- Source Apress Publishing
- Type Book
- URL `http://www.apress.com/book/bookDisplay.html?bID=402`

This book has a particularly nice coverage of Collaborative Application Markup Language (CAML) for site and list definitions. It also has some excellent chapters on web part development.

SharePoint Products and Technologies

- Topic All
- Source Microsoft Learning
- Type Book
- URL `http://www.microsoft.com/MSPress/books/6454.asp`

This is the encyclopedic "must-have" resource for any SharePoint developer. The content is written and organized for system administrators rather than developers, but if I know what I'm looking for, I can usually find it. Many of the programming examples are superficial. The book includes a CD of utilities and examples.

Backup and Restore Options for WSS

- Topic Backup/Restore
- Source Microsoft
- Type Website
- URL `http://www.microsoft.com/resources/documentation/wss/2/all/adminguide/en-us/stsf20.mspx`

This is the section of the online version of the WSS Administrator's Guide that deals with backup and restore. The guide provides a good discussion of all backup and restore options.

Configuring Authentication in WSS

- Topic ISA/SSL
- Source Microsoft
- Type Website
- URL `http://www.microsoft.com/resources/documentation/wss/2/all/adminguide/en-us/stse10.mspx`

This article, which is part of the WSS Administrator's Guide, provides a survey of the methods for configuring authentication in Internet Information Server (IIS) and WSS, including anonymous, basic, integrated, and Secure Sockets Layer (SSL).

Installing and Configuring a Windows Server 2003 Enterprise Certification Authority

- Topic ISA/SSL
- Source Training, Authoring, Consulting Team
- Type Website
- URL `http://www.tacteam.net/isaserverorg/exchangekit/2003createenterpriseca/createenterpriseca.htm`

Step-by-step instructions for installing and configuring Windows 2003 certificate authority (CA), as well as a discussion of the use of Windows Certificate Services with Internet Security and Acceleration (ISA).

Microsoft on SSL Certificates

- Topic ISA/SSL
- Source Microsoft
- Type Website
- URL `http://www.microsoft.com/technet/security/topics/cryptographyetc/certs.mspx`

This paper introduces digital certificates and how to use them on the Windows platform. The paper covers certificates, CAs, the certificate life cycle, certificate storage, and an overview of applications using certificates.

Publishing Windows SharePoint Services with ISA

- Topic ISA/SSL
- Source Microsoft
- Type Website
- URL `http://www.microsoft.com/technet/prodtechnol/isa/2004/plan/isawss.mspx`

This site covers configuration of ISA Server 2004 to publish WSS. Topics include configuring WSS and known limitations, configuring secure web publishing rules for SSL bridging, and information about configuring certificates.

Reverse Proxy Configurations for Windows SharePoint Services and Internet Security and Acceleration Server

- Topic ISA/SSL
- Source Microsoft
- Type Website
- URL `http://www.microsoft.com/technet/prodtechnol/sppt/wss/revproxy.mspx`

This white paper describes the reverse proxy configurations that work with WSS and includes procedures for publishing SharePoint sites using ISA Server 2004.

Reverse Proxy Configurations for Windows SharePoint Services and Internet Security and Acceleration Server

- Topic ISA/SSL
- Source Microsoft
- Type Website
- URL `http://office.microsoft.com/en-us/assistance/HA011915121033.aspx`

This site provides systematic instructions on how to configure ISA 2004 and WSS.

Yahoo! SharePoint Group

- Topic SharePoint 2003
- Source Multiple
- Type Discussion Group
- URL `http://groups.yahoo.com/group/sharepoint/`

This is a discussion list for Microsoft SharePoint Portal Server 2001, Microsoft Office SharePoint Portal Server 2003 (previously known as SPS v2.0), and related technologies.

Yahoo! SharePointDiscussions Group

- Topic SharePoint 2003
- Source Multiple
- Type Discussion Group
- URL `http://groups.yahoo.com/group/sharepointdiscussions/`

This group is dedicated to discussions surrounding the development, administration, and implementation of SharePoint Products and Technologies 2003 and the next version, currently called "V3." This group is monitored by SharePoint Resource Kit authors Bill English and Todd Bleeker. Both Todd and Bill are on the Beta team for the next version of SharePoint.

Document Library Browser 1.2

- Topic TreeView
- Source Stramit's SharePoint Blog
- Type Blog
- URL `http://blog.spsclerics.com/articles/9253.aspx`

This home site for a shareware Document Library TreeView demonstrates some of the more advanced possibilities.

Note This web part was the original inspiration for the TreeView web part developed in this book. Although the document library TreeView available at the site is quite useful, its author has chosen not to make source code available.

SharePoint Products and Technologies Web Component Directory

- Topic Web Parts
- Source Microsoft
- Type Website
- URL `http://www.microsoft.com/sharepoint/downloads/components/default.asp`

The directory was designed to provide a place in which thousands of developers and users who use WSS and Office SharePoint Portal Server 2003 can download and submit custom extensions. The site provides access to a gallery of web parts that Microsoft makes available without charge. Some of the web parts are trial versions of commercial products, whereas others are free and often include source code.

Adding Web Parts Programmatically in SharePoint

- Topic Web Parts, Object Model
- Source Jan Tielens
- Type Blog
- URL `http://weblogs.asp.net/jan/archive/2005/06/22/414283.aspx`

This article provides a nice discussion of how to programmatically add web parts to a web part page using .NET.

Architectural Overview of WSS

- Topic WSS
- Source Microsoft
- Type Website
- URL `http://msdn.microsoft.com/library/default.asp?url=/library/en-`

Examines the architecture implemented in WSS, including what happens on the server when users issue page requests and how WSS responds. Also discusses the role of managed and unmanaged code.

SharePoint Products and Technologies

- Topic WSS
- Source Microsoft
- Type Website
- URL `http://msdn.microsoft.com/library/default.asp?url=/library/en-us/odc_2003_ta/html/sharepoint.asp`

This article provides a good discussion of the differences between WSS and SharePoint Portal Server. The relative positioning of these two products is often a point of confusion for new SharePoint users, and an understanding of which is a prerequisite to making the right choice in terms of when to deploy one or the other of the two products.

WSS Administrator's Guide

- Topic WSS
- Source Microsoft
- Type Download
- URL `http://www.microsoft.com/downloads/details.aspx?FamilyID=a637eff6-8224-4b19-a6a4-3e33fa13d230&displaylang=en`

This is the place to go to download a Windows help file version of the WSS Administrator's Guide. Among other things, this guide provides an authoritative reference for the `STSADM` command.

WSS with Service Pack 2

- Topic WSS
- Source Microsoft
- Type Download
- URL `http://www.microsoft.com/downloads/details.aspx?FamilyID=b922b28d-806a-427b-a4c5-ab0f1aa0f7f9&DisplayLang=en`

This is the download site for WSS Service Pack 2.

WSS Software Development Kit (SDK)

- Topic WSS
- Source Microsoft
- Type Download
- URL `http://www.microsoft.com/downloads/details.aspx?FamilyID=1C64AF62-C2E9-4CA3-A2A0-7D4319980011&displaylang=en`

The WSS SDK provides information about the languages, protocols, and technologies used to customize a deployment of WSS. This Windows help file provides a wealth of information about customizing WSS using the object model and .NET.

XML Spy Home Site

- Topic XML/XSLT
- Source Altova
- Type Website
- URL `http://www.altova.com/`

This is the vendor website for an excellent XML/XSLT editor.

Stylus Studio Home Site

- Topic XML/XSLT
- Source Progress Software
- Type Website
- URL `http://www.stylusstudio.com/xml_product_index.html`

This is my tool of choice for XML and XSLT development. It allows you to easily design and debug XSLT files using a WYSIWYG editor and intelligent code completion. The vendor offers a free trial download.

W3 Org Home Site

- Topic XML/XSLT
- Source W3 Schools
- Type Website
- URL `http://www.w3schools.com/`

At W3Schools you will find all the web-building tutorials you need, from basic HTML and XHTML to advanced XML, multimedia, and Wireless Application Protocol (WAP).

W3 Schools Home Site

- Topic XML/XSLT
- Source W3.org
- Type Website
- URL `http://www.w3.org/TR/xslt`

This specification defines the syntax and semantics of XSLT, which is a language for transforming XML documents into other XML documents.

Index

Apress
eBookshop

ASP Today

Apress
THE EXPERT'S VOICE™